An Introduction to the Chansons de Geste

NEW PERSPECTIVES ON MEDIEVAL LITERATURE: AUTHORS AND TRADITIONS

UNIVERSITY PRESS OF FLORIDA

Florida A&M University, Tallahassee
Florida Atlantic University, Boca Raton
Florida Gulf Coast University, Ft. Myers
Florida International University, Miami
Florida State University, Tallahassee
New College of Florida, Sarasota
University of Central Florida, Orlando
University of Florida, Gainesville
University of North Florida, Jacksonville
University of South Florida, Tampa
University of West Florida, Pensacola

AN INTRODUCTION TO THE
Chansons de Geste

❖ ❖ ❖

Catherine M. Jones

Foreword by R. Barton Palmer and Tison Pugh

UNIVERSITY PRESS OF FLORIDA

Gainesville · Tallahassee · Tampa · Boca Raton

Pensacola · Orlando · Miami · Jacksonville · Ft. Myers · Sarasota

This book may be available in an electronic edition.

19 18 17 16 15 14   6 5 4 3 2 1

Library of Congress Cataloging-in-Publication Data
Jones, Catherine M. (Catherine Mary), 1956– author.
An introduction to the chansons de geste / Catherine M. Jones ;
foreword by R. Barton Palmer and Tison Pugh.
pages cm
Includes bibliographical references and index.
ISBN 978-0-8130-4989-2
1. Chansons de geste—History and criticism. 2. Epic poetry, French.
I. Palmer, R. Barton, 1946– II. Pugh, Tison. III. Title.
PQ201.J66 2014
841'.1—dc232013051137

The University Press of Florida is the scholarly publishing agency for the State University
System of Florida, comprising Florida A&M University, Florida Atlantic University, Florida
Gulf Coast University, Florida International University, Florida State University, New
College of Florida, University of Central Florida, University of Florida, University of North
Florida, University of South Florida, and University of West Florida.

University Press of Florida
15 Northwest 15th Street
Gainesville, FL 32611-2079
http://www.upf.com

This book is dedicated

to the memory of my brother,

Larry Jones

(1959–2009)

◈

CONTENTS

FOREWORD

As the general editors of New Perspectives on Medieval Literature: Authors and Traditions, it is our great pleasure to introduce students and other interested readers to some of the greatest authors and most noteworthy literary traditions of the Middle Ages. Undeniably remote in time, language, and custom, the Middle Ages may appear inaccessible, but this period brims with intellectual and artistic vitality for those willing to undertake just a bit of study. Each volume in this series is prepared by a leading scholar in the field according to the highest academic standards, and we are particularly pleased to introduce Catherine M. Jones as the author of this volume on the chansons de geste—a collection of Old French epic poems. The author and editor of four books and more than twenty articles, Professor Jones has expanded the field of medieval studies through her work on the chansons de geste and other works of medieval French literature, probing their treatments of genre, society, and culture. She begins this volume by detailing the historical and poetic context of the chansons de geste, then explores more deeply the contours of the genre in the masterpieces *La Chanson de Roland*, *Le Charroi de Nîmes*, *Raoul de Cambrai*, *Ami et Amile*, and others. The chansons de geste created a rich legacy for future writers and romancers of the Middle Ages and beyond, and Professor Jones concludes this volume by meditating on the influence of this literary tradition.

In developing the New Perspectives in Medieval Literature: Authors and Traditions series, we seek accomplished scholars who also excel in teaching, in the belief that the harmonious union of scholarship and teaching builds deeper, more robust, and more enjoyable engagements with the literature of the past. In this regard, Professor Jones has proved herself a cherished teacher of medieval literature, as evidenced by the numerous awards she has won at her home institution, the University of Georgia, which has bestowed upon her the Josiah Meigs Distinguished Teaching Professorship, the Lothar Tresp Outstanding Honors Professor Award, the General Sandy Beaver Teaching Professorship, and the Richard B. Russell Teaching Award, among numerous others. These awards testify to Professor Jones's great successes in the classroom, which, with her lively and engaging prose, she transfers to the book in your hands.

New Perspectives in Medieval Literature: Authors and Traditions, it is our hope, will help readers grasp the continuing relevance and appeal of medieval literary masterpieces, a body of work that ages yet never dies. Professor Jones's contribution to this endeavor, with this outstanding introduction to the chansons de geste, will inspire new generations of readers to appreciate the wonders and delights of medieval literature.

R. Barton Palmer
Tison Pugh
Series Editors

PREFACE

Why should a twenty-first-century reader delve into the stories and rhythms of the Old French chansons de geste? I ask this question in undergraduate and graduate classes before we launch into the *Chanson de Roland* or the *Charroi de Nîmes*—and I ask it again when we complete our study. The initial responses are generally accurate but uninspired. Students anticipate that these texts will teach them something about French history; since the stories are part of the Western canon, they serve as an important cultural reference point. After engaging with the works, however, students see beyond their value as literary artifacts, recognizing modes of conflict that continue to surface in the modern world. They draw fruitful comparisons with other bodies of literature founded upon oral traditions. Like their teachers, students must grapple with crucial moral and aesthetic questions, notably the difficulty of reconciling the incantatory beauty of the chansons de geste with their aggressive messages of intolerance and celebrations of violence. Finally, modern readers are often pleasantly surprised to discover that these timeworn epics contain gripping narratives capable of moving and amusing, as well as provoking thought and lively discussion.

The present study is thus designed to initiate the modern nonspecialist reader into a vibrant tradition of epic narrative that flourished in the Francophone world and spread throughout the cultures of the medieval West. It is neither an encyclopedia nor an exhaustive study of the genre, which comprises more than one hundred extant texts and numerous adaptations. Rather, I have sought to provide an overview of the tradition as well as a closer reading of selected individual works. Whenever possible, I have let the texts speak for themselves by including quotations in the original language (followed by English translations) in order to convey the poetic patterns specific to the Old French epic. These citations are drawn from canonical works as well as lesser-known poems, so as to give readers a broader sense of the tradition as a whole. Although it has been necessary to include key information found in traditional manuals, this study also takes into account recent critical approaches inspired by feminist, postcolonial, and cognitive theory. It questions the validity of certain "master narratives" of French literary history, particularly with respect to the relationship between the chanson de geste and verse romance.

Chapter 1 situates the chansons de geste in their historical and cultural context. In addition to poetic form and dominant themes, this section surveys the ongoing and spirited debates about origins, modes of composition and transmission, and the nature of the medieval audience. Chapter 2 provides an overview of the textual tradition itself, describing the principal groups or "cycles" of Old French epic as well as works that fall outside these clusters. Chapter 3 analyzes in more detail six individual works, which were selected on the basis of both medieval and modern reception. Here I have privileged texts that were widely disseminated and appreciated in the Middle Ages, representative of a dominant type or phase of Old French epic narrative, frequently taught in modern literature courses, and, whenever possible, available in English translation. An epilogue traces the various forms of adaptation that continued to assure the dissemination of Old French epic material in new media and across various languages and cultures. The back matter provides a listing of approximate dates and versification patterns for the chansons de geste cited in this volume, as well as a glossary of terms and proper names and a select bibliography. Since scholarship on the chansons de geste is quite abundant, the bibliography is restricted to works cited, works devoted to the selected texts, and general studies that touch upon the tradition as a whole.

The term "Old French epic" is used here interchangeably with "chanson de geste," despite the unique place of the French medieval epic tradition with respect to "epic" in its broadest literary and historical sense. Titles of individual chansons de geste, many of which were bestowed by their modern editors, are given in French according to established usage. A bit thornier is the matter of character names and historical personages. Once again I adhere to common usage, noting, for example, that in English-language scholarship, Roland's companion Olivier is typically called Oliver, and Pépin le Bref is commonly known as Pepin the Short. When speaking of characters who are not eponymous heroes, I translate the particle "de" as "of" (e.g., Ernaut of Douai).

ACKNOWLEDGMENTS

This project has benefited from the expertise and generosity of many colleagues in the field of Romance epic. In particular I am deeply grateful to William C. Calin and Leslie Zarker Morgan for their insightful reading and critique of the book manuscript. Others provided valuable suggestions, information, and resources, especially François Suard, Bernard Guidot, Jean-Charles Herbin, Joseph J. Duggan, Jean-Pierre Martin, William W. Kibler, Jean-Claude Vallecalle, Keith Busby, and Simon Gaunt. I am indebted to Bernard Ribémont for organizing a series of stimulating colloquia on law and epic at the Université d'Orléans: his vast erudition is matched only by his extraordinary hospitality. It is impossible to name all those who contributed to my appreciation for the chansons de geste during the triennial congresses of the Société Internationale Rencesvals. In addition to those listed above, I wish to mention Philip Bennett, Alice Colby-Hall, Mary Jane Schenck, Emanuel Mickel, Edward Heinemann, Norris Lacy, and Sarah Kay. Special thanks are due to Françoise Denis for ideas shared on life and literature during countless rambles through Naples, Poitiers, Granada, and Oxford. In a more general sense, I am infinitely grateful to Douglas Kelly, whose scholarship and teaching continue to guide my formation as a medievalist.

I wish to acknowledge the Office of the Provost at the University of Georgia for a summer research grant that greatly facilitated the final phase of this book project. Additional funding was provided by the Willson Center for the Humanities and Arts and the Franklin College of Arts and Sciences. Among my colleagues at UGA, I thank in particular Noel Fallows, Alex Sager, Steven Grossvogel, Patrick Reidenbaugh, and Kristin Nielsen, who furnished crucial bibliographical references. Others offered advice and much-needed encouragement, particularly Debbie Bell, Francis Assaf,

Jan Pendergrass, Jonathan Krell, Stacey Casado, Diana Ranson, Nina Hellerstein, Doris Kadish, Sarah Spence, Betty Jean Craige, Tim Raser, and Rachel Gabara. I also owe a tremendous debt to the many undergraduate and graduate students who have contributed to my thinking, reading, and teaching of the chansons de geste over the last twenty-six years.

This book would not have come to fruition without the intellectual initiative and professional guidance provided by Barton Palmer and Tison Pugh: I thank them for inviting me to submit the manuscript and for replying to my frequent queries with patience and alacrity. It was a pleasure to work with Amy Gorelick, Shannon McCarthy, Nevil Parker, Ale Gasso, and the rest of the staff at the University Press of Florida; their tremendous kindness and efficiency facilitated the review and production stages of this project. Special thanks go to Ann Marlowe for her meticulous copyediting; the book benefited immeasurably from her erudition and attention to detail.

I am grateful to my daughter Sophie for her smiling words of encouragement and solemn inquiries into the progress of the manuscript. Finally, I reserve my most profound expression of gratitude to Richard Neupert, who has endured innumerable musings on Old French epic narrative and style for nearly three decades. I am sincerely thankful for his sound critical judgment and unwavering support.

1

The Historical and Poetic Context

Qui veust oïr chançon de biau semblant,
Si face paiz, si se traie en avant,
S'orra la flor de la geste vaillant
Du fiz Pepin, le riche roi poissant,
Des .XII. pers, qui s'entramerent tant.

[Let those who wish to hear a fine song be silent and come forward,
to hear the flower of the valiant *geste* of Pepin's son, the rich and
powerful king, and of the twelve Peers, who so loved each other.]

OTINEL

Definitions

The chansons de geste, or Old French epics, constitute a rich and distinc-
tive poetic tradition that enjoyed considerable popularity from the elev-
enth to the fifteenth century. The term *chanson de geste* comes down to us
from the Old French and reflects the dual nature of these texts.

(1) *Chanson* (song) refers to their musical dimension: the oldest poems
were originally sung by professional entertainers called jongleurs. While
there is ample evidence of this musical component in medieval narrative
and iconography, no extant manuscripts contain musical notation.[1] It is
generally believed that the melodies involved a monotonous chant, often
accompanied by a vielle, a medieval fiddle. Composed in "laisses," stanzas
of varying length, the chansons de geste retained their lyrical character to
some degree even in the later period, when they were no longer sung but
recited or read aloud.[2]

(2) *Geste* refers to the content or narrative dimension of the texts. A
feminine noun in Old French, *geste* derives from the Latin *gesta* (exploits)

and designates: (a) great deeds or feats of arms; (b) a chronicle or account; (c) a family or lineage; (d) a group of epic songs about a particular lineage.

Thus a chanson de geste is a song or stanzaic poem celebrating the exploits of a hero or clan. The texts tend to be lengthy, but there is a considerable range, from 870 lines in the *Voyage (Pèlerinage) de Charlemagne* (12th century) to 34,298 lines in the *Lion de Bourges* (mid-14th century). Although most of the narratives are set in the eighth and ninth centuries, they reflect the structure and values of the later feudal society that produced them. Heroes of the Old French epic belong almost exclusively to the noble warrior class. Their feats of arms are accomplished primarily in the context of "holy war" against Muslim and other non-Christian forces, but also involve conflicts arising within Christian society, such as territorial and matrimonial disputes, relations between lords and their vassals, and other questions of feudal justice.

Although medieval vernacular genres were not defined by a prescribed set of norms or criteria, poets and audiences did conceive of the chansons de geste as a coherent textual tradition distinguished by its formal properties as well as the provenance of its subject matter. The prologue of the late twelfth-century *Chanson des Saisnes* (Song of the Saxons), attributed to Jehan Bodel, classifies the prevailing text types by the nature of their sources:

> Ne sont que .III. matieres a nul home antandant:
> De France et de Bretaigne et de Rome la grant;
> Et de cez .III. matieres n'i a nule samblant.
> Li conte de Bretaigne sont si vain et plaisant,
> Cil de Rome sont sage et de san aprenant,
> Cil de France de voir chascun jor aparant. (vv. 6–11)

> [For anyone who understands, there are only three matters: of France, of Britain, and of Rome the great. And among these three matters there is no resemblance. The tales of Britain are thus insubstantial and pleasant, those of Rome are wise and instructive, those of France are true, as is every day apparent.][3]

Jehan Bodel thus associates the Breton *lais* and Arthurian romances with light entertainment, the romances of antiquity with moral instruction, and the chansons de geste—derived from indigenous source material—with veracity. Epic narrators frequently assert the antiquity and truth value of the material, exhorting audiences to participate in the celebration of a collective past.

The chansons de geste display many characteristics of the "epic" or the "heroic" as a transhistorical and transcultural mode. They are among the first texts in the French vernacular, emerging at the dawn of a national literature. Lengthy verse narratives devoted to martial subjects, they fuse history and myth in the interest of social cohesiveness. However, the Old French epic is somewhat less concerned with universal human values than works such as the Homeric epics or the Indian *Mahâbhârata*. The chansons de geste are firmly rooted in the specific struggles of the French medieval warrior aristocracy as it responded to the threats of Muslim dominance abroad and the rising power of the monarchy within.[4]

The earliest surviving chansons de geste date from the late eleventh or early twelfth century, with a period of intense production during the late twelfth and thirteenth centuries. The fourteenth and fifteenth centuries saw a decline in the composition of verse epic, but the tradition was perpetuated by prose "translations" of older works. While most of the chansons de geste are anonymous, some are attributed to known authors, such as the aforementioned Jehan Bodel of Arras, who is credited with lyric poems, fabliaux, and dramatic works in addition to the *Chanson des Saisnes*. Indeed, the distinction between author, performer, and scribe is often unclear: the earliest version of the *Chanson de Roland*, for example, is attributed to a certain Turoldus, whose identity and role in the transmission of the song remain unknown. For the purposes of this study, the "poet" will designate the person or persons, generally unknown, who composed a given chanson de geste, with the stipulation that authorship was a collective enterprise involving oral antecedents, written composition, and scribal intervention. When referring to the voice speaking in the text, I use "narrator" as a general designation and "narrator-jongleur" with regard to passages in which the voice of the performer intervenes to comment upon the tale or its telling.

Origins: The Traditionalist/Individualist Debate

Many chansons de geste contain a "kernel of truth," a connection to a documented historical event or authentic historical figure(s). The *Chanson de*

Roland, composed in the late eleventh or early twelfth century, is loosely based on an actual ambush that decimated Charlemagne's rear guard in 778. Guillaume d'Orange, hero of several twelfth-century epics, is highly reminiscent of Guillaume, Count of Toulouse (ca. 755–812). Indeed, modern scholars have unearthed numerous historical allusions in the epics, revealing prototypes for protagonists and minor characters, tracing itineraries and topographical references, and matching territorial conflicts from the Carolingian era to the wars depicted in the later poems. Between these historical antecedents and the surviving chansons de geste, however, lies a chronological gap of several centuries. Moreover, the songs radically transform both events and personages, all of which undergo various forms of poetic distortion. It is precisely this temporal and imaginative hiatus that has preoccupied scholars of the chansons de geste since the mid-nineteenth century. What was the nature of the poetic process leading to the flowering of epic poetry in the twelfth century? Who composed the extant poems and under what circumstances? What was occurring during the long centuries between the defeat of Charlemagne's rear guard and its appearance in Old French epic?

Scholars in the Romantic period conceived of epic poetry as a collective effort springing from the soul of the people. Drawing upon this notion, the renowned medievalist Gaston Paris (1839–1903) theorized that certain momentous events in the earlier Middle Ages were quickly commemorated in *cantilènes*, short lyrico-narrative pieces, perhaps composed by warriors, that were subsequently reworked and amplified over the ages by generations of oral poets.[5] According to this paradigm, the chansons de geste represent the culmination of a long oral tradition—originally Germanic—that was absorbed and elaborated by the itinerant jongleurs of northern France. Paris's student Joseph Bédier (1864–1938) vigorously opposed his mentor's "traditionalist" account. Given the absence of extant *cantilènes* or of any concrete proof of their existence, Bédier proposed a different scenario to explain the "silence of the centuries."[6] According to his "individualist" theory, the chansons de geste were composed by individual poets of genius who drew their inspiration from local legends preserved in churches and monasteries along the pilgrimage routes. In a solemn and now famous pronouncement, Bédier declared: "In the beginning was the route, the route lined with sanctuaries."[7] As evidence, he cited the numerous references to such sanctuaries in the poems, as well as the extraordinary beauty and artistry of works such as the *Chanson de Roland*. Obviously, Bédier's theory also had the advantage of supposing a French origin for the epics, an important point in the wake of the Franco-Prussian War (1870–71).[8]

The debate between partisans of these two positions continued throughout the twentieth century. "Neo-traditionalists" such as Ramón Menéndez Pidal maintained that the epic texts preserved in manuscripts attest to a succession of oral reworkings.[9] The neo-traditionalists adduced evidence pointing to the existence of stories and traditions that predate the oldest surviving epic texts. The late tenth- or early eleventh-century *Fragment de la Haye*, a Latin prose transposition of a hexameter verse work, mentions heroes from the Guillaume d'Orange cycle. The *Nota Emilianense*, dating from 1065–75, is a Latin summary of what may be a lost Spanish *Cantar de Rodlane*, and recounts Charlemagne's 778 expedition to Saragossa; among his men are Roland, Oliver, and Turpin, the most prominent warriors in the *Chanson de Roland*. Finally, archival evidence shows that the names Roland and Olivier were frequently given to brothers from the beginning of the eleventh century, suggesting that the heroic companions of the *Chanson de Roland* were already fixed in the popular imagination before the appearance of the "Oxford version" celebrated by Bédier.[10]

Advocates of the traditionalist position began to build upon the work of the Hellenists Milman Parry and Albert B. Lord, who studied actual performances of orally composed epic songs in Yugoslavia. Because they had developed a repertory of stock units of content and formulaic phrases, the Yugoslavian bards were able to re-create long verse narratives spontaneously.[11] While Lord and Parry had applied their findings to the Homeric epic, the Swiss scholar Jean Rychner examined oral-formulaic style in the chansons de geste in his groundbreaking 1955 study *La Chanson de Geste: Essai sur l'art épique des jongleurs*. With the advent of computer-generated concordances, scholars were able to examine the intricacies of formulaic language and to make a case for oral composition as a plausible explanation for the artistry of the earliest Old French epic songs.[12] The earlier manuscripts were believed to represent transcriptions of oral performances. These findings were not universally accepted. In 1981 *Olifant*, a journal devoted to the Romance epic, published a spirited debate between the American scholars William Calin and Joseph J. Duggan.[13] Responding to Duggan's research on formulaic style in the *Chanson de*

Roland, Calin rejected the notion that a high density of repeated phrases might serve as a reliable indicator of oral composition; furthermore, he questioned the applicability of the so-called "living epic" to the study of the chansons de geste. Duggan countered with a mordant justification of the merits of statistical analysis and a defense of the aesthetic value of oral literature.

Many scholars today espouse a synthesis of the traditionalist and individualist positions. The best articulation of such a compromise came from Pierre Le Gentil, who envisioned a lengthy period of disorganized, orally transmitted material—chants or proto-epic narratives—followed by a "sudden mutation" in the eleventh century.[14] This mutation was brought about by a convergence of circumstances: a changing society's desire to reestablish ties with its past and the advent of a crusading mentality, as well as the intervention of learned, talented poets whose composition preserves the formulaic patterns of oral poetry. Dominique Boutet maintains that while improvised performances likely continued in twelfth- and thirteenth-century France, we must keep in mind that the poems that have come down to us are in manuscript form and bear the marks of literate culture.[15] Indeed, it is not rare for epic narrators to cite the authority of written sources, and some present their works as clerical versifications of written historical documents.[16]

One may thus reasonably conclude that surviving written versions of the earliest chansons de geste were preceded by and based upon some form of popular oral tradition that was reworked by individual poets. The precise nature of this reworking and the relationship between oral composition, performance, and written documents are tantalizing questions that remain unresolved.

Medieval Reception

Medieval accounts suggest that in the twelfth and thirteenth centuries the chansons de geste were performed in a variety of contexts, fulfilling a number of moral and aesthetic functions. One oft-cited scenario is described in the treatise *De musica* by the late thirteenth-century musicologist Johannes de Grocheio, known in French as Jean de Grouchy:

> We call that kind of *cantus* a *chanson de geste* in which the deeds of heroes and the works of our ancient fathers are recounted. . . . This

kind of music should be laid on for the elderly, for working citizens and for those of middle station when they rest from their usual toil, so that, having heard the miseries and calamities of others, they may more easily bear their own and so that anyone may undertake his own labour with more alacrity. Therefore this kind of *cantus* has the power to preserve the whole city.[17]

Johannes thus envisions the chansons de geste as a tool for the inspiration and moral edification of working people. The epic heroes serve as magnifying mirrors allowing the masses to channel their suffering for the benefit of the public good. The ancestors' deeds were also believed to motivate knights preparing for battle. William of Malmesbury in his *Gesta regum Anglorum* (ca. 1125) reports that a song of Roland was sung at the Battle of Hastings "to fire them as they went into battle with the example of a heroic warrior."[18] In 1095 Pope Urban II is said to have cited the deeds of Charlemagne and his son Louis in his sermon exhorting Christian knights to join in the First Crusade.[19]

Fictional performances of the chansons de geste suggest that the songs served as entertainment for aristocratic audiences. In *Flamenca*, a thirteenth-century Occitan romance, jongleurs sing tales of Charlemagne during the wedding feast of Count Archambaud and the princess Flamenca.[20] The *Roman de la Rose ou de Guillaume de Dole* (ca. 1230) depicts a jongleur singing an excerpt from *Gerbert de Metz* for the emperor Conrad.[21] The epic *Raoul de Cambrai* (ca. 1200) relates that the noble Bertolai, eyewitness to an important battle, composed a song about it that was later heard in "many great halls."[22] Finally, there is textual and codicological evidence to suggest that the songs were known and appreciated in the monastic and ecclesiastical communities. Although the Church generally condemned jongleurs for their profligate lifestyle and barred them from the sacraments, references from sermons, penitentials, and other sources indicate greater tolerance toward those jongleurs who performed chansons de geste and saints' lives.[23] The chansons de geste thus had broad appeal and were disseminated to popular, courtly, and clerical audiences. By the end of the Middle Ages, there is evidence that certain epic texts were owned or circulated by women and by bourgeois patrons.[24]

It has often been supposed that oral performance, either singing or recitation, was the dominant model through the thirteenth century. Indeed,

the epic poems themselves occasionally allude to the interaction between
jongleur and audience. In the thirteenth-century *Huon de Bordeaux*, for
example, the narrator-jongleur pauses his tale to address his listeners:

> Segnor preudomme, certes, bien le veés,
> Pres est de vespre, et je sui moult lassé.
> Or vous proi tous, si cier com vous m'avés
> Ni Auberon ne Huon le membré,
> Vous revenés demain aprés disner;
> Et s'alons boire, car je l'ai desiré.
> . . . .
> Et si vous proi cascuns m'ait aporté
> U pan de sa chemise une maille noué. (vv. 4976–88)

[Worthy lords, surely you see well that it is nearly evening, and I
am very tired. Thus I pray all of you, out of esteem for me and for
Auberon and the valiant Huon, to return tomorrow after dinner, and
let us go and have a drink, for I have been wanting one. . . . And I beg
each of you to bring me, tucked in your shirttail, a bronze coin.][25]

Such passages are, however, problematic. On the one hand, they have led
scholars to posit that the chansons de geste were performed in sittings or
séances, an argument that is supported by narrative articulations in some
of the texts.[26] The jongleur's invitation to the tavern may thus be imagined
as a scripted pause for an oral performance. On the other hand, one must
be careful to avoid an overly literal interpretation: the epic narrators' calls
for silence, remuneration, and sustenance may very well be mere literary
artifices intended to punctuate the lengthy narrative and maintain contact
with the listener. In any case, by inscribing a performance context in the
works themselves, such interventions dramatize the complicity between
the audience and the narrator-jongleur, both of whom have a stake in the
tale and its telling.

The hypothesis of oral transmission as the predominant reception model
was long bolstered by the existence of modest, small-format manuscripts
that were believed to be "jongleur manuscripts" suitable for the itiner-
ant performer. However, codicological research has recently questioned
this model of ownership and performance. Many scholars now believe
that even the earliest manuscripts belonged to a more literate culture,
with more significant clerical participation than was previously thought.[27]

Keith Busby's research shows that manuscripts containing chansons de geste often display rhythmical marking, such as the "interpunct" or raised period at the caesura. Such notations may well have served as aids for oral performance or individual reading.[28] Produced at a time when oral and literate cultures coexisted and overlapped, the chansons de geste self-consciously engage in a nostalgic re-creation of archaic signifying practices.[29] Even if one posits the loss of the performer's physical presence—the traditional tale's principal guarantor of truth—the texts preserve the fiction of oral performance in the discourse of the narrator-jongleur, which regularly enjoins the audience to "listen," to "pay attention," to "be silent," that they may "hear" a "song" worthy of commemoration.

Sources and Relationship to History

We have seen that many chansons de geste draw upon distant historical figures and battles from the "matter of France."[30] A relatively small number of epics draw their material from more recent history, notably the late twelfth-century *Chanson d'Antioche*, which relates events from the First Crusade (ca. 1098) and purports to be a reworking of a song composed by an eyewitness. Links between the epics and documented events and personages are, however, extremely variable. While the *Chanson de Roland* and *Raoul de Cambrai* deploy and transform verifiable episodes from Carolingian history, the bitter and prolonged feud between the lineages of Lorraine and Bordeaux in *Garin le Lorrain* appears to have no basis in fact. The chansons de geste, particularly those of the later period (13th–15th centuries), drew their material from a wide range of sources, including folklore motifs. *Huon de Bordeaux* propels its hero from Charlemagne's court into the marvelous world of the fairy Auberon. *Hervis de Metz* and *Lion de Bourges* both incorporate the popular legend of the Grateful Dead, in which a spendthrift pays the debts of a dead man to ensure the latter's proper burial; the grateful spectre returns later to reward the hero in his hour of need. The fourteenth-century *Belle Hélène de Constantinople* is a version of the Handless Maiden tale, in which a persecuted heroine flees her father's incestuous desire. A number of epics include Arthurian motifs and even interludes situated in the Arthurian world.[31] Thus, while the "matter of France" serves as the framework for the Old French epic narrative, the genre was permeable to a variety of source materials, many of which it shared with romances of the period.

The main historical interest of the chansons de geste does not, however, reside in the strength of their ties to actual events. Rather, the ways in which the poets deform and rewrite history reveal the interactions between epic narratives and their immediate historical context. As Sarah Kay has written, the chansons de geste are "political fictions" whose "narratives are bounded by assumptions about the nature of the personal and the social, the licit and the illicit, the ethical and the unethical."[32] When a weak and unjust Charlemagne is trumped by the fairy king Auberon in *Huon de Bordeaux*, the real "kernel of truth" lies in the poet's response to contemporary problems, notably the conflicts opposing Louis IX and the high aristocracy.

Another historical perspective is provided by comparative studies that seek to establish traces of Indo-European ideological structures in the chansons de geste. Basing his research upon the anthropologist Georges Dumézil's work on "trifunctionality," Joël Grisward has identified avatars of the Indo-European tripartite division of societal functions: the sacred, represented by the sovereign/priest; the warrior function; and fertility or abundance, represented by characters associated with nourishment or riches.[33] This approach has met with some skepticism, partly because it privileges "deep structures" over the specifically feudal underpinnings of the Old French epics, and partly because it fails to account for the transmission and reception of the trifunctional model.[34] Nonetheless, Grisward's research has yielded some fascinating rereadings of individual works, portions of which correspond quite closely to Indo-European mythical structures.[35]

Form and Style

Verse Structure

While the chansons de geste share some thematic features with other medieval genres, their distinctive form sets them apart from other Old French narrative traditions. Most surviving epics of the first generation—that is, the twelfth century—are composed in assonanced decasyllabic laisses.[36] An excerpt from laisse 41 of *Garin le Lorrain* illustrates this basic structure:

maint cor d'olif i peüssiez oïr.
Ne puis cele hore que nasqui Jhesu Crist
ne fu nul jor nul si fier chapleïz.

. . . .
Se Dex ne fust, n'en eschapast un **vif**! (vv. 1793–1800)

[You would have heard many ivory horns. Not since the hour of Jesus Christ's birth was there ever so fierce a battle. . . . Were it not for God, no one would have escaped alive.][37]

The decasyllabic line typically exhibits "epic caesura," or a division into two parts, 4+6 syllables: "ne fu nul jor // nul si fier chapleïz." Much less frequent is the division 6+4. "Assonance" refers to the identical stressed (tonic) vowel at the end of each line. Although the words *oïr, Crist, chapleïz*, and *vif* do not rhyme (having different final consonants), they all share the stressed vowel *i*. In this case, the assonance is said to be "masculine," because the stressed vowel *i* is the final vowel in the line. When the stressed vowel is followed by the unstressed (atonic) vowel *e*, the assonance is said to be "feminine," for instance in lines ending in *mise, sire*, and *merite*, again with the stressed vowel *i*. Normally a change of assonance signals the beginning of a new laisse, whether or not the boundaries of the laisses are marked in the manuscripts.

From the thirteenth century on, the preferred metrical structure became alexandrine verse—twelve-syllable lines—with a regular division after the sixth syllable. At the same time, rhyme began to replace assonance, but there are many hybrid poems in which rhyme and assonance coexist.

Three early chansons de geste are noteworthy for the presence of a refrain. In the *Chanson de Roland*, the letters "AOI" appear 180 times, usually at the end of a laisse. Scholars have proposed numerous interpretations for this mysterious notation, including a war cry, a musical symbol, a scribal or recitational cue, a lamentation, and an abbreviation for "amen" or "alleluia."[38] The *Chanson de Guillaume* (mid-12th century) contains an intermittent refrain that articulates the chronological and affective progress of the narrative.[39] A four-line refrain occurs sporadically in the fragmentary *Gormont et Isembart* (late 11th or early 12th century), where it functions as an incantatory conclusion to a series of single combats. Because they occur in the oldest texts, these recurring phrases may represent vestiges of an ancient tradition of refrains in the Old French epic. In addition, a number of more recent epics contain a six-syllable feminine *vers orphelin* or "orphan verse" at the end of the laisse. Like the refrains, these short lines emphasize the boundaries of the laisse and have a distinct lyric quality. Though Jean

Frappier believed that the *vers orphelins* were modified versions of archaic refrains, it is more likely, as François Suard supposes, that they are later imitations of the older refrain device.[40]

Laisse Techniques

The epic laisse is a remarkably flexible structure that allows the chanson de geste to modulate between its narrative and lyric functions. Jean Rychner's influential study of epic artistry, *La chanson de geste: Essai sur l'art épique des jongleurs*, has shaped our modern understanding of the compositional techniques associated with the laisse. The following presentation owes a great deal to the classifications and terminology proposed by Rychner, as well as to Edward A. Heinemann's more recent study, *L'art métrique de la chanson de geste: Essai sur la musicalité du récit*.[41] In the epics that have come down to us, whether they are the products of oral or written composition, the laisse unites narrative movement with musical effects.

The length of the laisse varies considerably within a given text, and the average laisse length tends to be greater in later works. The *Chanson de Roland*, for example, averages 14 lines per laisse, with the shortest laisse containing 7 lines and the longest 26. The thirteenth-century *Hervis de Metz* averages 129 lines per laisse, with a range of 3 to 1,443. Rychner distinguishes between unified laisses, which recount one narrative event, and composite laisses, which incorporate multiple story elements. He privileges the shorter, unified stanzas in which strophic boundaries coincide with narrative junctures, believing that this is the only truly authentic epic structure. However, Old French epic poets did not conform to a predetermined set of norms, and this supposed generic "integrity" is present only in portions of the oldest extant poems, particularly in the much venerated *Chanson de Roland*. Most of the epics make wide use of the composite laisse, but this does not detract from the vital relationship between rhythm and meaning. As Heinemann insists,

> strophic structure *is* narrative movement: the initial position *marks* the beginning of a metrical incident; the passage from final position in one laisse to initial position in the following laisse *expresses* the movement from one incident to the next.[42]

Thus the laisse is a coherent metrical unit that imposes its own narrative organization.

The poets emphasize the boundaries of the laisse in a number of ways. Many laisses begin with an "intonation verse."[43] Typical phrases in the initial position include a protagonist's name or designation and the "epic" inversion of subject and verb, as in these examples:

> Li quens Guillelmes a la chiere hardie [Count Guillaume of the bold face][44]
>
> Grans fu la joie a Riviers la cité [Great was the joy in the city of Riviers][45]
>
> Halt sunt li pui e li val tenebrus [High are the hills and the valleys dark][46]

Similarly, the final line of a laisse can have a "concluding" timbre.[47] Following a deliberation or discourse, a character or group often expresses a closing opinion or decision, as in "Et cil respont: 'Tot a vostre plaisir!'" [And he responds: "As you wish!"].[48] Anticipatory or moralizing statements may also be placed at the end of a laisse for dramatic effect: "Tez fet la guerre ne la puet afiner" [He who wages war cannot put an end to it][49] or "Des or cumencet le cunseill qu'en mal prist" [Now begins the council that turned to grief].[50]

Epic laisses are often connected by patterns of repetition that create lyric pauses in the narrative. Among the most frequent forms of echo are the following:[51]

(a) The device known as *enchaînement* or linking is the narration of the same action at the end of one laisse and the beginning of the following laisse. The repetition may cover multiple lines or be limited to a single line, as in this example from *Hervis de Metz*:

> Passent les tertres, s'ont lo val avaleit,
> **Tant chevachait Hervis li baicheler.**
>   [laisse change]
> **Tresor chevache li damoisiax Hervis.**
> Ses oncle ataint qui en vont le chamin. (vv. 1771–74)

> [They pass the hills and descend into the valley; so far rode Hervis the young nobleman. Henceforth rides the young nobleman Hervis; he reaches his uncles who are continuing on their way.][52]

Although the action itself, Hervis riding after his uncles, is repeated, the repetition is not literal: it is a poetic reformulation. In the first occurrence the verb *chevacher* is in the past tense,[53] but the new laisse uses the present tense, giving the action more immediacy. Hervis's name is accompanied by two different epithets, *baicheler* and *damoisiax*, with roughly the same meaning—a young nobleman who has not yet entered knighthood—but one follows the name and the next precedes it. And of course, the change of laisse requires a change of assonance. The linking device creates a bridge between two laisses, lingering briefly over an action before revealing its aftermath.

(b) "Parallel laisses" are defined as a series of two or more laisses presenting an analogous action in a similar form. In laisses 17–19 of the *Chanson de Roland*, for example, Charlemagne consults his council of barons on the choice of an ambassador to King Marsile's court. In each successive laisse, distinguished knights come forward to offer their services, and in each case Charlemagne angrily rejects their offers. The *Roland* poet also uses parallel laisses to construct battle scenes: laisses 96–103 present analogous instances of single combat between high-ranking Christian and Saracen knights, with each laisse representing a new pair of adversaries. Despite their resemblances, "parallel" laisses are distinguished not only by a new assonance but also by the introduction of new narrative elements; this usually involves the substitution of new characters in the same narrative template. The device allows the poet to evoke parallel events occurring simultaneously (the set of single combats) or sequentially (the barons' offers of service). In neither case does the poet linger over the exact same event; rather, the same types of events are represented in roughly the same way.

(c) The term "similar laisses," on the other hand, is used to describe a series of two or more laisses presenting the same action in a slightly different perspective, with little or no narrative progress. This device, employed for moments of significant dramatic or emotional significance, reveals the full lyric potential of the laisse. The most celebrated examples are found in the *Chanson de Roland*, which uses similar laisses to represent Ganelon's treason, the quarrel between Roland and Oliver, and Roland's death. In each of these scenes, narrative time nearly stands still. When Oliver entreats Roland to sound his horn in three successive laisses, Roland's tripartite refusal contains subtle variations on the same basic notion: honor.[54] It is impossible to determine whether the sequence presents three separate exchanges between the two companions or three versions of the same event, each furnishing additional nuances. Reconstructing the "actual" fictional sequence is futile and beside the point, because similar laisses obscure narrative logic and chronology. For Rychner, such passages represent the chanson de geste at its finest: the poet's virtuosity consists in transforming story into song through the use of short, incantatory laisses.[55] However, the oft-praised strophic technique of the *Chanson de Roland* is quite exceptional. Rather than measuring other epics against this exemplar, more recent scholarship has come to appreciate the wide array of compositional devices applied to the epic laisse.[56] Common variations on the similar laisses include consecutive laisses with similar beginnings or extended similar passages whose parameters are not defined by laisse boundaries.

In addition to the patterns associated with consecutive laisses, parallel or similar passages may link stanzas that are separated by intervals of dozens or hundreds of lines. Heinemann refers to this device as "disjunctive echo."[57] It appears in both early and late chansons de geste and constitutes an irregular refrain that transcends strophic boundaries. In *Garin le Lorrain*, for example, the Bordelais Fromont asserts his innocence in the death of the Lorraine hero Begon, claiming that the act was performed without his knowledge or consent: "Puis li jurrai .xx. foïes ou .x. / que je nel vols, ne je nel consenti, / ne la ne fui ou li dus fu ocis" (vv. 10157–59) [Then I told him twenty or ten times, that I didn't wish this, nor did I consent to it, nor was I there when the duke was killed]. The disclaimer is repeated three times with only slight variations over a span of more than 1600 lines. Here the disjunctive echo is a recurring signal of impending doom: Fromont's declaration of innocence is predictably and consistently met with disbelief, culminating in a renewal of hostilities. While some scholars are skeptical about an audience's ability to process such widely spaced repetitions, Paula Leverage, in her study of memory and reception in the chansons de geste, outlines the cognitive processes that explain how audiences recognize disjunctive echo and perceive its aesthetic effects.[58]

For Rychner and other staunch traditionalists, the techniques associated with the epic laisse are closely tied to the conditions of oral composition and transmission. The linking device and similar laisses allowed the jongleur to pause before continuing his story and also highlighted essential passages for an audience that might be ambulatory or noisy. Whether or not one accepts the oral composition theory, it is clear that, at the very least, laisse technique was adapted to oral recitation and functioned to preserve the heritage of the oral tradition. The same may be said of the oral-formulaic modes of composition discussed next.

Formulaic Style

Old French epic poets made use of the compositional practices associated with oral-formulaic style. Their stories are conventional, constructed around typical episodes such as council scenes, battles, trials, pilgrimages, or the death of a hero. Within these larger units, stereotypical elements of narrative are treated in much the same way within a given text and across the genre. These stereotypical narrative units are known as *motifs*. Motifs serve as molds or templates that can be adapted to different characters and contexts.[59] The highly stylized "single combat with lances" is often used to demonstrate how epic motifs are constructed and adapted. This motif displays a number of basic elements: a knight spurs his horse, brandishes his lance, strikes his adversary with the lance, pierces the adversary's shield, pierces the adversary's hauberk, kills him, and utters a cry of victory, insult, or encouragement to his companions.[60] This basic configuration may be expanded or condensed and used in any epic confrontation; its versatility is well demonstrated in the parallel laisses 96–103 of the *Chanson de Roland*, mentioned above. Other common motifs include the mobilization of troops, the boast, the prayer uttered in extreme danger ("prière du plus grand péril"), the lament intoned upon the death of a hero, and the premonitory dream.

Within the framework of the motif, which spans a number of lines, content is rendered by means of *formulas*. The definition of a formula has been a matter of debate for many decades. Milman Parry's broad definition applies to oral-formulaic texts in general: "a group of words which is regularly employed under the same metrical conditions to express a given essential idea."[61] In the case of the chanson de geste, we will consider the formula to be a hemistich or line that is employed at least twice within the same poem to express a given narrative detail.[62] In the *Chanson de Roland*, for example, the slaying of the adversary at the end of single combat may be rendered by a four-syllable formula, "que mort l'abat" [he strikes him dead] with fourteen occurrences, or a six-syllable formula, "el camp mort le tresturnet" [he knocks him dead on the ground] with two occurrences.[63]

Other stock formulas, such as proper names or epithets ("li quens Rollant" or "Carles li reis"), may be inserted into any motif or any action falling outside the confines of conventional motifs.

Oral-formulaic style may initially strike the modern reader as unimaginative and tedious. It is important to remember, however, that medieval audiences appreciated conventional modes of discourse and perceived subtle variations and innovations in the use of motifs and formulas. Duggan points out:

> The long sequences of battle motifs, appearing similar to the point of excess to the modern reader, must have been appreciated by the audience of twelfth-century fighting men, and the differences expressed in substitute formulas, or the inclusion and exclusion of typical movements, are no less real for being difficult for us to appreciate.[64]

Other Stylistic Traits

The composition of individual verses and sentences, particularly in the earlier epics, is largely paratactic: that is, the poets frequently juxtapose ideas and clauses without using subordinating conjunctions. (Hypotaxis, the use of complex sentences with subordinate clauses, is more characteristic of romances.) Paratactic composition suppresses the logical links between phrases, as in "Nostre empereres les a oï tancier, / Celle part vint, ne s'i volt atargier" [The emperor heard them arguing; he went there; he did not wish to delay].[65] The poet does not specify that the emperor moved quickly *because of* the argument. As Duggan observes, parataxis does not often lead to ambiguity; rather, "the syntax itself, by its lack of explicit connectives, tends to draw the audience into the logical texture of the verse movement."[66]

The chansons de geste tend to represent characters through their external actions and words and thus make abundant use of direct discourse. Utterances are generally emphatic, privileging war cries, expressions of defiance, moral convictions, laments, and declarations of victory or revenge. Female-voiced discourse is no less forceful. In *Gerbert de Metz*, Queen Blanchefleur reacts vigorously to an accusation of adultery: "Puis dist en haut: 'Fel viez, tu as menti! / Se je fuisse hom, par le Dieu qui me fist, / Ja te feïsse l'arme du cors partir'" (vv. 1697–99) [Then she said loudly: "Treacherous old man, you lied! If I were a man, by God who made me, I would make your soul leave your body!"][67] Although there are instances of self-addressed monologue, particularly in the later epics, the chansons de geste are much less interested in the characters' interior life than are romances.

The narrator's voice also distinguishes epic style. As we have seen, the narrator-jongleur's interventions inscribe vestiges of performance, establishing contact and complicity with the audience. In the early chansons, the narrator gestures toward listeners by emphasizing shared values, as by using "nostre" in the opening line of the *Chanson de Roland*: "Carles li reis, nostre emperere magnes" (v. 1) [Charles the king, our great emperor]. There is no prologue to introduce the tale; the narrator plunges into the material in medias res, forging an immediate bond between past and present, jongleur and audience. According to Dominique Boutet, prologues became necessary when the audience's relationship to the past ceased to be clear and immediate.[68] These preambles typically begin with a *captatio benevolentiae*, exhorting the audience to listen. Guaranteeing the excellence of the song may entail a denunciation of other versions or other performers, as in this prologue from the thirteenth-century *Vivien de Monbranc*:

> Segnors, or escoutez, se Deus vous beneïe,
> Bonne canchon qui bien doit estre oïe.
> . . . .
> Chil autre jougleor ne vous en chantent mie,
> Quer il n'en sevent pas la monte d'une alie;
> Mes je vous en diroi, j'en soi toute la vie,
> La vraie estoire, or weil qu'el soit oïe. (vv. 1–18)

> [Lords, now listen, may God bless you, to a good song that deserves to be heard. . . . Other jongleurs won't sing about [Vivien's story], for they don't know beans about it. But I will tell you the true story; I've known it all my life, and now I want it to be heard.][69]

By preserving the direct address and ritual verbs of singing and listening, even a playful prologue such as this one locates itself within the traditional epic context of celebration.[70] For Paul Zumthor, the jongleur's performative discourse provides a glimpse of the text's "vocality," its historical grounding as an object of sensory perception.[71]

The narrator-jongleur's voice occasionally intervenes to comment upon the action. In the *Chanson de Roland*, when Charlemagne's rear guard is about to be attacked by 400,000 Saracens, the narrator exclaims: "Deus! quel dulur que li Franceis ne l' sevent!" (v. 716) [Oh God, how sad! The Franks know nothing of it!]. Anticipatory passages are frequent, particularly in older works. The narrator in the *Chanson de Roland* gives advance warning that Ganelon will betray and that Roland will die. To be sure, these events were well known to medieval audiences. However, the tendency to foreshadow is also an aesthetic choice. Hans-Robert Jauss distinguishes between the "if-suspense" of romance and the "how-suspense" of the chansons de geste. Romance narrators tend not to reveal the story's outcome in advance, while epic narrators adumbrate events to come with a good dose of foreboding: the narrative interest thus lies not in what will be told but how it will be presented.[72]

Epic Narratives

This section provides a broad outline of the epic narrative repertory. The closer readings of selected texts in chapter 3 illustrate in greater detail the components of the epic fictional world.

The chansons de geste are deeply rooted in the feudal society that took shape after the dissolution of the Carolingian empire. As the influential historian Georges Duby has shown, the Indo-European trifunctional model took on a particular form in the medieval Christian West, which envisioned a society divided into three groups: those who wage war (*bellatores*), those who labor (*laboratores*), and those who pray (*oratores*). The epic poems principally address the duties, tensions, and values associated with the first group, the warrior aristocracy. Feudal society depended on a system of interpersonal relations and mutual obligations linking the overlord to his vassals. Lords (including kings) owed their vassals protection and, increasingly, a fief that gradually became a hereditary possession. Vassals were obligated to provide counsel, military service, and unswerving loyalty. Many epic narratives are generated by the breakdown of these reciprocal obligations. How can a vassal remain loyal when his lord neglects to give him a fief (*Charroi de Nîmes*)? What are the stakes involved in betraying one's lord (*Chanson de Roland*)? Questions of feudal justice and the regulation of disputes abound in the chansons de geste.

A good number of these disputes are informed by the rivalry between an increasingly strong French monarchy and the great feudal lords who were threatened by royal power. It is important to note that feudalism was not a static or codified system to be "reflected" in the epics; attitudes and customs varied from region to region and changed over the course of the period. Moreover, the poems do not present a unified response to the problems posed by society; rather, individual texts grapple with these issues in different ways, imagining various responses to the pressures and disorders of feudalism. In the *Charroi de Nîmes*, Guillaume d'Orange responds to royal injustice by conquering his own fiefs from the Saracens; though he sharply rebukes King Louis, Guillaume remains ever loyal. In other epics, such as *Raoul de Cambrai* and *La Chevalerie Ogier de Danemarche*, the hero actively rebels against the monarch. These works constitute a thematic subgenre known as the "epic of revolt" or the "cycle of rebellious barons."[73]

Crime and punishment loom large in the plots of the chansons de geste.[74] Homicide, betrayal, land seizure, and rape are among the infractions depicted in the narratives. During the twelfth and thirteenth centuries, medieval France did not yet have a codified legal system; customs for settling conflicts varied from one region to another in a patchwork of interrelated practices, many of which were inherited from Germanic law. The chansons de geste, though preoccupied with legal customs and procedures, do not necessarily reflect contemporary legal practices but often hark back to earlier customs inherited from Germanic criminal justice. The regulation of conflict is a function of narrative and ideological imperatives and generally takes place in three principal contexts: seigneurial and royal power, divine justice, and familial solidarity.[75] This last category most often takes the form of the *faide* or blood feud, in which the wronged party initiates a private war of revenge. The Lorraine cycle generates a substantial portion of its narrative by renewing the cycle of violence that opposes two prominent lineages.[76] The *judicium Dei* (judgment of God) resolves conflict by pitting two knights against each other in a duel whose outcome is determined by God. The judicial duel was introduced into France by Germanic tribes and was still practiced during the time when most chansons de geste were composed—from the eleventh to the thirteenth century—though its use began to decline in the twelfth century.[77] Like other forms of ordeal, the *judicium Dei* assumes the immanence of divine power in human affairs. Since divine judgment wills the outcome of the battle, the role of the presiding judge in this feudal procedure is limited: he mainly serves to ensure the fairness of the proceedings and pronounce sentence.[78]

The majority of epics were composed during the Crusades (1095–1291). Drafted into the service of a universal Christian ideal, the warrior class was called upon to channel its aggression into the defense of the Church. A crusading ethos required new models of conduct and conviction, and many chansons de geste fulfill that role, portraying Christian knights dedicated to the reconquest of Spain, the defense of the Holy Land, and the general struggle against the military and cultural forces of Islam. Certain epics, such as the *Chanson de Roland*, may well have served a propagandist function. The famous line 1015 asserting that "Pagans are wrong, and Christians are right" reflects a Manichean stance and has led many to suppose that the chansons were composed in part to inculcate Christian knights with the crusading spirit. In fact, the representation of the Other in the Old French epic is anything but simple. The chansons de geste attest to the complexities of French medieval attitudes toward the Muslim world and its inhabitants.

Non-Christian adversaries in the poems are typically designated as "pagans" or "Saracens." The term "Saracen" is not used with any ethnic specificity and may refer to Vandals and Saxons as well as Arabs, Berbers, and Turks.[79] In most of the epics, Saracens are associated with Islam. The epic poets notoriously misrepresent the Islamic faith, depicting Muslims as polytheistic and the prophet Muhammad as a god. Portraits of Saracen knights often reveal demonic traits such as flaming red eyes and horns. They may bark like dogs, be covered in fur, or appear black as pitch. They are prone to treachery, barbarism, and deceit. Marked as morally, ethnically, and culturally Other, they often come from infernal lands plagued by obscurity and sterility. Their alterity serves in part to justify Western hegemony and the notion of "holy war" celebrated in so many epic works.

This sharply drawn portrait of the Saracen adversary is, however, attenuated by several factors. First of all, a "good Saracen" character type appears in a number of texts including *Aspremont*, *Aye d'Avignon*, and *Les Chétifs*; to be sure, such characters are on the path to conversion, and thus their "goodness" effectively aligns them with the Christian protagonists. Secondly, there is a tendency toward greater religious tolerance and cultural understanding in some later epics.[80] Finally, the impulse to construe the Other as alien is counterbalanced by a tendency to domesticate the foreigner.[81] The Saracens' sociopolitical structure strongly resembles that of the Christians; their religion is in some respects patterned after Christianity, with a "trinity" of pagan gods (Apollo, Tervagant, and Muhammad), a popelike caliph of Baghdad, and Mecca as an Islamic version of Jerusalem. The stock character of the Saracen Princess is a product of Western male wish-fulfillment: passionate and assertive, framed by an Oriental decor, she nonetheless corresponds to the Western ideal of feminine beauty, and she forsakes her faith and family for love of a Christian knight.[82] Thus the real (or imagined) Muslim world, resistant to religious conversion, is subject to narrative and cultural conversion in many of the epics. As Gérard Brault has demonstrated, the Saracens function as projective images: haunted by a rival civilization, the West projected its own faults onto the Saracen, fashioning the Other as a scapegoat.[83]

The chansons de geste marginalize other groups as well, including peasants, merchants, Lombards, and Jews. Because the poems are preoccupied with relationships between aristocratic males, women tend to play a subordinate role. Their function is, however, far from negligible. As Sarah Kay has written, female characters in epic "occupy the blank spaces created by the tangled lines of force among men. But a space, even a blank space, gives form to what surrounds it."[84] Indeed, though women are relegated to very minor roles in early epics such as the *Chanson de Roland*, female characters—mothers, sisters, wives, objects of desire—intervene in most chansons de geste to cement relationships between males or to circumvent and disrupt them. It is true that one might read epic women as mere pawns in the male competition for land and power. At the same time, many of these characters are sources of what Kay terms "counternarratives," alternative stories and discourses that run against the grain.[85] Notable examples include Marsent, the nun in *Raoul de Cambrai* who articulates a critique of violence, and Beatrice, the wife of *Hervis de Metz*, who compensates for the hero's deficiencies by means of craftsmanship and craftiness.[86] Guibourc, wife of Guillaume d'Orange, is a particularly strong and complex female epic figure: though she steadfastly supports her husband's mission, she assumes traditionally masculine roles and does not hesitate to challenge Guillaume's heroic identity.[87]

The chansons de geste are deeply concerned with kinship and lineage. Genealogy is one of the underlying principles of "cycle" formation, according to which epics were generated and organized around a particular lineage or *geste*.[88] The Guillaume d'Orange cycle, for example, originated in a core of poems devoted to Guillaume himself, but branched out to include his forebears, brothers, and nephews.[89] The epics as a whole place considerable emphasis on the uncle-nephew relationship. Maternal uncles in particular may substitute for an absent or deceased father, as in the *Chanson de Roland* and *Raoul de Cambrai*. W. O. Farnsworth attributed this tendency to the vestiges of a Germanic matrilineal system, but Jack Goody and others maintain that maternal uncles play an important role within the patrilineal system: whereas the father is a figure of authority, the uncle may appear as a nurturing mentor.[90] For their part, nephews often function as key allies, as in the songs devoted to the childless Guillaume d'Orange. The narrator in *Aye d'Avignon* formulates the value of this bond in terms of a proverbial truth: "Por ce dit on encore: Ainz venge niez que fiz" [For this reason it is still said: better a nephew than a son].[91]

Epic narratives are often described in terms of their opposition to the characteristics of Arthurian romance. The chanson de geste is said to portray collective action, with heroes operating in the public sphere, surrounded by their peers and members of their lineage; conversely, the Arthurian knight undertakes a solitary quest in view of individual growth. Epic heroes perform exploits; romance heroes have adventures. Romance heroes undergo an initiation process and tend to develop over the course of the quest, while epic heroes have a more fixed identity, becoming ever more like themselves.[92] The chivalric ideal of romance combines martial prowess and courtly love; epic chivalry privileges prowess, placing erotic love in the service of territorial conquest and conjugal love in the interest of lineage. Chansons de geste eschew the Celtic marvels of romance, favoring divine interventions such as miracles and premonitory dreams.

This table of binary oppositions is not without merit, since chansons de geste and romances did fulfill different sets of audience expectations. However, the stark contrasts apply only to the very earliest works; both textual traditions continually tested out new narrative possibilities and influenced each other. In the case of epic, the most striking generic innovations appear in the works William Kibler has dubbed the *chanson d'aventures*.[93] Beginning in the thirteenth century, there appeared a substantial group of works that preserved the epic form and general framework but incorporated narrative ingredients associated with romance; the innovations in content coincided with a progressive lengthening of the laisse and an attenuated lyricism. *Huon de Bordeaux*, for example, includes not only the aforementioned fairy interlude but also a set of exotic Oriental adventures. *Parise la Duchesse* and *Lion de Bourges*, among others, construct their narratives around the "family romance" plot, in which a lost child is reunited with his family after a lengthy separation teeming with adventures. Many of the thirteenth-century *chansons d'aventure* exhibit a bipartite or tripartite structure, with more conventionally "epic" plots being resolved by romance narrative strategies, or vice versa.[94] Such innovations do not, however, signal a degradation of Old French epic or herald its demise. As Simon Gaunt has written, "Generic boundaries are not defined in influential, but unwritten rule-books; they are constructed and transformed through textual production."[95] One of the greatest misconceptions about the chanson de geste is that it peaked with the *Chanson de Roland* and was then supplanted by romance, the latter being deemed a more "complex" textual tradition.[96] In fact, the epic tradition continued to thrive throughout the Middle Ages, engaging in a productive dialogue with its competing genre.[97] Like romance, the chanson de geste experienced a renewal in the later medieval period thanks to a wave of prose adaptations that appealed to changing tastes.[98]

French medieval narrative traditions, therefore, exhibit some degree of generic overlap. The chansons de geste share many traits not only with romance but also with saints' lives. Hagiographic works, which Johannes de Grocheio does not distinguish from chansons de geste, also celebrate exemplary figures in a highly stylized form. The late eleventh-century *Vie de Saint Alexis* is composed in assonanced decasyllabic stanzas whose tonality has often been compared to the *Chanson de Roland*. In some instances the same narrative was adapted to both traditions. The legend of *Ami et Amile*, for example, survives in a number of versions, including hagiographic texts, romances, and a miracle play, as well as a chanson de geste.

One of the Old French epic's closest relatives in modern times is the classic Hollywood western genre. Though one cannot speak of direct influence, both traditions involve foundational myths that seek to elaborate a collective national (or proto-national) identity. Like the early chansons de geste, many westerns are loosely based on historical events; they promulgate a white male ideology of conquest and social order, with a clear delineation between good and evil and highly stereotyped versions of the nonwhite adversary; and they offer at once a critique and a poetics of violence, staging large-scale confrontations between opposing societies or clans. Both genres expanded and endured by questioning the very tenets and techniques that engendered them.

We cannot champion many of the values celebrated by the chansons de geste, and thus their ritual, participatory function is largely lost to us today. What we can appreciate, however, is the combination of "good song" and "great story" so justly vaunted by the epic narrators.

2

The Texts—An Overview

N'ot que trois gestes en France la garnie;
ne cuit que ja nus de ce me desdie.
Des rois de France est la plus seignorie,
et l'autre aprés, bien est droiz que jeu die,
fu de Doon a la barbe florie,
cil de Maience qui molt ot baronnie.
. . . .
De ce lingnaje, ou tant ot de boidie,
fu Ganelon, qui, par sa tricherie,
en grant dolor mist France la garnie.
. . . .
La tierce geste, qui molt fist a prisier,
fu de Garin de Monglenne au vis fier.
. . . .
Einz roi de France ne vodrent jor boisier;
lor droit seignor se penerent d'aidier,
. . . .
Crestïenté firent molt essaucier.

[There were only three *gestes* in wealthy France; I don't think any-
one would ever contradict me on this. The most illustrious is the
geste of the kings of France; and the next, it is right for me to say, was
the *geste* of white-bearded Doon de Mayence. . . . To this lineage,
which was full of disloyalty, belonged Ganelon, who, by his duplic-
ity, plunged France into great distress. . . . The third *geste*, remarkably
worthy, was of the fierce Garin de Monglane. . . . Those of his lineage
never once sought to deceive the king of France; they strove to help
their rightful lord, . . . and they advanced Christianity.]

BERTRAND DE BAR-SUR-AUBE, *GIRART DE VIENNE*

Since the Middle Ages, the corpus of chansons de geste has been di-
vided into groups based on various criteria. In the above prologue to the
thirteenth-century *Girart de Vienne*, Bertrand de Bar-sur-Aube classifies

epics according to their heroes' lineage. He uses the word *geste* to refer to the lineage itself, the deeds attributed to members of this lineage, and the songs commemorating these deeds. The first *geste* is associated with Charlemagne and members of his family, including his renowned nephew Roland. The second grouping revolves around the lineage of traitors that produced Ganelon, who betrayed Roland at Roncevaux. Bertrand's own chanson belongs to the *geste* of Guillaume d'Orange, named here for his illustrious ancestor Garin de Monglane.

Modern scholars use the term "cycles" to categorize the chansons de geste as well as other vernacular narrative assemblages such as the prose Tristan and Lancelot-Grail cycles. When applied to the epic, the notion of cycle takes into account the genealogical component inherent in Bertrand's taxonomy. A typical process of cyclic formation involved an initial song whose popularity led to sequels and prequels featuring the same hero as well as his forebears, descendants, or other relations. Epic cycles, then, proliferated in much the same way as the *Star Wars* films, by a gradual amplification of existing material through accretion. Cyclic prequels may relate the hero's early exploits (*enfances*), while sequels may include a hero's death or retirement to a monastery (*moniage*); the cycle of Guillaume d'Orange exemplifies this form of cyclicity. Moreover, many works in the *geste* of Guillaume are preserved in "cyclical" manuscripts that group the related texts materially. When individual works were gathered into cyclical manuscripts, they often required adjustments to link separate source texts and resolve contradictions. (Often, however, compilers dispensed with the fine-tuning and did not attempt to eliminate narrative inconsistencies among texts.)[1] Cyclification was part of a larger intellectual movement in the thirteenth century that sought to categorize vast bodies of knowledge in an attempt to achieve encyclopedic wholeness.[2]

The other two cycles cited by Bertrand do not display the same kind of "organic" integrity as the Guillaume cycle. The *geste* of the King(s) could theoretically encompass any works featuring Charlemagne, his father Pepin the Short, his grandfather Charles Martel, or his son Louis the Pious. Modern scholars, however, speak of a more limited "Charlemagne cycle," which François Suard divides into two thematically coherent subgroups: works pertaining to the disaster at Roncevaux and works in which Charlemagne figures prominently.[3] Unlike the Guillaume cycle, the Charlemagne cycle is not characterized by a clear cyclical manuscript tradition.

Similarly, the *geste* of Doon de Mayence is a problematic category that imposes a genealogical unity upon disparate works portraying barons who rebel against royal authority. This group, commonly known today as the "cycle of rebellious barons" or the "epic of revolt," includes works devoted to Ganelon's lineage as well as autonomous texts such as *Raoul de Cambrai*. Other significant epic clusters not mentioned by Bertrand are the Lorraine cycle and the Crusade cycle.

As the epic tradition developed, poets sought to promote their tales and characters by forging links with those of other, more prestigious cycles. Thus *Hervis de Metz*, a prequel to the Lorraine cycle, identifies its heroine Beatrice as the great-aunt of Charlemagne.[4] Moreover, some poems partake of multiple cycles: in *Girart de Vienne*, Charlemagne and Roland play a significant role, the heroes are part of the lineage of Garin de Monglane, and they rebel against Charlemagne.[5]

This overview begins with the principal French epic cycles outlined above, followed by discussion of notable works that fall outside these broad categories. Separate sections are devoted to the French epics of the later period (14th–15th centuries) and Occitan texts. An appendix before the endnotes provides a list of the chansons de geste cited, with approximate dates, number of lines, and type of versification.

The Charlemagne Cycle

> Li premiers des enfans, de ce ne doutez mie,
> Que Pepins ot de Berte, la blonde, l'eschevie,
> Orent il une fille, sage et bien ensaignie,
> Fenme Milon d'Aiglent, molt ot grant seignorie,
> Et fu mere Rollant qui fu sans couardie,
> Ains fu preus et hardis, plains de chevalerie.
> Aprés ot Charlemaine a la chiere hardie,
> Qui puis fist seur paiens mainte grant envaie. (vv. 3473–80)

[The first of the children—do not ever doubt this—that Pepin had from the blonde and elegant Bertha was a daughter, wise and cultivated, the wife of Milon d'Aiglent, who had great power; she was the mother of Roland, who was without cowardice; on the contrary, he was valiant and bold, full of chivalry. Then there was Charlemagne of the bold countenance, who launched many great attacks on the pagans.]

BERTE AS GRANS PIÉS

The chansons de geste played a significant role in the elaboration of the medieval Charlemagne legend. The point of departure for the Charlemagne cycle is the *Chanson de Roland*, which dates from the late eleventh or early twelfth century and is one of the oldest specimens of Old French epic poetry. This text, examined in greater detail in chapter 3, recounts the tragic loss of Charlemagne's rear guard at Roncevaux. Charlemagne's nephew Roland incurs the wrath of his stepfather Ganelon, who plots with the Saracen king Marsile to ambush Roland and his companions. Though they defend themselves valiantly, the knights of the rear guard all perish, including the twelve Peers, the elite of the imperial army. They are avenged when Charlemagne and his army return to wage a second battle and when Ganelon, found guilty of treason, is executed.

A number of later songs constitute preludes to the Battle of Roncevaux. *Gui de Bourgogne* (early 13th century) relates Charlemagne's earlier Spanish expeditions, alluded to in the first laisse of the *Roland*: "Set anz tuz pleins ad estét en Espaigne" (v. 2) [He [Charles] had been in Spain seven long years].[6] During the absence of Charlemagne and his barons, a new generation comes of age in France. They join their fathers in Spain and are instrumental in a number of victories against the Saracens. While Charlemagne is on a pilgrimage to Compostela, Gui de Bourgogne captures the city of Luiserne, but Roland challenges him for the honor of presenting it to Charlemagne. The emperor quells the dispute and prays God to destroy Luiserne; Charlemagne's prayer is answered, and his army sets out toward Roncevaux. *Aspremont* (late 12th century) is less directly related to Roncevaux but does invent a partial backstory for Roland. The tale opens with the arrival of a Saracen envoy, Balant, who announces that the pagan king Agolant threatens to have his son Aumont crowned in Rome. Charlemagne and his troops undertake an expedition to Aspramonte in southern Italy, but the emperor first imprisons his impetuous nephew Roland, deemed to young to participate. Eventually Roland breaks free, and he and his companions help the Frankish forces to defeat the Saracens. A portion of the poem is thus devoted to Roland's *enfances*: in his first great exploit, the defeat of Aumont, Roland conquers the emblematic objects that will accompany him to Roncevaux—his horn (*olifant*), his horse Veillantif, and his mighty sword Durendal. The "good Saracen" envoy Balant, persuaded of the superiority of Christianity by Charlemagne's trusted adviser Naimes, converts after the Frankish victory. Other pre-Roncevaux Spanish expeditions are related in *Otinel* and *Fierabras*, both from the twelfth century.

The well-known *Voyage* (or *Pèlerinage*) *de Charlemagne à Jérusalem et à Constantinople* presents a very different image of Charlemagne and the twelve Peers. This short twelfth-century epic is a mostly comic tale that mocks elements of the heroic tradition. In an attempt to prove his superiority to the emperor Hugo of Constantinople, Charlemagne undertakes a voyage, stopping first in Jerusalem, where he receives relics from the patriarch. He then proceeds to Constantinople, a city so dazzling in its riches that it outshines all of Charlemagne's possessions. The twelve Peers indulge in drunken boasts (*gabs*), the most outrageous of which is Oliver's sexual boast with regard to Hugo's daughter. With God's help, the Peers are able to accomplish their rash boasts, terrifying Hugo. In the end, Hugo pays homage to Charlemagne, and Oliver declares his love to the Byzantine princess. The latter relationship comes to the fore in *Galien le Restoré*, which survives only in a fifteenth-century reworking but is thought to date from about 1200.[7] Galien, the bastard son of Oliver and Hugo's daughter Jacqueline, participates in the Battle of Roncevaux, where he encounters his dying father. The narrative multiplies the adventures of Galien and reconfigures the Roncevaux material around the restoration of Galien's family honor.

Several songs depict Charlemagne's reign in the wake of Roncevaux. The *Chanson des Saisnes* by Jehan Bodel (late 12th century) relates Charlemagne's campaigns against the Saxons. The Saxon king Guiteclin invades Charlemagne's lands in the hope that the emperor and his troops have been weakened and demoralized by the loss of the twelve Peers. The hero Baudouin, nephew of the emperor, and his companion Berart are strongly reminiscent of Roland and Oliver. In accordance with the prologue, which promises a song "de chevaleries, d'amours et de cembiaus" (v. 26) [of chivalry, of love, and of combat],[8] the narrative recounts Baudouin's military and amorous exploits. When Charlemagne slays Guiteclin, Baudouin marries Guiteclin's widow, Sebile, who converts to Christianity. Later in the poem, however, Baudouin and Berart are killed in battle and mourned by Charlemagne. Saxony is conquered at last, and a converted Saxon is crowned king. The thirteenth-century song *Gaydon* prolongs the tale of Thierry, who prevailed in the judicial combat against Ganelon's relative Pinabel at the end of the *Chanson de Roland*. Thierry, now the Duke of Angers, has taken the name Gaydon because a jay alit on his helmet during that famous duel. Ganelon's brother poisons one of Charlemagne's men and accuses Gaydon of the crime. Gaydon proves his innocence in a judicial combat, but Charlemagne continues to have dealings with the traitors in his court. Gaydon rebels against Charlemagne, and after a series of unsuccessful diplomatic missions and military operations, Gaydon saves the emperor's life and the two are reconciled. The chanson *Gaydon*, therefore, is also associated with the cycle of rebellious barons. In *Anseïs de Carthage* (= Cartagena), also from the thirteenth century, the emperor conquers all of Spain and has Anseïs crowned king. Marsile, who has survived the Battle of Roncevaux in this version, invades the newly reconquered Spain but is eventually defeated. When he refuses to convert to Christianity, the emperor, recalling the demise of his twelve Peers, has Marsile beheaded. In the closing lines the aged Charlemagne returns to Aachen, falls ill, and dies.

Other works seek to expand the poetic biography of Charlemagne and his forebears. *Berte as grans piés* (Bertha of the Big Feet), a late thirteenth-century *chanson d'aventures* by Adenet le Roi, is a reworking of a lost poem that draws upon folklore motifs to invent the tale of Charlemagne's mother. Bertha, daughter of the king of Hungary, is engaged to Pepin, but an evil nurse substitutes her own daughter for the future queen and accuses the real Bertha of murder. The persecuted heroine finds refuge and remains hidden for nine years, until her mother unmasks the false queen, who does not have large feet like the real Bertha. Pepin and Bertha are united, and the poem's epilogue announces the birth of Charlemagne. *Mainet*, which survives only in a late twelfth-century fragmentary reworking, relates Charlemagne's early exploits or *enfances*. When traitors force the young Charlemagne to flee Pepin's court, he offers his services to the emir Galafre of Toledo. He changes his name to Mainet (diminutive of *magne*) and falls in love with Galafre's daughter Galienne.

At the very end of the thirteenth century, Girart d'Amiens composed—at the behest of his patron Charles of Valois, brother of Philip the Fair—the *Istoire le Roy Charlemaine*, a compilation in rhymed alexandrine laisses that draws upon both chansons de geste and chronicles. This lengthy work of 23,348 lines aims to provide a complete portrait of Charlemagne's reign. Here the wise and valiant emperor of the *Chanson de Roland* is portrayed as a pragmatic and visionary leader.[9] Other epic narratives pertaining to Charlemagne survive in Franco-Italian versions.[10]

The Cycle of Guillaume d'Orange

> Bone chançon plest vous a escouter
> Del meillor home qui ainz creüst en Dé?
> C'est de Guillelme, le marchis au cort nes,
> Conme il prist Nymes par le charroi monté;
> Aprés conquist Orenge la cité
> Et fist Guibor baptizier et lever
> Que il toli le roi Tiebaut l'Escler;
> Puis l'espousa a moillier et a per,
> Et desoz Rome ocist Corsolt es prez.
> Molt essauça sainte crestïentez.
> Tant fist en terre qu'es ciels est coronez. (vv. 3–13)

[Would it please you to hear a good song about the best man who ever believed in God? It is about Guillaume, the marquis with the short nose: how he captured Nîmes with the carts, and then conquered the city of Orange, and captured Guibourc from the pagan King Tibaut and had her baptized, and then took her as his wife, and killed Corsolt in the fields outside Rome. He greatly exalted holy Christendom. He accomplished so much on earth that he is crowned in heaven.]

LE CHARROI DE NÎMES

The cycle known as the *geste de Guillaume*, the *geste de Monglane*, or the *geste des Narbonnais* is a group of twenty-four poems devoted to an illustrious family.[11] At the core of the cycle is Guillaume d'Orange, a colorful hero based loosely on Guillaume, Count of Toulouse (ca. 755–812), who was defeated by the Saracens at Orbieu but subsequently captured Barcelona.[12] The historical Guillaume eventually founded the abbey of Gellone, which was later renamed Saint-Guilhem-le-Désert; he died in 812. The epic hero Guillaume follows a similar trajectory, devoting his chivalric career to war against the Saracens in the South before withdrawing to a monastery in his old age. The epic and historical figures appear to have fused early on and were already assimilated by the early twelfth century.[13] The monastic *Vita sancti Wilhelmi* (ca. 1125), for example, appropriates the epic hero's exploits to enhance the reputation of the saintly Count of Toulouse. The cycle originated with a cluster of songs about Guillaume and then branched out to include tales of his vast lineage, including brothers, brother-in-law, nephews, father, uncles, great-uncles, and great-grandfather

Garin de Monglane. It is the largest cycle of Old French epic poetry, with most of its works preserved in vast "cyclical manuscripts" that group individual songs according to fictional chronology.[14]

In the cyclical manuscripts, the core of Guillaume's epic biography is represented in three related works, all composed in the mid-twelfth century: the *Couronnement de Louis* (Coronation of Louis), the *Charroi de Nîmes*,[15] and the *Prise d'Orange* (Conquest of Orange). The *Couronnement de Louis* initiates the tenuous but enduring vassalic bond between the hero and Louis the Pious, son of Charlemagne. In order to ensure the proper succession to the throne, Charlemagne has Louis crowned as a young boy, though he recognizes the child's weak character. When Arneïs of Orléans threatens to usurp young Louis's power, Guillaume "Fierebrace" (of the Mighty Arms) kills the traitor with his bare hands. He then sets out for Rome, where he rescues the pope from the Saracens. It is here that Guillaume vanquishes the giant Corsolt, who slices off a piece of his nose; the hero thus earns the sobriquet "Guillaume of the Short Nose."[16] In the remaining episodes, Guillaume saves both Louis and the pope from would-be usurpers, and he gives his sister Blanchefleur in marriage to Louis. The opening of the *Charroi de Nîmes* further illustrates Guillaume's valor and Louis's shortcomings. In distributing fiefs and wives to his vassals, the king has forgotten Guillaume, his most trusted and valuable knight. Furious, Guillaume leaves the court and manages to take Nîmes from the Saracens by deploying a ruse of the Trojan-horse variety. In the *Prise d'Orange*, he proceeds to conquer the city of Orange and its Saracen queen Orable, wife of King Tibaut. Orable is baptized, taking the name Guibourc, and she and Guillaume marry. The *Charroi de Nîmes* and the *Prise d'Orange* are analyzed in more detail in chapter 3.

Guillaume's later exploits appear in the *Chanson de Guillaume*, a song that does not figure in the cyclical manuscripts. It survives in a single Anglo-Norman manuscript from the thirteenth century, and though it contains some of the most primitive elements of the Guillaume legend, the text shows evidence of considerable reworking.[17] Scholars generally divide the work into two main parts, G1 and G2. The first part relates a battle at l'Archamp between the forces of the Saracen Desramé and a much smaller Christian army that includes Guillaume's nephew Vivien. Abandoned by the cowardly Tedbalt of Bourges, Vivien, who has vowed never to retreat in the face of the enemy, falls on the battlefield. Guillaume sets out for l'Archamp to aid Vivien, but instead loses two more nephews in battle. Guibourc raises an army to support Guillaume's efforts at l'Archamp, and eventually Desramé is slain. At the beginning of G2, Guillaume finds Vivien lying beneath an olive tree beside a fountain, his hands crossed, his body exuding a sweet odor. Overcome, Guillaume pronounces a *planctus* and gives communion to his martyred nephew, who perishes. Vivien's poignant and highly charged death scene has often been compared to the death of Roland in the *Chanson de Roland* and that of Begon in *Garin le Lorrain*. The greater part of G2, however, is devoted to the heroicomic exploits of Rainouart, a scruffy giant who wields a large club with considerable success. At the end of the poem, the Saracen forces are vanquished thanks to Rainouart, who turns out to be Guibourc's long-lost brother. A striking formal feature of the *Chanson de Guillaume* is the presence of an intermittent refrain that serves both a chronological and an incantatory function. The refrain takes three forms—"lunsdi al vespre" (Monday at vespertide), "joesdi al vespre" (Thursday at vespertide), and "lores fu mecresdi" (then it was Wednesday)—with the first occurring most frequently.

The material from the *Chanson de Guillaume* appears in the cyclical manuscripts as well, but it is distributed over two songs, *Aliscans* and the *Chevalerie Vivien*. Other works in Guillaume's epic biography are the *Enfances Guillaume* (13th century), which recounts the hero's youth, and the *Moniage Guillaume* (later 12th century), which tells of his uneasy transition to religious life. The *Moniage*, which exists in both a short and a long version, portrays an aging Guillaume, desolate after the death of his wife and repenting of the numerous lives he has taken. Though he withdraws first to the monastery of Aniane and then to a hermitage, his chivalric instincts and loyalties cause him to emerge repeatedly from retirement. It is only after he has slain the giant Ysoré that Guillaume retreats definitively from the world. He builds a bridge over the river Hérault to allow pilgrims easier passage to Santiago, successfully fighting a demon who would undo his work. The narrator assures us that the bridge may still be seen by visitors to the place henceforth known as Saint-Guilhem du Désert.

Spin-offs from *Aliscans* include two works about Rainouart (the *Bataille Loquifer* and the *Moniage Rainouart*) as well as the story of Vivien's earlier adventures (*Enfances Vivien*), all dating from the thirteenth century. Another group of poems forms a sub-cycle that revolves around Guillaume's father Aymeri de Narbonne and his progeny and also forges links with the Roncevaux material. *Aymeri de Narbonne* (13th century) relates the conquest of Narbonne, represented as vengeance for the Roncevaux disaster. In the *Narbonnais* (13th century), Aymeri sends six of his seven sons into the world to embark on their chivalric careers; they return to repel a Saracen invasion. A younger Aymeri appears in *Girart de Vienne* (late 12th century), and his final adventures and death are the subject of the *Mort Aymeri de Narbonne* (late 12th century). Other branches are devoted to Guillaume's brothers and nephews, notably the thirteenth-century *Siège de Barbastre*, *Guibert d'Andrenas*, and *Prise de Cordres et de Sebille*.[18] The cycle reaches back to the founding of the lineage with *Garin de Monglane* (13th century, largely unedited) and to younger generations with *Foucon de Candie* and the *Enfances Renier* (both 13th century).

The Rebellious Baron Cycle

> "Je suis uns hon c'on m'a fait escillier
> De doche France et banir e cachier;
> Che m'a fait Kalles qi France a a baillier,
> Ne m'a laissié qi vaille un suel denier." (vv. 3378–81)
> ["I am a man exiled from sweet France, banished and driven away. Charles, who governs France, did this to me; he left me nothing worth a single cent."]
>
> LA CHEVALERIE D'OGIER DE DANEMARCHE

This section considers the works associated with the family of Ganelon's grandfather Doon de Mayence as well as other major poems representing a baron in conflict with his king. The epics of revolt are generally sympathetic to the rebellious baron, who suffers at the hands of an unjust or weak monarch. Nonetheless, as William C. Calin explains, "due to the never-diminished aura of the royal ideal, the official philosophy of the Church, and a very real desire for order among the people, revolution is never allowed to succeed."[19]

Ogier le Danois

Ogier le Danois (the Dane) was one of the most popular epic heroes of the French Middle Ages. The Ogier legend may be traced to the historical figure Autcharius, a vassal of Charlemagne's brother Carloman who fled after Carloman's death to the court of the Lombard king Desiderius, where he fought against Charlemagne on behalf of Carloman's sons. An early Ogier legend is attested in an eleventh-century clerical text, the *Conversio Othgerii militis*, in which a certain Othgerius, one of Charlemagne's warriors, entered the monastery at Meaux.[20] The epic hero Ogier has a dual identity, appearing in some texts as a loyal vassal and in others as a rebel baron. He is mentioned at the beginning of the *Chanson de Roland*, in the same line as the archbishop Turpin, as one of the barons convened by Charlemagne in the council scene (v. 170); he is also present at the judicial combat that determines Ganelon's guilt (v. 3937). Ogier's revolt narrative is preserved in *La Chevalerie Ogier de Danemarche*, attributed to Raimbert de Paris; this composite text is an early thirteenth-century reworking of an older, lost poem. The first 3,100 lines represent a later addition recounting the hero's *enfances*. This preamble is followed by the core narrative, a bitter conflict that arises when Charlemagne's son Charlot flies into a rage during a chess game and beats Ogier's son to death with a chessboard. Ogier refuses any reparation other than Charlot's death, to which Charlemagne cannot consent. Ogier, furious, kills the queen's nephew and is obliged to flee. He makes his way to Pavia, where he offers his services to the Lombard king Desier and receives the fief of Castelfort, to which Charlemagne lays siege. Ogier is eventually captured by the archbishop Turpin, who grants him protection while keeping him in captivity. When Charlemagne is menaced by the giant Saracen Brehier, Ogier is released, saves the realm, and marries a princess. The poem's epilogue foreshadows Ogier's death and burial at Meaux (v. 12342).

The Geste de Doon de Mayence

A cyclical manuscript from the fourteenth century joins the originally independent *Chevalerie Ogier* to two later poems, artificially linking the rebellious baron material to the *geste de Doon de Mayence*.[21] *Doon de Mayence* (later 13th century) begins, like the *Chevalerie Ogier*, with the *enfances* of its hero. Subsequently it relates a temporary conflict between Doon and Charlemagne. Hearing that the proud Doon has neglected to pay his respects at court, an irate Charlemagne declares that Doon is a poor, unknown rascal with no right to Mayence. When Doon's cousin speaks up to defend him, Charlemagne strikes the man to the ground. Doon arrives at court with seven hundred armed men and threatens Charlemagne, who is unarmed. The angry vassal demands and receives the fief of Vauclère in Saxony, ruled by the pagan Aubigant, as well as Aubigant's daughter Flandrine. An angel commands Charlemagne to assist Doon in his war against the Danes. In the ensuing battles, Doon is also joined by Garin de Monglane and his companion, the giant Robastre. It is important to note that *Doon de Mayence* in its surviving version does not link Doon's lineage with Ganelon. Moreover, Doon's rebellion is brief; the bulk of the narrative depicts him as Charlemagne's ally against pagan forces.[22] *Doon de Mayence* also relates the conception and birth of Doon's son Gaufrey, who will rule Denmark. It is the sequel *Gaufrey*, also from the later thirteenth century, that depicts Gaufrey as the father of Ogier le Danois and uncle of Ganelon. A rather jumbled *chanson d'aventures*, *Gaufrey* generally presents the members of Doon's lineage as loyal vassals, with the notable exception of Gaufrey's brother Griffon, the father of Ganelon.[23] Griffon is an almost comical villain who gleefully declares that he despises loyalty, loving only those who delight in treason and duplicity (vv. 3995–99). Like *Doon de Mayence*, *Gaufrey* includes characters from the Garin de Monglane cycle, devoting segments of the narrative to the captivity of Garin and Doon in a Saracen prison and the adventures of the giant Robastre. The end of the poem provides a transition to the *Chevalerie Ogier*, as Gaufrey's treacherous second wife turns him against Charlemagne. Gaufrey mistreats the king's messengers and paves the way for the future conflict between his son Ogier and Charlemagne.

Renaut de Montauban

The enduring success of *Renaut de Montauban*, also known as the *Quatre Fils Aymon*, is attested by the number of manuscripts, translations, and reworkings of the story throughout the Middle Ages and beyond; the tradition has continued almost without interruption to the present day. The tale presents striking similarities to that of Ogier le Danois, notably the nature of the event that triggers the protracted conflict between Charlemagne and his vassal, the rebellious baron's lengthy exile, and the protagonists' eventual reconciliation.[24] Although there is evidence that a song of Renaut existed at least as early as the twelfth century, the oldest surviving manuscripts contain thirteenth-century reworkings of varying length.[25]

In most versions, Renaut's story is preceded by that of his uncle Beuves d'Aigremont, who kills Charlemagne's son Lohier and is himself killed in an ambush prepared by traitors including Griffon and Ganelon. A war of revenge ensues, led by Beuves's son Maugis the Sorcerer, Girart de Roussillon, and Doon de Nanteuil (all of whom are eponymous heroes of chansons de geste). The rebellious barons negotiate peace with Charlemagne, who holds a great feast to celebrate the reconciliation. Present, in addition to Maugis, are Aymon, Duke of Dordone, and his four sons Renaud, Alard, Guichard, and Richard. During a chess game, Charlemagne's nephew Bertholet quarrels with Renaud and strikes him. When Charlemagne takes his nephew's side, Renaut kills Bertholet with a chessboard and is forced to flee the court with his brothers. The sons of Aymon take refuge in the Ardennes, where they secretly build the fortress of Montessor. Aymon himself is forced to join forces with Charlemagne against his sons in the siege of Montessor. When the castle falls, the brothers make their way to the deepest forest of the Ardennes, where they spend seven years living off the land and enduring great hardship. After a brief respite in their parents' palace, they go to Gascony and deliver King Yon from the Saracens. Renaut builds the castle of Montauban, marries Yon's sister Clarisse, and fathers two sons.

In the remaining episodes of their conflict with Charlemagne, the brothers are assisted by the sorcerer Maugis as well as the marvelous horse Bayard. At one point, Renaut does battle with Roland; they are equally matched, and eventually Roland takes part in the reconciliation between Renaut and Charlemagne. The peace settlement requires Renaut to make a pilgrimage to the Holy Land. With the help of Maugis, he liberates Jerusalem from the Saracens, after which Maugis retires from chivalric life to do penance as a hermit. The end of the poem relates Renaut's own retreat into a hermitage, from which he emerges to help build a church in the city of Cologne. There he is savagely murdered by treacherous masons, but his funeral service and burial are accompanied by great miracles. Henceforth he is known in that region as Saint Renaut.

It is possible to speak of a Renaut de Montauban cycle, since the core poem gave rise to two prequels, *Maugis d'Aigremont* and *Vivien de Monbranc*. A brief sequel, appearing in only one manuscript, relates the death of Renaut's brothers at the hands of the Saracens Marsile and Baligant, as well as the death of Maugis in his hermitage. The marvelous horse Bayard is said to be still roaming the Ardennes forest.[26]

A fifteenth-century verse reworking of *Renaut de Montauban* considerably amplifies Renaut's pilgrimage.[27] By the sixteenth century, when prose versions of *Renaut de Montauban* appeared in print, Renaut and his brothers were equally prominent in the popular imagination, and the legend became known henceforth as the *Quatre Fils Aymon*.[28] It is by this title that the work is still known today in France, where the story continues to thrive in popular culture.[29]

Girart de Roussillon

Dating from the second half of the twelfth century, *Girart de Roussillon* is composed in an artificial hybrid language, Occitan with strong northern French characteristics. Its decasyllabic verses are formally distinguished by their use of the relatively unusual 6+4 caesura. The hero is loosely based on the ninth-century Gerardus, a vassal of Charles the Bald, who was also the prototype of two other epic characters: the eponymous hero of *Girart de Vienne* and Girart de Fraite in *Aspremont*.[30]

Girart and his king, Charles Martel, deliver Rome from the Saracens, and the emperor of Constantinople rewards them by promising his two daughters in marriage. It is solemnly agreed that Elisant will be granted to Girart, and Berte to the king. When Charles Martel learns that Elisant is the more beautiful of the two, he insists on taking her as his wife over the protests of his vassal. A papal intervention leads to an agreement whereby Girart relinquishes Elisant but is freed from his vassalic obligations to Charles. Elisant pledges her everlasting (but chaste) love to Girart, igniting Charles's jealousy. Thus begins a bitter and lengthy struggle. The Battle of Vaubeton, intended to settle the dispute once and for all, fails to produce the desired result when a heavenly thunderbolt causes both banners to go up in flames. After a five-year period of peace, the war is rekindled and rages with an extraordinary ferocity. As Sarah Kay observes, the differences between antagonists in *Girart de Roussillon* and other epics of revolt are gradually blurred by the all-consuming passion of revenge. Even if the rebel baron initially appears to be the victim of an unjust and vindictive monarch, the righteous cause fades with the constant renewal of violence: "Girart in *Girart de Roussillon* and Ogier in *La Chevalerie Ogier* are sucked into the warlike frenzy of their respective texts, becoming increasingly more like Charles Martel and Charlemagne respectively."[31]

After a particularly fierce battle at Roussillon, Girart is forced to flee with his wife Berte to the Ardennes forest. There they meet a hermit who persuades Girart to abandon his grudge against the king and relinquish both horse and armor until he has repented of his sins. Girart and Berte endure a twenty-two-year exile, living first as fugitives in the forest and then engaging in menial labor. Like Tristan and Iseut in the forest of Morrois, Berte begins to miss the aristocratic life the couple has abandoned, and she persuades Girart to attempt a reconciliation. With the help of Elisant, Girart and Berte return to court, and periods of uneasy peace alternate with renewed hostilities. Girart and Berte found an abbey at Vézelay, where Berte also supervises the building of a church dedicated to Saint Mary Magdalene. At the end of the narrative, Berte is falsely accused of adultery, but she is exonerated by a miracle, which prompts Girart to relinquish his landholdings and devote himself to God.

Scholars have often underscored the profoundly religious nature of *Girart de Roussillon*.[32] Representatives of the Church—the pope, the hermit, and others—are portrayed in a positive light and act in the interest of reconciliation. Unlike the *Chanson de Roland*, which glorifies martial exploits in the service of crusading ideology, *Girart* portrays extreme violence to promote ecclesiastical values of pacifism and humility.[33] Also noteworthy is the crucial role of women in the narrative. Even if Berte and Elisant are somewhat effaced during the long episodes devoted to battle, they jointly effect the resolution of the conflict and the redemption of the hero: "Elisant, the beautiful queen, offers a benign image of secular power, using wealth and physical attributes to good effect. Berte, Girart's wife, endowed with unusual wisdom and education, opens up a more radical path to social reversal and sanctity."[34]

Gormont et Isembart

The song *Gormont et Isembart* survives in a 661-line fragment from a late twelfth-century Anglo-Norman manuscript.[35] Scholars date the poem itself to the late eleventh or early twelfth century, and thus it is one of the earliest chansons de geste, roughly contemporary with the *Chanson de Roland*. The text's formal structure is archaic: rather than the decasyllabic verse characteristic of most early epics, *Gormont et Isembart* is composed in octosyllabic laisses, most of which conclude with a four-line refrain.[36] The fragment begins with a series of parallel laisses in which the Saracen

Gormont (of "Oriente") defeats a series of Christian knights in the service of King Louis. Fighting on Gormont's side is the renegade Isembart. The king slays Gormont after a three-day battle; Isembart rallies the Saracen troops and strikes his own father in single combat without recognizing him. Eventually Isembart is mortally wounded and repents, uttering a conventional prayer of greatest peril. Thanks to more complete versions found in later reworkings, scholars have been able to reconstruct the fragment's place in the larger story. Isembart's rebellion began when he found his position threatened by a conspiracy among King Louis's men. He not only entered the service of Gormont in England but also renounced his religion and assisted Gormont in invading France. The legend of Gormont and Isembart may be traced back to a Viking invasion in 881 that was successfully repelled by King Louis III at the Battle of Saucourt.[37]

Raoul de Cambrai

The late twelfth- or early thirteenth-century poem *Raoul de Cambrai* relates the hero's fanatical struggle to take possession of the fief of the Vermandois, which is also claimed by the family of his companion Bernier. When Raoul's troops attack Origny and set fire to the church, Bernier's mother, the abbess Marsent, perishes in the blaze. Bernier subsequently slays Raoul, and the feudal conflict is inherited by Raoul's nephew Gautier. *Raoul de Cambrai* is examined more closely in chapter 3.

The Lorraine Cycle

> Granz fu la guerre qui ja ne prendra fin.
> Aprés les mors la reprennent li vif;
> Aprés les peres la racuellent li fil.
> Aprés la mort al Loheren Garin,
> La reconmence li dus Gerbers, ses fiz. (vv. 2471–75)

> [Long was the war that never would end; after the dead, the living took over; after the fathers, the sons carried on; after the death of Garin le Lorrain, his son Duke Gerbert began it anew.]

> *GERBERT DE MEZ*

The five poems commonly classified under the rubric *geste des Lorrains* enjoyed tremendous popularity throughout the Middle Ages, as evidenced by the large number of manuscripts preserving all or part of the cycle. The French verse versions survive in more than fifty manuscripts and fragments, and a number of lost documents are attested.[38] Unlike most Romance epics, the works in the Lorraine cycle do not revolve around the struggle between Christians and Muslims; rather, the conflict is sustained primarily by interlineal hostilities. The core of the cycle, *Garin le Lorrain* (12th century), is attributed to a certain Jehan de Flagy in four of the extant manuscripts; although Jehan's identity and authorial status are not known, it is likely that he was responsible for reworking earlier versions of *Garin*. The first thousand lines are devoted to the exploits of Hervis, Duke of Lorraine. Hervis faithfully serves Charles Martel in his battles against invading Vandals and other "pagan" forces and, upon the king's death, ensures the coronation of Pepin the Short. The bulk of the narrative, however, is devoted to the onset of a fierce and protracted conflict between two feudal houses, the worthy "Lorrains" and the treacherous "Bordelais." Hervis's sons, Garin le Lorrain and his brother Begon, must contend not only with the insidious clan led by Fromont of Lens but also with the weak and vacillating King Pepin, who shifts his loyalties from one faction to the other according to his own interests. Because the Lorraine heroes are often forced to abandon their allegiance to Pepin, or to defy him outright, *Garin le Lorrain* has often been classified with the rebellious baron cycle.[39] The merciless rhythm of battles, sieges, duels, and pillage is interrupted by rare moments of truce that serve only to sow the seeds of renewed conflict. During one such time of peace, Begon hunts a legendary wild boar in a forest belonging to Fromont and is slain by Fromont's men. Following the Lorraine allies' brutal campaign of revenge, a penitent Garin vows to take up the cross, but he is ambushed in a chapel and murdered by his enemies.

The feud is inherited by the succeeding generation. *Gerbert de Metz* (late 12th century), which immediately follows *Garin le Lorrain* in nearly all of the surviving manuscripts, depicts the revenge exacted by Garin's son Gerbert and his cousins Hernaut and Gerin.[40] The cousins and their allies benefit from the unwavering support of Queen Blanchefleur but are frequently abandoned by Pepin. Gerbert and Gerin are more richly rewarded for their service to other sovereigns and acquire titles through powerful marriages: Gerin becomes king of Cologne and Gerbert is crowned king of Gascony. Hernaut marries Fromont's daughter Ludie, but rather than calming the feud, this alliance only fosters more discord. Although the poet's sympathies remain with the Lorraine heroes, the age-old rivalry degenerates into savagery on both sides. In a particularly gruesome episode, Gerbert secretly removes from its grave the skull of his deceased enemy Fromont, has it fashioned into an elaborate goblet, and serves wine from this very goblet to Fromont's son, Fromondin. Enraged, Fromondin murders his young nephews, the twin sons of Ludie and Hernaut, hurling them against a pillar and dashing out their brains. At the end of this branch, Fromondin, who has retired to a hermitage, plots to murder Gerbert and his cousins but is instead slain by them.

Subsequent branches of the cycle build upon the *Garin-Gerbert* core, extending the narrative to both past and future generations. The first continuation, *Hervis de Metz* (early 13th century), does not directly pertain to the conflict between the houses of Lorraine and Bordeaux. Rather, in the tradition of *enfances*, the poem goes back in time to relate the youthful adventures of the Lorraine heroes' illustrious ancestor. Like many chansons de geste of the thirteenth century, *Hervis* incorporates a number of traits typically associated with romance, particularly in the first half of the poem.[41] It may thus be classified as a *chanson d'aventures*. The product of a "mixed marriage" between a noblewoman and a wealthy bourgeois, Hervis struggles with the opposing value systems he has inherited. He fails miserably as a cloth merchant, disdaining the thriftiness and bargaining skills prized by his father.[42] He does succeed in purchasing the slave Beatrice, who is in reality the Princess of Tyre; abducted by a band of mercenary squires, the maiden was put up for sale at the fair in Lagny. After marrying Beatrice, who conceals her royal identity, Hervis accomplishes great feats of chivalry, winning the tournament of Senlis and slaying the giant Hinbaut. The second half of the story effects a return to more conventional epic patterns. Succeeding his maternal grandfather as Duke of Metz and Lorraine, Hervis engages in warfare to preserve his territorial and matrimonial rights. His union with Beatrice produces the future heroes Garin and Begon, who are related through their mother to the lineage of Charlemagne.

The fourth and final branch of the cycle resumes the narrative of the great feud after the events of *Gerbert de Metz*. This branch survives in two different versions, *La Vengeance Fromondin* and *Anseÿs de Metz* (recently rebaptized *Anseÿs de Gascogne*),[43] both dating from the mid-thirteenth century. Here the poets develop the disastrous consequences of intermarriage between the two warring families. In both accounts Gerbert is murdered by the son of Hernaut and his treacherous wife Ludie. To avenge a personal affront as well as the death of Fromondin and other members of Ludie's lineage, the boy crushes Gerbert's skull with a chessboard. The imperative of revenge thus falls to Gerbert's son, named Yon in the *Vengeance Fromondin* and Anseÿs in the lengthier *Anseÿs de Metz/Gascogne*. *La Vengeance Fromondin* is noteworthy for its annexation of an episode from *Raoul de Cambrai*: the poet incorporates Raoul's burning of the abbey of Origny and the death of Bernier's mother into the conflict between the Lorraine and Bordeaux families.[44] Among the salient episodes in *Anseÿs de Metz/Gascogne* is the devastating Battle of Santerre, in which 20,000 women take up arms and ensure the victory of the "Bordelais" and the Flemish.[45] Jean-Charles Herbin has persuasively argued that neither of these versions bears an organic relationship to the cycle.[46] *La Vengeance Fromondin* surprisingly transforms Pepin into a worthy ruler, and the poem as a whole serves to promote the Capetian monarchy. *Anseÿs de Metz/Gascogne* diverts sympathy from the heroes of the Lorraine lineage in order to glorify the Flemish aristocracy. These texts must therefore be considered spin-offs that appropriate the narrative framework of the cycle for very specific ideological purposes. There is, however, evidence of a lost version, *Yonnet*, preserved in Philippe de Vigneulles's sixteenth-century prose adaptation. More closely connected to the earlier branches of the cycle, *Yonnet* takes its characters back to the landscapes of *Garin le Lorrain* and ends in their ancestral city of Metz.[47]

The development of this corpus thus exemplifies the flexibility of the genealogical model of cyclical formation. Indeed, lineage not only serves to unify the four branches but also informs the name given to the cycle by its nineteenth-century editors. While the *geste des Lorrains* is the commonly accepted designation, Lorraine is not the principal theater of action in the cycle as a whole; nor do the terms "Lorrains" and "Bordelais" systematically designate characters from Lorraine and Bordeaux. At the same time, the cycle—and *Garin* in particular—is characterized by the remarkable precision of its geographical references.[48]

The Lorraine cycle's relationship to historical events and figures is problematic. A number of characters, including of course Pepin the Short, have historical antecedents. Moreover, the death of Begon, so charged with mythical resonance, may represent a poeticized version of an actual incident that formed the ancient kernel of *Garin le Lorrain*.[49] However, there appears to be no historical basis for the great feud, a conflict so memorable for medieval audiences that it gave rise to the expression "as long as the wars fought by Garin le Lorrain."[50] While the cycle is most notorious for its depictions of enmity and bloodshed, other aspects are equally striking, including the representation of strong female characters. François Villon celebrates Alice and Beatrice, the heroines of *Garin le Lorrain* and *Hervis de Metz*, in his renowned "Ballad of the Ladies of Yesteryear."[51] Admittedly, the most frequently cited passage from *Garin le Lorrain* refers to the predominantly male bonds that offer protection and security against feudal aggression. True riches, Begon assures his wife, have nothing to do with material wealth: "mes c'est richece de parenz et d'amis: / li cuers d'un home valt tot l'or d'un païs" (9575–76) [rather, riches come from family and friends: a man's heart is worth the gold of an entire country].[52]

The Crusade Cycle

> De la sainte cité vous volrai anoncier,
> U Dex laisa son cors pener et travillier
> Et ferir de la lance et navrer et plaier;
> Et li jentius barnajes, que Dex viut essaucier,
> S'en ala outre mer pour sa honte vengier. (vv. 35–39)
>
> [I would like to tell you of the holy city where God allowed his body to suffer pain and torture and to be pierced with the lance and injured and wounded. And the noble barons whom God wished to exalt went across the sea to avenge his shame.]
>
> *LA CHANSON D'ANTIOCHE*, ED. NELSON

Until the second half of the twentieth century, the narrative poems devoted to the First and Second Crusades were largely neglected by scholars of the epic, many of whom excluded the works from the category of chansons de geste.[53] It is now generally recognized that although the Crusade poems derive their material from more recent history, they weave historical events, legends, and pure invention in much the same way as the epics set in Carolingian or Merovingian times and bear witness to similar processes of cycle formation.[54] Moreover, their formal structure situates them squarely in the French epic tradition, as all of the texts are composed in rhymed alexandrine laisses.

The structure of the Crusade cycle has been most aptly described as a series of stages unfolding over the course of the late twelfth to the four-teenth century.[55] The nucleus of the Crusade epic material is the *Chanson d'Antioche* (late 12th century), attributed in the prologue to a certain Graindor de Douai, who is said to have "renewed" or reworked the song in keeping with its true origins (vv. 12–15).[56] Later in the text, the narrator cites "Ricars li pelerins" (Richard the Pilgrim) as an eyewitness source for the Battle of Antioch and the author of the original song (vv. 10886–87). Scholars long took this declaration at face value, considering the *Chanson d'Antioche* as a more or less historical document. In his 1980 study of *Antioche*, Robert Francis Cook discredited this approach, demonstrating the remarkable lack of evidence linking the text to an eyewitness account. Indeed, in many respects, the poem is inconsistent with the historical events of Antioch as they have been reconstructed from other sources.[57] *Antioche* must therefore be read and judged as a literary work, evoking and trans-forming events already distant in the collective memory. Bernard Guidot, its most recent editor, deems the poem a "pure literary gem in a cycle that, in many ways, renewed the epic genre without losing sight of tradi-tion."[58] Moreover, as Carol Sweetenham has shown, framing the events of the First Crusade within the signifying practices of the chanson de geste had very specific aesthetic and political advantages. Composed on the eve of the Fourth Crusade, the *Chanson d'Antioche* gives special prominence to heroes from northeastern France and Flanders, who were important participants in the Fourth Crusade. By providing heroic antecedents for present political actors, the poem may have functioned as a renewed call to arms. Like chansons de geste set in the more distant past, the *Antioche* employs a historical framework to stage contemporary concerns.[59]

The *Chanson d'Antioche* presents the crusading enterprise as a revela-tion of divine will. Before launching into the narrative proper, the poet flashes back to Christ on the cross, who predicts the eventual conquest of the Holy Land by an avenging army who will exterminate "les paiens desfaés" (v. 173) [the infidel pagans]. The story begins with an initial expe-dition to Jerusalem, undertaken by Peter the Hermit at God's urging. That mission ends with the disastrous Battle of Civetot, where Christians are massacred in great numbers and survivors endure harsh captivity. Notably, Corbaran of Oliferne (based on Kerbogha, the Turkish governor of Mosul) imprisons Richard of Chaumont, Harpin of Bourges, and their companions, whose plight will be recounted in a later branch, *Les Chétifs*. The poet then recounts the preparations and departure of the crusaders, led by Godfrey of Bouillon; the troops' arrival in Constantinople and resulting tensions with the emperor; the capture of Nicea; and the siege and conquest of Antioch. Even by the standards of the Old French epic, the *Chanson d'Antioche* is remarkable in its depiction of horrific acts of violence perpetrated by both Christians and Muslims. Imbued with the crusading spirit, the narrator denounces the savagery of the enemy but generally condones or implicitly excuses the Christians' brutality.[60] The perpetrators of the worst atrocities are the Tafurs, a notorious band of rogues serving the Christian forces who rape Muslim women and cannibalize the bodies of dead Turks. The oft-cited cannibalism episode is treated with dark humor, when Godfrey of Bouillon arrives on the scene and offers fine wine to accompany the meal. Faced with the outraged emir of Antioch, Bohemond of Sicily shrugs off the offense and attributes full responsibility to the cruel Tafurs. Like other crusading narratives of its time, the *Antioche* projects the Christian forces' acts of barbarism not only on the Muslim adversary but on the marginal elements of Christian society. As Norman Daniel points out, the low-ranking Tafurs, with their ferocious appetite for violence, women, and wealth, bear no small resemblance to the aristocratic leaders of the Crusade."[61]

The first sequel to *Antioche*, the *Chanson de Jérusalem* (late 12th century), relates the capture of the Holy City. The newly released Christian captives arrive in time to participate in the battle. Before the siege proper, the Christian knights assemble on the hill overlooking Jerusalem, where Peter the Hermit offers a description of the city steeped in sacred history and dogma. The crusaders fight valiantly, aided by the Tafurs, with armies of saints led by Saint George providing occasional reinforcements. After the triumphant entry into Jerusalem, the crusaders choose Godfrey of Bouillon as king, an honor he declines until a miracle designates him as God's chosen leader. Godfrey acquiesces, but he refuses to wear a crown of gold, preferring a crown of leaves from Saint Abraham's garden in memory of Christ's passion.[62] Further battles ensue as the Saracens return to reclaim the city, but Christian forces succeed in driving them back to Acre.

Composed after *Antioche* and *Jérusalem* but inserted between them in the fictional chronology and cyclical manuscripts is *Les Chétifs* (The Captives), which relates the adventures of the Christians taken prisoner by Corbaran. While the two earlier songs bear at least a tenuous relationship to historical events, *Les Chétifs* is primarily a *chanson d'aventures* complete with a dragon, hidden treasures, and a child kidnapped by a lion and a wolf. In this branch the Christian/Saracen dichotomy is greatly attenuated by temporary alliances: Richard of Chaumont defends Corbaran against a charge of treason in judicial combat, and Harpin of Bourges saves Corbaran's nephew from wild animals.

The earliest continuations, dating from the late twelfth century, go back in time to elaborate a mythical genealogy for Godfrey of Bouillon. *Le Chevalier au cygne* (The Swan Knight) and its prequel, *La Naissance du Chevalier au cygne* (The Birth of the Swan Knight, late 12th century), draw upon a legend already in circulation by 1175–80, which would later be known in German versions as the Lohengrin tale.[63] In its epic adaptation, the story relates the plight of seven children engendered by a fairy and a mortal king. The children are born with golden chains, without which they assume the form of swans, a transformation that comes to pass through the machinations of the king's wicked mother. All but one of the children are able to recover their human form when their golden chains are restored. The remaining swan-child becomes the faithful companion of his brother Elias, who is dubbed the Swan Knight. Elias saves the Duchess of Bouillon from the Duke of Saxony and marries the duchess's daughter, Beatrice, expressly forbidding his wife to inquire about his origins. The couple produce a daughter, Ida, who will give birth to Godfrey of Bouillon. Eventually Beatrice asks her husband the forbidden question, and he disappears in the company of the swan. The Swan Knight legend is closely related to the tale of the fairy Mélusine, the half-woman, half-serpent figure appropriated by the house of Lusignan in the late fourteenth century.[64] Both of these emblematic figures served the interests of aristocratic families eager to enlist marvelous ancestors in the service of political ambition.[65]

Other continuations include the *Fin d'Elias*, which relates the Swan Knight's further adventures; the *Enfances Godefroi*, devoted to the youthful exploits of the future king of Jerusalem; the *Retour de Cornumaran*, a prelude to the *Antioche*; and continuations of the *Chanson de Jérusalem*, namely the *Chrétienté Corbaran*, the *Prise d'Acre*, the *Mort Godefroi*, and the *Chanson des Rois Baudouin*, all dating from the thirteenth century. The fourteenth century produced an elaborate reworking of the earlier material, the *Chevalier au cygne et Godefroi de Bouillon*. Also dating from the fourteenth century are *Baudouin de Sebourc* and *Le Bâtard de Bouillon*, which Cook places in the "margins" of the cycle.[66] Although its hero is loosely based on Baldwin II, third king of Jerusalem, the lengthy *Baudouin de Sebourc* is not properly speaking a Crusade epic, but rather a *chanson d'aventures* revolving around Baudouin's search for his identity and his lost family.[67] The Crusade does serve as a backdrop for the final episodes of the narrative, in which the hero is granted the fief of Edessa and serves King Baldwin I in his military campaign against the kings of Mecca. Similarly, *Le Bâtard de Bouillon* imagines the adventures of an illegitimate son of King Baldwin I; despite references to the Latin Kingdom of Jerusalem, the poem is essentially ahistorical.[68]

As Cook points out, the poetic history of the Crusades begins with the myth of origins and ends with the myth of the fall.[69] The early continuations of the Crusade cycle do not treat the fall of Latin Jerusalem, though the crusader kingdom had already been lost by the time of their composition. There is, however, evidence of a lost poem devoted to Saladin, which survives in a fifteenth-century prose version.[70] Saladin, a model knight with Christian ancestry, conquers Persia and Jerusalem, participates in tournaments, and converts to Christianity before his death. Though the dream of a Latin Christendom had been shattered, the medieval imagination found redemption by absorbing the conquering Muslim hero into the cultural and spiritual ideals of the Western Christian aristocracy.

Other Notable Works: The Thirteenth Century

Although each chanson de geste is "notable" in its own way, I am able to include here only a handful of works. The following texts were selected because of their enduring success among medieval and modern audiences and/or because they represent certain tendencies in the development of the genre. All of them are generically "hybrid," conjoining motifs from romance, folklore, and/or hagiography to the thematics and formal structure of the chanson de geste.

Ami et Amile

Composed about 1200, *Ami et Amile* is but one version of a legend that enjoyed tremendous popularity in the Middle Ages. Like a number of chansons de geste, including the *Chanson de Roland*, it explores the homosocial bonds between two knights. Rather than being subordinate to a larger plot, however, the remarkable friendship of Ami and Amile is the central focus of the narrative.[71] Born on the same day and bearing a remarkable physical resemblance to each other, Ami and Amile develop a profound relationship that weathers the machinations of the traitor Hardré, the malevolence of Ami's wife Lubias, a dangerous seduction scheme hatched by Charlemagne's daughter Belissant, and Ami's leprosy. *Ami et Amile* is analyzed in more detail in chapter 3.

Auberi le Bourguignon (*Auberi le Bourgoin*)

The eponymous hero of *Auberi le Bourguignon* makes his first appearance as one of the most prominent secondary characters in *Garin le Lorrain*. A nephew of Garin, Auberi is represented as a faithful and dutiful vassal and thus worthy of extraction as a hero in his own right.[72] In the poem devoted to his adventures, Auberi loses his mother as a child, is persecuted by a wicked stepmother, and is betrayed by a malevolent uncle. Forced to kill his cousins, he leaves his native Burgundy with his loyal nephew Gasselin. Auberi's narrative trajectory combines military exploits and amorous adventures: he helps the king of Bavaria to defeat the Huns and the Count of Flanders to repel the Danes, but he is obliged to flee both courts because of dangerous liaisons with his lords' wives. Auberi marries the queen of Bavaria but is tragically killed by Gasselin, who mistakes him for the traitor Lambert. After defeating Lambert in judicial combat, Gasselin marries Senehaut, Princess of Bavaria; from this union is born Naimes, Duke of Bavaria and wise and faithful councilor to Charlemagne. For Isabelle Weill, *Auberi le Bourguignon* is a surprisingly "modern" text for the thirteenth century, depicting an intrepid, womanizing hero whose honor is occasionally compromised by the temptations of the flesh and a lust for power and riches.[73]

Aye d'Avignon

One of a very few chansons de geste named after a female protagonist,[74] the early thirteenth-century *Aye d'Avignon* recounts the complex and shifting rivalry for the hand and lands of its eponymous heroine, niece of Charlemagne. As Sarah Kay affirms, Aye "acts as an absent centre, frequently immobilized and rarely an agent."[75] When Charlemagne marries Aye to the worthy Garnier of Nanteuil, the match is disputed by various traitors of Ganelon's lineage. Aye is abducted and imprisoned by the traitors and removed to Aigremore in Spain. There the Saracen king Ganor becomes enamored of the lady and sequesters her in the marvelous tower of Aufalerne. Garnier liberates his wife and they return to Avignon, where Aye gives birth to a son, Gui, whom King Ganor kidnaps and raises in Aigremore. When Garnier is slain in battle by traitors, Charlemagne promises Aye to Ganelon's nephew Milon, but Aye manages to delay the marriage. Eventually she is reunited with her son Gui, who has promised to unite her with the "good Saracen" Ganor. Aye agrees to the marriage when Ganor obligingly converts to Christianity. *Aye d'Avignon* thus begins as a conventional epic conflict, somewhat reminiscent of the Lorraine cycle: powerful barons compete for royal favor and matrimonial advantage, and interlineal disputes are complicated by shifting alliances. In this *chanson d'aventures*, conflict is resolved by means of a "family romance" plot, in which Aye's son Gui improves his status (and that of his mother) by replacing his biological father with an exotic fantasy father.[76]

Aye d'Avignon is part of a group of poems often labeled the "small cycle of Nanteuil." Although the works are not assembled in a cyclical manuscript, their protagonists are linked by genealogy.[77] *Doon de Nanteuil*, the tale of Garnier's father, survives only in a 220-line fragment and is also associated with the *geste de Doon de Mayence*.[78] *Gui de Nanteuil* relates the story of Aye's and Garnier's son, and *Parise la Duchesse* invents a daughter for the couple. *Tristan de Nanteuil*, a lengthy continuation composed in the mid-fourteenth century, weaves together multiple adventures, including numerous separations and reunions, interventions by a fairy and King Arthur, and a miraculous sex change.

Beuve de Hantone (Boeve de Haumtone)

One of the most popular and enduring stories of the French epic tradition, *Beuve de Hantone* survives in an Anglo-Norman version and three lengthier Continental versions, all from the first half of the thirteenth century.[79] Perhaps more than any other hybrid work of the period, *Beuve* has been said to blur the boundaries between epic and romance traditions.[80]

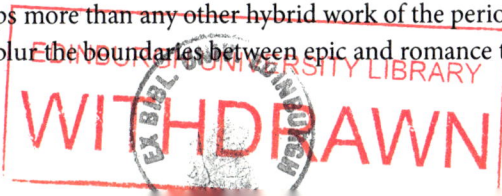

The story is launched by the treachery of Beuve's mother, who plots with the German emperor Doon de Mayence to have her husband Gui killed during a wild boar hunt. Beuve escapes with the help of a faithful servant, but is sold into slavery. Purchased by Saracen merchants, he is transported from England to Egypt and brought before the Saracen king Hermine. Beuve steadfastly refuses to abandon his faith, but he grows up in the Egyptian court and serves Hermine valiantly. However, when it is discovered that Beuve is in love with the king's daughter Josiane, the lovers are subjected to a lengthy series of separations and reunions. Beuve eventually returns to England, defeats his stepfather Doon, and recovers his lands; his mother commits suicide. Josiane and Beuve marry and have twin sons before enduring a new separation and further adventures. During her long search for Beuve, Josiane disguises herself as a jongleur. All four family members are ultimately reunited. Beuve and Josiane die on the same day; one of their sons is crowned king of England and the other inherits the kingdom of the converted Saracen Hermine.

Beuve de Hantone's intertextual network includes close thematic ties with a number of chansons de geste, including *Horn*, an Anglo-Norman "romance" composed in the form of a chanson de geste,[81] and the Occitan *Daurel et Beton*.[82] Comical sequences involving a Saracen giant named Escopart are highly reminiscent of Corsolt and Rainouart from the Guillaume d'Orange cycle.[83] *Beuve* enjoyed success throughout Europe, particularly in Italy, where it appears in Franco-Italian and Tuscan verse versions. Translated into French prose in the fifteenth century, the tale was also reworked in English, Welsh, Irish, Norwegian, Russian, and Yiddish.[84]

Huon de Bordeaux

A *chanson d'aventures* of the later thirteenth century, *Huon de Bordeaux* opens with a conventional revolt epic plot that subsequently gives way to a romance-like quest. The victim of an ambush, young Huon unwittingly kills Charlemagne's malevolent son Charlot. The emperor banishes Huon, who undertakes an expiatory journey to the Orient, where he encounters marvelous adventures and finds an ally in the fairy king Auberon. *Huon de Bordeaux* is analyzed in more detail in chapter 3.

The Fourteenth and Fifteenth Centuries

The chansons de geste of the later period were long disdained as unwieldy, confusing, and long-winded compositions with little to commend them other than their status as literary artifacts. In the 1980s François Suard and Robert Francis Cook, among others, undertook a serious reevaluation of the late epics, concluding that while these works do not display the simplicity and coherence of an Aristotelian plot, they do correspond to certain aesthetic and compositional principles of the later Middle Ages.[85] Cook points out that the lengthy interlaced narratives produced in the final decades of epic production reflect some of the same aspirations that led to the formation of cycles, notably the desire to relate a total story that embraces multiple trajectories. Moreover, there is every reason to believe that these long, interlaced compositions were not meant to be recited or read in their entirety, but rather in segments.[86] Although their narrative content is at times indistinguishable from that of romance, the persistence of epic form (the rhymed alexandrine laisse) suggests a conscious desire to situate the works in the epic tradition.

Some chansons de geste of this period are reworkings of earlier texts; others are continuations of existing *gestes* and are mentioned above in conjunction with their respective cycles. The works listed below are among the new compositions produced during the fourteenth century.

La Belle Hélène de Constantinople

Composed in the mid-fourteenth century, *La Belle Hélène de Constantinople* is based in part upon a folktale common to a number of medieval narratives, the Handless Maiden tale (T. 706 in the Aarne-Thompson classification).[87] The motif is found in other fourteenth-century epics, such as *Lion de Bourges* and *Tristan de Nanteuil*, as well as the thirteenth-century romance *La Manekine* by Philippe de Beaumanoir. The Handless Maiden tale is characterized by this basic structure: the heroine's hands are cut off as the result of a family conflict; a king finds her in the woods and marries her in spite of her mutilation; when a letter to her husband is intercepted and falsified, she and her children are banished; she miraculously recovers her hands and is reunited with her husband. This framework belongs to a series of tales staging the trials and tribulations of a persecuted heroine.[88]

In *La Belle Hélène*, a variation on the Handless Maiden core narrative is joined to the thematics of the chanson de geste and hagiography.

Hélène, daughter of the emperor of Constantinople, flees her father's incestuous desire, embarking on a tumultuous journey that brings her to England, where she is united in marriage with King Henry, all the while concealing her true identity. While Henry is in Rome fighting a Saracen invasion, she gives birth to two sons, but she is persecuted by her evil mother-in-law, who sends a false letter to Henry claiming that Hélène has given birth to two monsters. Hélène narrowly avoids execution but has her arm amputated before escaping with her sons; the severed arm, wrapped in a precious cloth, is attached to one of the boys. When they arrive on a desert island, one son is carried off by a wolf and the other by a lion; they are eventually raised by a saintly hermit. Characters and narrative threads multiply, with mirror episodes that figure the central plot. (A Saracen king, for example, vows to marry his daughter, who is secretly a Christian, and is saved—ironically—by Hélène's father.) Hélène and Henry's sons, Martin and Brice, mature and join the struggle against the Saracens. Hélène's father, who has repented of his sinful desire, seeks his daughter for thirty-four years, often in the company of Henry. The family is finally reunited in Tours, where a voice instructs Hélène's son Martin (the future Saint Martin) to restore his mother's severed arm. Hélène and Henry die in Rome and are buried at Saint Peter's. Martin eventually becomes archbishop of Tours and is succeeded by Brice's son, the future Saint Brice.

La Belle Hélène de Constantinople was adapted into prose by Jean Wauquelin in the mid-fifteenth century, and it remained popular into the nineteenth century as a staple of the Bibliothèque Bleue.[89]

La Chanson de Bertrand du Guesclin

Produced by an otherwise unknown poet named Cuvelier, the *Chanson de Bertrand du Guesclin* was composed between 1380 and 1385, shortly after the death of this celebrated hero of the Hundred Years' War. Du Guesclin, a minor Breton nobleman, distinguished himself on the battlefield, defeating the English in a number of important battles. Appointed Constable of France by Charles V, he captured the popular imagination with his military prowess and reputed physical ugliness. Cuvelier's poetic biography combines features of epic and chronicle, adapting the form and hyperbolic register of the chanson de geste to events of the recent past:

> tant fu redoubtez
> Que chascuns se tenoit desconfiz et matez,
> Aussi tost qu'en assault estoit ses cris levez.
> . . . .
> En mains lieux disoit on aux enfans nouveaux nez:
> "Taisiez vous, taisiez vous, ou ja le comparrez,
> Bertran de Glaiequin est deça arrivez!" (vv. 37–45)

[So feared was he that everyone considered himself vanquished and defeated as soon as he raised the battle cry. . . . In many places, people told newborn babies: "Hush, hush, or you will pay for it: Bertrand du Guesclin has arrived here!"][90]

The *Chanson de Bertrand du Guesclin* enjoyed considerable success and was adapted into prose almost immediately after its appearance in verse.

Lion de Bourges

Numbering 34,298 alexandrine lines, *Lion de Bourges* is the lengthiest extant chanson de geste. Its interlaced narrative incorporates conventional epic themes (a baron's quarrel with the king and subsequent banishment), romance commonplaces (otherworldly intervention by a fairy king), and folklore motifs (the Handless Maiden, the Grateful Dead).[91]

Harpin de Bourges, unjustly accused of disloyalty to Charlemagne, enters into exile with his pregnant wife Alis. Deep in a forest, while Harpin seeks a midwife, Alis gives birth to a son and is soon kidnapped by bandits. The child, who bears the mark of a red cross on his shoulder, is rescued by fairies and cared for by a lioness. Bauduyn of Monclin discovers the child, names him Lion, and raises him as his own son. The protagonists encounter numerous adventures as they follow their separate trajectories. Alis disguises herself as a man and finds her way to Toledo, where she learns Arabic and works as a cook in the emir's kitchen under the name of Ballian of Aragon. When the emir's daughter becomes enamored of "Ballian," Alis is forced to reveal that she is a woman and immediately attracts the attention of the emir, who resolves to marry her, prompting Alis to escape. Lion's father Harpin spends eighteen years in a hermitage before emerging to battle the Saracens in Rome. Lion, for his part, frequents tournaments and develops his chivalric potential. In an episode based on the Grateful Dead motif, he spends his last coins to bury a knight who died indebted to an innkeeper; later Lion is helped by a White Knight who proves to be none other than the spirit of the man whose burial expenses he so generously paid. The family is reunited and Lion claims his rightful fief of Bourges, after which the poem embarks on the story of Lion's sons. Allusions to *Lion de Bourges* in other late French epics suggest that this lengthy *chanson d'aventures* was fairly well known in the fourteenth century.[92] In the fifteenth century, Elisabeth of Nassau-Saarbrücken composed a German prose version entitled *Herpin*.

Occitan Works

The Occitan epic tradition is characterized by a small number of surviving texts as well as some tantalizing allusions to lost models and versions.[93] Like so many questions related to textual origins and genealogy, the relationship between French and Occitan epic production has been a matter of considerable debate. Some have argued that all Occitan epics derive from northern French works; others have maintained that the epic tradition originated in the South and was absorbed by the Old French chansons de geste. A third position attempts to bypass the question of anteriority, positing that "Occitan epic represents an independent tradition, with an undefined amount of northern French influence."[94]

Most of the extant works appear in a single manuscript or fragment and display strong ties to northern French material. *Ronsasvals* and *Rollan a Saragossa*, as well as an Occitan version of *Fierabras* (*Fierabratz*), likely date from the thirteenth century. The fragmentary *Canso d'Antioca* was probably composed in the late twelfth century but attests to a lengthy and complex Occitan tradition of epics on the Battle of Antioch; its relationship to the Old French *Chanson d'Antioche* is difficult to ascertain, since both texts are reworkings of older material.[95]

Daurel et Beton, a late twelfth-century work, mirrors in many ways the plot of *Beuve de Hantone*. In the Occitan text, the pact of companionship between Bove of Antona and Guy of Aspremont is severed when Guy, driven by desire for Bove's wife and estate, murders his friend during a boar hunt. Bove's son Beton is rescued by the faithful jongleur Daurel, and the two escape to Babylonia. The text is noteworthy for its portrayal of the hero-jongleur Daurel, who, though of lowly birth, is granted a hereditary fief for his service to Bove.[96] Later in the story, the downfall of the treacherous Guy is brought about by the combined skills of jongleur and knight: accompanied by Beton, himself disguised as a minstrel, Daurel entertains Guy and his knights with a song of the latter's misdeeds. The *mise-en-abyme* showcases epic artistry and directly leads to a decisive battle, in which Beton cuts off Guy's right arm and leads his troops in the annihilation of Guy's army.

Two other Occitan epics have received well-deserved critical attention in recent years. *Girart de Roussillon*, composed in a highly Gallicized Occitan, is discussed above in conjunction with the rebellious baron cycle. The *Canso de la Crozada* (*Chanson de la Croisade Albigeoise*) is a poetic chronicle of the first part of the Albigensian Crusade, the series of military expeditions initiated by the papacy and undertaken between 1209 and 1229 to extirpate the Cathar heresy in what is now southern France. The first 130 laisses were composed by Guilhem de Tudela, a poet from Navarre residing in the Montauban region. Guilhem espouses the official position condemning heresy without denouncing the southern barons; sympathetic to the Crusade, he nonetheless deplores the infamous massacre at Béziers.[97] His portion of the *Canso*, composed during the years 1212–13, contains 2,749 lines and relates the events of the crusade until the beginning of 1213. Guilhem thus adapts traditional epic form to the immediacy of an ongoing conflict. His poem was later taken up by an anonymous continuator from the region of Toulouse. The second poet's sympathies clearly lie with the southern noblemen—though he does not condone heresy—and he is particularly vehement in his denunciation of Simon of Montfort, whom he characterizes as "mals e cozens" (laisse 141, v. 34) [evil and cruel]. The anonymous poet's contribution of 6,811 lines is substantially longer than Guilhem's and covers the period from 1213 to June 1219. Although the date of composition is uncertain, this portion of the *Canso* was likely written between 1218 and 1219.[98] Both parts are composed in rhymed alexandrines and make use of a six-syllable *vers orphelin* or short line at the close of the laisse.

◈

This brief survey can afford only a glimpse into the scope and variety of the chanson de geste corpus. The tradition proliferated largely under the impulse of cyclicity, with poets generating new works by locating spaces in the genealogical structures of existing narratives. Perceived as open-ended, the foundational texts invited continuation and imitation. By their very nature, the conflicts depicted in the chansons were conducive to sequels and preludes: the threat of Saracen invasion was infinitely renewable, and great feudal rivalries were apt to be rekindled with each new generation. These principles also operated within individual texts, particularly in the later period, when poets sought to represent a protagonist's trajectory within the totality of his or her sphere of influence.

3

Selected Works

Six works have been selected for more detailed analysis. They are among the best known and most frequently taught chansons de geste and together are representative of the tradition's narrative and stylistic range.

La Chanson de Roland (late 11th or early 12th century)

> "Ben devuns ci estre pur nostre rei:
> Pur sun seignor deit hom susfrir destreiz
> E endurer e granz chalz e granz freiz,
> Si'n deit hom perdre e del quir e del peil.
> Or guart chascuns que granz colps i empleit,
> Male cançun de nus chantét ne seit!
> Paien unt tort e chrestïens unt dreit.
> Malvaise essample n'en serat ja de mei." (vv. 1009–16)

> ["It is our duty to be here for our king: / For his lord a vassal must suffer hardships / And endure great heat and great cold; / And must lose both hair and hide. / Now let each man take care to strike great blows, / So that no one can sing a shameful song about us. / The pagans are wrong and the Christians are right. / No dishonourable tale will ever be told about me."]

The Oxford version of the *Chanson de Roland*,[1] since its rediscovery in the early nineteenth century, has occupied a privileged place in the French national consciousness and the canon of Western literature.[2] For general readers as well as most specialists, the *Roland* is the undisputed masterpiece of the Old French epic. With evocative language and stark grandeur, it grapples with numerous issues at the heart of feudal society, including the viability of the heroic ethos, the stakes involved in loyalty and adherence to one's word, the power of homosocial bonds, the threats posed by internal discord, and political and religious confrontation with the Muslim world. Roland, nephew of Charlemagne, is a particularly vivid and controversial figure, both in the poem itself and in the abundant critical works devoted to it over the last 175 years. It should be noted, however, that the Oxford manuscript bears no title. In his 1837 *editio princeps*, Francisque Michel provided the hesitant designation *La Chanson de Roland ou de Roncevaux*, underlining the text's dual emphasis on the hero and the site of his demise.

One of the earliest chansons de geste, the Oxford *Roland* is relatively short, with 4,002 decasyllabic lines arranged in assonanced laisses. The narrative may be roughly divided into three parts: Ganelon's betrayal of the rear guard, the two battles of Roncevaux, and Ganelon's trial. The text closes with an enigmatic reference to a certain Turold ("Ci falt la geste que

Turoldus declinet," v. 4002). Because of the highly ambiguous nature of the verse's vocabulary and syntax, it is impossible to determine the identity and the role of this figure, who may have been the poem's author, scribe, jongleur, source, translator, or continuator.

Summary

Ganelon's Betrayal of the Rear Guard (vv. 1–702)

The emperor Charlemagne and his troops have been at war in Spain for seven years, conquering many castles and towns. Marsile, the Saracen king of Saragossa, knows that he cannot defeat Charlemagne by force. Upon the advice of his baron Blancandrin, he resolves to rid Spain of the Christians by means of a ruse. A Saracen delegation bears olive branches and costly gifts to the emperor, falsely promising that Marsile and his subjects will convert to Christianity if Charlemagne returns to Aix-la-Chapelle. Marsile pledges to follow him there and become his vassal. When Charlemagne consults the full council of barons, his nephew Roland, one of the Twelve Peers, vehemently opposes the offer, citing Marsile's past duplicity. Ganelon, Roland's stepfather, angrily rejects Roland's reasoning as pure folly. Duke Naimes, the emperor's most trusted adviser, points out that the Saracens have offered hostages as security. Charlemagne is ultimately persuaded to accept the proposal, and on Roland's suggestion, Ganelon is sent to Marsile's court to conclude the arrangement. Ganelon, furious, issues a challenge to Roland in the presence of Charlemagne.

Once in Saragossa, Ganelon deviates from his diplomatic mission and suggests to Marsile that Charlemagne would cease all warfare were it not for the bellicose Roland. Ganelon and Marsile devise a plot to eliminate Charlemagne's nephew: Ganelon will see to it that Roland is named to the emperor's rear guard, and the Saracens will ambush the rear guard as Charlemagne leaves Spain. Ganelon convinces Marsile that Roland's death will so weaken Charlemagne's army that Marsile will never again fear war. The betrayal is sealed with an oath, a kiss, and lavish gifts.

The Battles of Roncevaux (vv. 703–3674)

Roland leads a rear guard composed of 20,000 of Charlemagne's worthiest knights, including Oliver, Roland's closest companion, and Turpin, archbishop of Reims. At Roncevaux, Oliver is the first to perceive the approach of the sizable Saracen army, 400,000 strong. Realizing that the Christians are vastly outnumbered, Oliver urges Roland to blow his *olifant*, his ivory horn, to recall Charlemagne and his forces. To Oliver's dismay, Roland emphatically refuses, citing his own honor as well as that of his family and France. In the ensuing battle, the rear guard fights valiantly but eventually begins to sustain serious losses. Roland now resolves to sound his horn to inform Charlemagne of the battle, thus provoking a new quarrel with Oliver. Blaring his horn with all his might, Roland bursts his temples. Still he carries on, slaying hundreds of Saracens and dealing a fatal blow to Marsile. Eventually, however, the entire rear guard perishes. Before his death, Roland mourns Oliver and Turpin and pays tribute to his sword Durendal. He offers his glove to God, and Saint Gabriel, Saint Michael, and Cherubin bear his soul to heaven.

When the grief-stricken Charlemagne returns, God prolongs the daylight so that the emperor's forces may avenge the rear guard. All of Marsile's remaining troops are annihilated. Charlemagne must now confront the army of Marsile's overlord Baligant, emir of Babylon. With the help of the angel Gabriel, Charlemagne prevails in single combat against Baligant. The emperor enters Saragossa, destroys the pagan idols, and forces the city's inhabitants to convert to Christianity. The Saracen queen Bramimonde is taken captive, but Charlemagne wishes her to convert by choice, out of love for God.

Ganelon's Trial (vv. 3675–4002)

During the return journey, Charlemagne deposits Roland's horn at Saint-Seurin in Bordeaux and has Roland, Oliver, and Turpin buried in Blaye. In Aix-la-Chapelle, Roland's fiancée Aude learns of his death and perishes on the spot. Charlemagne convenes his barons for Ganelon's trial. Charged with treason, Ganelon asserts that he justifiably sought Roland's death, but he denies betraying the emperor. The barons, intimidated by Ganelon's imposing relative Pinabel, advise Charlemagne to exercise clemency. However, the Angevin knight Thierry offers to prove Ganelon's guilt in judicial combat. Though unevenly matched against the towering Pinabel, Thierry triumphs, and Ganelon is executed along with thirty of his family members. Queen Bramimonde embraces Christianity and is baptized under the new name Julianne. That night Saint Gabriel brings Charlemagne a message from God: a new battle awaits him in Imphe, where King Vivien is besieged by Saracens. Here ends Turold's song.

Origins

The Battle of Roncevaux has its roots in a documented historical event that has been radically transformed by the poetic imagination.[3] By comparing Carolingian annals and Arabic historiography, scholars have established with reasonable certainty that in the spring of 778, Charlemagne undertook an expedition to Spain at the request of the Muslim ruler of Barcelona, Suleiman ibn al-Arabi, who was attempting to rebel against the emir of Cordoba. When Charlemagne arrived in Saragossa, however, the city refused him entry, perhaps because of a change of heart on Suleiman's part, and Charlemagne laid siege to the city. Two months later, unable to take Saragossa, Charlemagne learned of a Saxon uprising in the North and headed back through the Pyrenees, taking Suleiman as hostage. At this point the sources give diverging accounts, but it seems clear that Charlemagne's rear guard was ambushed in a mountain pass at or near Roncesvalles (Roncevaux in French), probably by al-Arabi's sons aided by Basque forces. Al-Arabi was freed, and Charlemagne lost high-ranking warriors and important supplies. The earliest Latin account, the Royal Annals to 801, does not mention the Roncevaux disaster, perhaps in an attempt to suppress the humiliating defeat, but subsequent Carolingian histories acknowledge the ambush and provide further details. Einhard's 830 *Vita Karoli Magni* (*Life of Charlemagne*) contains the first reference to Roland's presence at Roncevaux: among the fallen is a certain "Hruodlandus Brittannici limitis praefectus" (Roland, prefect of the March of Brittany).[4] Roland's name is attested in an earlier document as one of Charlemagne's paladins.

The *Chanson de Roland* has always been at the center of the traditionalist-individualist debate.[5] Several twelfth-century sources report that a "song of Roland" was sung to the Norman troops before the Battle of Hastings. The Anglo-Norman chronicler Wace offers a lively account of this performance in his *Roman de Rou*, composed around 1160:

Taillefer, qui mult bien chantout,
sor un cheval qui tost alout,
devant le duc alout chantant
de Karlemaigne e de Rollant,
e d'Oliver e des vassals
qui morurent en Rencesvals.

[Taillefer, a very good singer, rode before the duke on a swift horse, singing of Charlemagne and of Roland, of Oliver and of the vassals who died at Rencesvals.][6]

Traditionalists have interpreted the reference to Taillefer's song as evidence of oral versions circulating before the Oxford manuscript. Many nineteenth-century medievalists believed that this manuscript even represented Taillefer's lost song, and thus the *Chanson de Roland* came to be identified with the origins of French national literature. Individualists posit a learned, clerical Anglo-Norman poet named Turold, perhaps Thorold, bishop of Bayeux in the late eleventh century.[7] In a provocative article published in 2001, Andrew Taylor challenged long-held notions that the unassuming, pocket-sized Oxford manuscript was a "jongleur manuscript" containing a song that might be sung by minstrels to a popular audience. Based on codicological evidence and research on medieval reading practices, Taylor argues for both clerical origins and a clerical audience. The Oxford manuscript is in fact a composite volume containing, in addition to the *Chanson de Roland*, a glossed copy of Chalcidius's translation of Plato's *Timaeus*. In response to the question "Was There a Song of Roland?" Taylor allows that there were short songs of Roland, a legend of Roland, and a poem of Roland, but he disputes the existence of a lengthy, orally circulating, 4,000-line song.[8]

Structure

A number of ingenious structural models have been proposed to describe and interpret the Oxford *Roland* narrative. Fern Farnham, for example, likened the poem's structure to that of the tympanum found at the Romanesque abbey-church of Moissac, which depicts Christ in Majesty flanked by the animal symbols of the four Evangelists.[9] Farnham discerns a similar five-part structure in the *Roland*, with Roland's death at the center of the narrative; occupying the lateral positions are Ganelon's treason and the first Roncevaux battle on one side and the second battle and Ganelon's trial on the other. Indeed, there has been much scholarly disagreement regarding the poem's division into parts: the tripartite division proposed above could be reconfigured to allow for four principal segments, depending on one's interpretation of the second Roncevaux battle or "Baligant episode."[10]

Some have questioned the authenticity of the Baligant section, which does not appear in all versions of the Roland story.[11] There is evidence that this episode is an interpolation, a later addition to a hypothetical "original" song of Roland. The episode begins rather abruptly in laisse 189 with overt markers of a textual juncture: the opening of the laisse echoes the very first lines of the poem, recalling Charlemagne's seven-year presence in Spain. The narrator then reports that Marsile had asked the emir's help in the first year of Charlemagne's Spanish campaign, though this circumstance was never mentioned previously. The battle narrative is organized differently from the rear guard's confrontation with Marsile's men: the encounter between Baligant's and Charlemagne's troops is preceded by a long series of parallel laisses enumerating the disposition of squadrons in each camp, which reflects a more modern military configuration. In a sense, the *Chanson de Roland* would still be a coherent work without the Baligant episode, with the action flowing in logical and linear fashion from Ganelon's betrayal to Roland's death to Ganelon's trial. On the other hand, scholars have found no significant linguistic differences or variations in formulaic style between the two battle episodes. Moreover, the inclusion of the Baligant episode corresponds to the narrative and ideological exigencies of feudal conflict. The Franks' triumph in the second battle compensates for the earlier defeat of the rear guard. As the overlords of Roland and Marsile, Charlemagne and Baligant must avenge their vassals' deaths. Perhaps most important, Charlemagne's victory over the supreme leader of the Muslim world imbues the battle with a transcendent value, a confirmation of the moral and spiritual superiority of the Christian worldview.

If one looks beyond the number and integrity of its episodes, other structural patterns emerge. The *Chanson de Roland*, like many Old French epics, is constructed upon an elaborate system of doubling and inversion.[12] To name the most obvious examples, the work opens with two parallel council scenes in which a feudal lord (Marsile, Charlemagne) consults his most trusted advisers; Roland's designation of Ganelon as Charlemagne's ambassador is countered by Ganelon's designation of Roland as the leader of the rear guard; Roland and Oliver quarrel in two parallel scenes, exchanging roles in the dispute over the sounding of the *olifant*; the second Battle of Roncevaux redeems the first; and the judicial combat between Thierry and Pinabel is a corrective to the failed judgment of Ganelon by Charlemagne's barons. This doubling pattern on the level of macro-narrative is complemented by the verbal echoes that saturate the text, creating multiple layers of repetition that engage the audience's memory and interpretive faculties.[13]

Christians and Saracens

An initial reading of the *Chanson de Roland* gives the impression of a profoundly dualistic universe in which righteous Christians and demonic Muslims are diametrically opposed. One of the most frequently cited lines is Roland's assertion "Paien unt tort e chrestïens unt dreit" (v. 1013) [The pagans are wrong and the Christians are right], a binary opposition frozen into the rhythm of the epic caesura. Saracen figures are overtly distinguished by onomastics, with numerous proper names connoting otherness: those with exotic sound combinations such as Escababi (v. 1512) or Aëlroth (v. 1188) and those with recognizable Latinate roots that connote malevolence or duplicity, such as Malquiant (v. 1594) [evil-seeking] or Falsaron (v. 1213). Certain names are conspicuous for their poetic resonance, notably the alliterative Turgis de Tortelose (v. 916) and the duo Esturganz and Estramariz (vv. 940–41).[14] The jongleur provides sinister portraits for some noteworthy Saracens: Chernuble of Muneigre's hair flows down to the ground; for sport, he carries more weight than seven mules could support; in his land, the sun never shines, wheat cannot grow, rain never falls, and all the rocks are pitch black: indeed, devils are said to dwell there (vv. 975–83). Archbishop Turpin slays Siglorel the magician, who once visited hell through Jupiter's sorcery (vv. 1391–92). The "Micen" fighters in Baligant's camp have enormous heads and piglike bristles along their spines (vv. 3221–23). The Saracens are said to worship a pagan trinity of false gods (Muhammad, Tervagant, and Apollo), whom they readily repudiate when Marsile is fatally wounded by Roland (vv. 2578–91). The Saracens are morally reprehensible, resorting to false promises and displaying casual disregard for their own progeny, whose lives they are willing to sacrifice in the interest of land and possessions. The fallacy of their religious beliefs is made abundantly clear by the emptiness of their false boasts: though Marsile's finest knights all vow to destroy Roland, the hero will not be slain by a Saracen, and despite their ominous predictions that Charlemagne will never recover from the loss of Roland and the rear guard, thousands of Christians rise up to take their places.[15]

At the same time, the radical alterity of the Saracens is somewhat attenuated by the inclusion of more admirable figures. Margariz of Seville is described as the finest of pagan knights, valiant, strong, nimble, and so handsome that all ladies who catch sight of him light up with joy (vv. 955–60, 1311–12). Both the emir of Balaguer and the emir Baligant are depicted as brave, worthy warriors with all the requisite qualities of a fine knight—save one: "Deus! quel baron, s'oüst chrestïentét!" (v. 3164, cf. v. 899) [O God, what a noble baron, if only he were a Christian!]. It is significant that the narrator employs a similar hypothetical locution to characterize Ganelon, who likewise lacks one essential trait: "S'il fust leials, ben resemblast barun" (v. 3764) [If he were loyal, he would seem the perfect baron]. This implicit comparison between the foulest Christian and the finest Saracens allows for a degree of mobility in the seemingly rigid partition between righteous Christians and evil Saracens. In addition to shared values in the domain of chivalry, Christians and Saracens have a similar sociopolitical structure, as emphasized in the parallel council scenes at the beginning of the text. To be sure, these parallels serve in part to illuminate fundamental moral and ideological differences, but they also suggest a certain permeability in the wall dividing the two imagined societies.

Sharon Kinoshita has sought to complicate the conventional argument that the *Roland* reflects a pervasive crusading ethos.[16] She interprets the Saracen proposition at the beginning of the poem as a reflection of the Iberian convention of *parias*, the tribute money exchanged between Christian and Muslim rulers whose alliances have often been overlooked by the conventional "clash of civilizations" master narrative. In Kinoshita's reading, the *Chanson de Roland* dramatizes the waning of the politics of negotiation in favor of an intractable stance founded on religious difference. Thus the poem gradually and purposefully constructs a crusading mentality, which reaches its fullest expression in the duel between Charlemagne and Baligant.[17]

Pivotal Episodes: Responsibility for Roncevaux

The *Roland*'s poetic artistry is perhaps most evident in the deployment of similar laisses at three crucial moments in the narrative: Ganelon's betrayal of the rear guard, the two-part quarrel between Roland and Oliver, and Roland's death. The question of responsibility for the Roncevaux disaster hinges largely on a close and contextualized reading of these pivotal sequences, which have been parsed in numerous commentaries.[18] Modern interpretations fall into two principal camps: those scholars who believe that Roland is guilty of excessive pride and those who have sought to counter this notion.[19] The following brief analysis is intended as a point of departure for further reading and reflection.

Ganelon's defense against the charge of treason at the end of the poem depends in part on a distinction between his responsibility for Roland's death and his alleged betrayal of Charlemagne. Setting aside Ganelon's problematic claim to revenge, we as readers or listeners have ample evidence to convict Ganelon of treason based on his pact with Marsile, a plot that begins to take shape in the similar laisses 40–42. Probing Ganelon's loyalty, Marsile opens the dialogue in each laisse with the same observations and the same question: Charlemagne is over two hundred years old; he has inflicted and received countless blows on the battlefield; when will he tire of waging war? Ganelon's tripartite response unfolds as a gradual slippage from proud allegiance to incipient treachery: in laisse 40 he stoutly defends Charlemagne's honor and refutes any claim that the emperor would desert his barons; in laisse 41 he declares that Charlemagne will never renounce war so long as his nephew (here unnamed) remains alive, since the nephew, along with Oliver and the entire vanguard of 20,000 Franks, constitutes the emperor's principal source of protection; in laisse 42 he reiterates the previous claim but pointedly names Roland. Thus each successive laisse brings the traitor's developing scheme into increasingly sharper focus; through patterns of repetition and subtle variation, the sequence links Charlemagne's military strength and security to the very knights Ganelon conspires to ambush in succeeding stanzas.

Robert Francis Cook has written, "One of the more misleading tics of *Roland* criticism is surely the habit of saying or implying that Ganelon . . . champions a course of action that will lead to peace and security."[20] In fact, Ganelon consistently behaves in ways that jeopardize the Christians' wellbeing. If he was merely imprudent in the council scene, when he was so eager to ignore Marsile's history of duplicity, he emerges as a consummate figure of Judas during his mission in Saragossa. Whether or not he has the right to avenge himself against Roland is beside the point; it is clear that Ganelon's retribution involves a fatal breach of his feudal bond with Charlemagne. The narrator-jongleur's verdict, which precedes the trial, is unequivocal: "Dés ore cumencet le plait e les noveles / De Guenelun, ki traïsun ad faite" (vv. 3747–48) [Then the trial and the case begin / Of Ganelon who committed treason]. Loyalty to Charlemagne must therefore transcend feudal particularism. William Calin sums up the poem's political philosophy: "that the individual be subordinated to the group, anarchy to order and hierarchy, feudal or clan honor to Christian duty, and that God's sacred mission and the supremacy of the royal person take priority over other calls."[21]

Another commonplace of *Roland* criticism is the notion that Roland is responsible for the Roncevaux disaster because of a tragic flaw of *démesure* or excessive pride.[22] Proponents of this argument typically point to the quarrel between Roland and Oliver, which unfolds in and around two series of similar laisses separated by some 620 lines. Standard literary histories tend to align themselves with Oliver's thrice-stated position that Roland should sound the horn, thus recalling Charlemagne to assist the rear guard.[23] Roland's three-pronged response, which cites his own good name, the reputation of his family, and the honor of France, has been interpreted as a prideful disregard of his duty to Charlemagne.[24] Roland's stance is admittedly somewhat alien to the sensibilities of the modern Western reader. After all, if Charlemagne had returned with his forces, might not the massacre of the rear guard have been avoided?

The narrator, however, is curiously reticent on the matter and does not pronounce in favor of either position. Though many have claimed that line 1093, "Rollant est proz e Oliver est sage" [Roland is brave and Oliver is wise], reflects the classic distinction between *fortitudo* and *sapientia*, the narrator's statement does not constitute a binary opposition, nor does it cast the quarrel in terms of Roland's heroic folly and Oliver's superior judgment.[25] The next line confirms that the two companions are united in their worthiness: "Ambedui unt mervellus vasselage" (v. 1094) [Both are marvelous vassals]. Moreover, the narrator never reproaches Roland for excessive pride; only Ganelon and Oliver do so. In the absence of explicit narratorial intervention, it is the audience who must consider the merits of each knight's argument. Oliver's position is grounded in the immediacy of his perception that the Christians are vastly outnumbered: "Dist Oliver: 'Paien unt grant esforz; / De noz Franceis m'i semble aveir mult poi'" (vv. 1049–50) [Oliver said: "There is a huge army of pagans, / But mighty few of our Franks, it seems to me"]. Roland's response, on the other hand, is framed in terms of feudal principles that would have been understood by medieval audiences. In invoking his reputation—and by extension that of his lineage and his homeland—he is not merely concerned with his personal "image," as we would understand that notion today. Rather, he is steadfastly observing the promise he made to Charlemagne, that he will lead the rear guard so that Charlemagne and his army can cross the mountains in safety (vv. 789–91). Requesting the return of the army would entirely defeat the purpose of the rear guard, which is precisely to protect the retreating troops. Sounding the horn would thus violate fundamental principles of trustworthiness and adherence to one's word. As Cook points out, Roland does not claim that he can save the rear guard; he does vow that the Saracens will all die (vv. 1058, 1069, 1081). This is not a rash boast, but rather a promise that will be fulfilled, just like his earlier assurance that Charlemagne will lose nothing that is not first vigorously defended by the sword (vv. 754–59).[26]

Because Roland seemingly reverses his position in the second horn scene (laisses 128–31), it is often assumed that he regrets his previous decision. Now it is Roland who repeatedly insists on sounding the horn and a bewildered Oliver who objects in the name of honor (vv. 1705–10). What Oliver fails to recognize, however, is that Roland invests the horn signal with an entirely new meaning, since the circumstances have changed dramatically since the companions' earlier exchange. Only sixty Christian knights remain, and their moments are numbered: Roland is not calling to ask for reinforcements, but rather to inform Charlemagne of the rear guard's imminent demise (v. 1699). Indeed, Charlemagne's duty as overlord is to avenge the death of his vassals and assure their proper burial, as Archbishop Turpin recognizes when he intervenes in the quarrel (vv. 1742–51). Charlemagne is able to exact revenge with little difficulty, thanks to the extraordinary losses inflicted upon the Saracens by the rear guard.

When it becomes clear that defeat is imminent, Roland laments the loss of his men, stating that they have died "pur mei" (v. 1863) [for me]. This passage has been offered as proof that Roland belatedly recognizes his error and is now prepared to begin the process of expiation.[27] The phrase "pur mei" is, however, ambiguous. While proponents of the *démesure* theory have translated it as "through my fault," Cook's revisionist reading, "because I am your leader," supports his view that Roland is merely expressing grief over his inability to protect those who have followed him into battle.[28] Jean-Charles Payen, in his study of the repentance motif in medieval French literature, finds that Roland's pride is heroic rather than sinful and that the hero does not regret or repent of his decision not to sound the horn.[29] Given the elliptical presentation of the horn debate and the lack of a narratorial verdict, neither position can be deemed authoritative, and it is likely that medieval audiences debated the matter as well. In any event, the age-old *démesure* theory should not be accepted without serious consideration of the textual and social context of Roland's decisions. Responsibility for the Roncevaux disaster ultimately lies with Ganelon, whose betrayal triggered the series of events leading to the hero's death.

Roland's death scene, occurring just past the midpoint of the poem and recounted in two consecutive series of similar laisses, masterfully combines the intensity of a lyrical pause with temporal thickness and spiritual progression. Sarah Kay has characterized the approaching death of an epic hero as a violent "storm of energy" that focuses on the dying man's life story.[30] In laisses 171–73, Roland's final burst of energy is concentrated upon his sword Durendal, which he vainly attempts to shatter against a rock so that no Saracen might possess it. As the sword crashes against the sardonyx, Roland vividly recalls his past exploits, evoking general victories in laisse 171 and proceeding to a litany of specific conquests in laisse 172. Laisse 173 shifts the focus to the sword's hilt, which enshrines holy relics commemorating Saints Basil, Peter, and Denis as well as the Blessed Virgin. In each laisse Roland concludes his reflections on the past with a fierce desire to control the future, begging God that Durendal might not fall into the hands of a pagan or a coward. In the second sequence (laisses 174–76), he painstakingly sets the stage for his own death, lying down on a steep hill under a pine tree and turning his face toward the enemy. Thus he orients future witnesses to the proper interpretation of his death: "Turnat sa teste vers la paiene gent: / Pur ço l'at fait quë il voelt veirement / Que Carles dïet e trustute sa gent, / Li gentilz quens, qu'il fut mort conquerant" (vv. 2360–63) [Towards the pagan host he turned his head, / Because it was his earnest wish that / Charles and all his men should say / That he, the noble count, had died victoriously]. This unusual deployment of hypotaxis draws attention to the process of transmission and translation set in motion by the hero's positioning of his body.[31] However, each laisse culminates with a more transcendent gesture, as Roland turns his thoughts from chivalric distinctions to eternal life, extending his right glove to God. By shifting his attention from feudal to heavenly lord, Roland completes his trajectory toward martyrdom.

The Figure of Charlemagne

The *Chanson de Roland* both reflected and perpetuated a legend of Charlemagne that began to develop soon after the emperor's death in 814.[32] The poem's opening line evokes the ideal of a universal Christian empire, crystallized in a ruler who transcends time: "Carles li reis, nostre emperere magnes" (v. 1) [Charles the king, our great emperor]. Although Charlemagne was not crowned emperor until 800, the chansons de geste routinely blur the distinction between king and emperor, choosing between the two titles largely on the basis of assonance and metrics. When he first appears in the *Roland*, Charlemagne is surrounded by the markers of power and majesty. Seated in a garden, on a throne of pure gold beneath a pine tree, the bearded, white-haired figure leaves no doubt as to his identity: "S'est ki l'demandet, ne l'estoet enseigner" (v. 119) [If anyone seeks him, there is no need to point him out]. In the medieval epic imagination, however, he is also represented as a distinctly feudal monarch, with all of the obligations and constraints imposed by that system. When confronted with Marsile's proposal, Charlemagne must consult his barons before arriving at a decision; later, at Ganelon's trial, he must convene the barons and state his case against the accused. This does not mean that the king is weak or ineffectual, only that feudal custom limits the scope of his authority.[33]

Emperor, king, military chief, and warrior, Charlemagne is also a saintly figure who enjoys a privileged relationship with the divine. God grants him protection by sending a holy interpreter in times of crisis:

Karles se dort cum hume traveillét.
Seint Gabriel li ad Deus enveiét,
L'empereür li cumande a guarder.
Li angles est tute noit a sun chef.
Par avisiun li ad anuncïét
D'une bataille ki encuntre lui ert:
Senefiance l'en demustrat mult gref. (vv. 2525–31)

[Charles sleeps like a weary man. / God sent Saint Gabriel to him; / He gives him orders to guard the emperor. / The angel spends all night at his head; / In a vision he announced to him / a battle to be waged against him / And showed him its grim significance.]

Through the divine intermediary, Charlemagne experiences premonitory dreams laden with violent animal imagery, in addition to an explicit prediction of imminent battle in the poem's closing lines. In this sense, Charlemagne recalls the Old Testament prophets.[34] A more specific allusion to the Old Testament may be discerned in the miracle performed for the emperor: God halts the course of the sun for Charlemagne just as he did for Joshua, allowing both to vanquish their enemies.[35] New Testament imagery is present not only in Ganelon's Judas-like betrayal, but also in the construct of the Twelve Peers, an obvious parallel with Christ's Apostles.

This majestic, hieratic figure alternates with a more human characterization, particularly in the scenes depicting the emperor's anguished reflection or suffering. These states of mind are rendered not by introspection but by stylized gestures: the pensive leader bows his head, and the bereaved uncle tugs his beard, weeps, and faints. The end of the poem evokes a weary and embattled Charlemagne lamenting a new call to war: "Li emperere n i volsist aler mie: / 'Deus!' dist li reis, 'si penuse est ma vie!' / Pluret des oilz, sa barbe blanche tiret" (vv. 3999–4001) [The emperor had no wish to go. / "God," said the king, "how wearisome my life is!" / He weeps and tugs at his white beard]. Finally, although it is not explicitly mentioned in the *Chanson de Roland*, the Charlemagne legend does include a tale of transgression: some medieval texts allude to an incestuous relationship between the emperor and his sister, a union that produced Roland.[36] There is no clear evidence that the Oxford *Roland* poet was aware of this legend, but some have argued that it informs the animosity between Roland and Ganelon, which is apparent from the beginning of the poem.[37] In any case, the incest narrative ultimately inscribes Charlemagne and Roland in a familiar mythical scenario in which the son is sacrificed to redeem the sin of the father.

Ganelon's Trial

Ganelon's trial and punishment have come under considerable scrutiny as indicators of the poem's date and provenance, as well as its overarching political message. In his 1936 study, Ruggero Ruggieri claimed that Ganelon's defense, as well as the legal procedures depicted in the trial, reflected archaic Germanic practices, and thus he argued for the text's early, Germanic origins.[38] According to Ruggieri, Ganelon's claim to private revenge has legitimacy because it derives from Germanic customs that privileged the rights of the clan; the *Roland* thus revolves around a conflict between ancient baronial rights and the central power of the Carolingian monarchy. A half century later, Emanuel Mickel refuted Ruggieri's claims by demonstrating that elements of the trial scene correspond quite well to later feudal judicial practices; in Mickel's view, Ganelon's defense is little more than a ruse and thus constitutes an entirely unjustified assault on royal authority, with Charlemagne standing in for the Capetian monarchy.[39] Mary Jane Schenck, introducing additional documentary evidence from the Anglo-Norman legal context, contends that the trial scene is a multilayered, multivoiced episode that affords glimpses into various legal practices.[40] A precise legal evaluation of the trial episode is greatly complicated by the lack of documentation of medieval customary law in northern France before the late twelfth century. As Mickel and Schenck recognize, the fictional trial does not serve as a mirror of contemporary legal procedures, but rather integrates aspects of such procedures into a political and poetic strategy.

The judicial system in the twelfth century was accusatory rather than inquisitorial, and motives for a crime were far less important than the deed itself. Ganelon's trial begins with the emperor's formal accusation:

"Seignors barons," ço dist Carles li reis,
"De Guenelon car me jugez le dreit!
Il fut en l'ost tresqu'en Espaigne od mei,
Si me tolit vint mil de mes Franceis,
E mun nevold, que jamais ne verreiz,
E Oliver, li proz e li curteis;
Les duze pers ad traït por aveir." (vv. 3750–56)

["Lord barons," said King Charlemagne, / "Give me a true judgment with regard to Ganelon. / He came with me in my army as far as Spain / And robbed me of twenty thousand of my Franks / And my nephew, whom you will never see again, / Oliver too, the brave and the courtly. / He betrayed the twelve peers for money."]

The barons are not called upon to give a verdict as the modern Western reader would understand it. Rather, there is a presumption of guilt, and Charlemagne is asking the barons to judge what consequences are dictated by the law in this case.[41] Ganelon responds to the accusation by attempting to redefine his deed as an act of justifiable vengeance. Claiming that he was wronged by Roland and challenged him openly, he declares: "Vengét m'en sui, mais n'i ad traïsun" (v. 3778) [I avenged myself, but there is no treason in it]. Charlemagne's council does not make any pronouncement on Ganelon's interpretation of his deed; instead, the barons recommend that Charlemagne drop the case and allow Ganelon to resume his loyal service (vv. 3809–13). While feudal justice did generally seek to reconcile parties, the barons' decision here is clearly in response to Pinabel's intimidation (v. 3797). Charlemagne declares them to be traitors ("felun," v. 3814), and the impasse is resolved when Thierry comes forward and formally challenges Pinabel to a judicial duel. Thierry asserts that any wrongdoing committed by Roland against Ganelon is entirely irrelevant: "Que que Rollant Guenelun forsfesist, / Vostre servise l'en doüst bien guarir. / Guenes est fels d'iço qu'il le traït" (vv. 3827–29) [Whatever Roland may have done to Ganelon, / The act of serving you should have protected him. / Ganelon is a traitor in that he betrayed him]. It is this judgment that will be tested by his battle with Pinabel. The *judicium Dei* proceeds according to established ritual: Pinabel formally accepts the challenge, pledges are secured, and each adversary presents his right gauntlet to the emperor. Before the battle, the combatants make confession, hear mass, and receive communion. Charlemagne invokes the essential principle of judicial combat, that is, God's immanence in the procedure: "'E! Deus!' dist Carles, 'le dreit en esclargiez!'" (v. 3891) ["Oh God," said Charles, "make justice shine forth!"]. Thierry's victory proves the veracity of his judgment, thus confirming the narrator's pretrial assessment.

Bramimonde and Aude

Preoccupied as it is with the bonds of fealty and companionship between males, the Oxford *Roland* famously devotes very little textual space to its two female characters. However, Bramimonde and Aude do command considerable attention in the post-Roncevaux episodes. As Kinoshita points out, the two figures "bracket" Ganelon's trial, which is preceded by Aude's death and followed by Bramimonde's baptism.[42] Each in her own way introduces an element of "counternarrative" into a male-dominated epic trajectory.[43]

Oliver alludes briefly to his sister Aude during the quarrel with Roland, threatening to prevent the physical union of his sister and his companion

(vv. 1720–21) and thereby placing the possession of Aude's body at stake in the male competition for superior military judgment. Subsequently, however, Aude is curiously de-eroticized. Her appearance is limited to 26 lines (vv. 3708–33), of which 14 relate her death, vigil, and burial. Her brief and pointed speeches reflect the language of feudal agreement rather than the agony of a bereaved lover: "O 'st Rollant le catanie, / Ki me jurat come sa per a prendre?" (vv. 3708–9) [Where is Roland the captain, who swore to take me as his bride?]. When Charlemagne offers his own son Louis in "exchange" for Roland, Aude categorically rejects the emperor's proposal as "strange" or "foreign" (vv. 3714–17) and promptly expires. Aude has often been contrasted with the lyric heroine Belle Doette, who copes with the death of her beloved Doon by commissioning an abbey for true lovers.[44] Unlike Doette, Aude displays little agency and appears to have no place in the world in the absence of her betrothed. She would seem at first glance to be nothing more than a female version of Roland, preferring death to the violation of cherished principles. Nonetheless, Aude does present a fleeting challenge to feudal marriage practice by removing herself from circulation. The *eschange-estrange* rhyme is particularly salient in the assonanced laisse and underscores her resistance to the notion of interchangeability. "Refusing her prescribed role in the feudal politics of lineage, she elects the dramatic gesture of absolute devotion over the option of a measured, longer-term advantage. . . . she demonstrates a loyalty to Roland that equals Roland's to Charles."[45]

Queen Bramimonde's reaction to her husband's imminent death is quite different.[46] When Marsile established his alliance with Ganelon earlier in the story, she functioned as her husband's loyal helpmate (vv. 634–41). Faced with the likely fall of Saragossa, however, she assumes the stance and the discourse of the typical Saracen Princess, rejecting the Muslim gods and touting Charlemagne's superior prowess (vv. 2600–2607). Unlike the typical Saracen Princess, however, she is motivated by disillusionment rather than desire for a Christian knight (vv. 2737–40). When she bitterly predicts a Frankish victory, her male interlocutors repeatedly attempt to suppress her unwelcome speech (vv. 2724, 2741). Bramimonde's resistance, of course, is contained within the other, Muslim arena. She ultimately gives voice to the ideology of the Christian adversary, and she freely joins their world in acknowledgment of its superiority. The solemn account of her baptism at the end of the poem both recognizes her enlightened conversion and reduces her to silence and passivity: "La baptizerent la reïne d'Espaigne; / Truvét li unt le num de Juliane. / Chrestïene est par veire conoisance" (vv. 3985–87) [There they baptize the Queen of Spain. They found for her the name of Juliana; She is a Christian, convinced of the truth].[47]

Beyond the Oxford Version

Succeeding Old French versions modify and amplify the Roland material. Notably, in the rhymed manuscripts, the episode of Aude's death is significantly more developed.[48] After the Roncevaux disaster, Charlemagne summons her to Blaye, but he initially hides the deaths of Roland and Oliver from her. En route she experiences premonitory dreams, which the cleric Amaugis falsely interprets as signs of impending good fortune. Charlemagne welcomes her to Blaye and claims that Roland and Oliver have remained with the Saracens. When the emperor offers to marry her to the Duke of Normandy, Aude refuses and demands to know the truth. Learning of the deaths of her brother and fiancé, she initially faints, but then regains consciousness and visits the bodies of Roland and Oliver in a church. An angel adopts Oliver's voice, and he invites his sister to join him in heaven. Aude soon dies and, like Roland, is transported to heaven by angels. She is buried at Blaye along with Roland and Oliver.

Earlier scholars who were passionately convinced of the Oxford *Roland*'s incomparable excellence took a dim view of such innovations.[49] More recent studies have embraced the inevitable *mouvance* or variation displayed by the textual tradition, demonstrating the poetic richness of later versions. Joseph J. Duggan, for example, notes the strong sexual overtones present in Aude's dream sequence and in her encounter with the dead Roland; by enhancing Aude's erotic value, the poet underscores her genealogical worth and the missed opportunity of a powerful alliance between her lineage and that of Charlemagne.[50] Giovanni Palumbo finds that Aude's association with motifs such as the premonitory dream and the miracle elevate her status; her expanded role in the rhymed versions makes her worthy of burial beside the greatest of epic heroes.[51]

The *Chanson de Roland* gave rise to a number of translations and adaptations during the Middle Ages. In the mid-twelfth century, the Roncevaux material inspired a Latin prose text, the *Historia Karoli Magni et Rotholandi*, known as the Pseudo-Turpin Chronicle.[52] Allegedly the Archbishop Turpin's eyewitness account of Charlemagne's Spanish expeditions, the *Historia* combines the Charlemagne tradition with that of Saint James of Compostela. A profoundly religious work, the *Historia* was immensely popular in the Middle Ages, with more than two hundred known manuscripts. It was translated into many European languages, including French (in five separate versions), Occitan, Welsh, Spanish, Old Norse, and English. Another, lesser-known Latin version of Roncevaux is the *De tradicione (prodicione) Guenonis*, which likely dates from the thirteenth century.[53] This work, composed in Latin hexameter verse, suppresses many episodes and focuses on the experience of Ganelon, who is represented "less as a transgressor of a social code and more as a victim of his own wrath."[54]

Other adaptations include the Middle High German *Rolandslied* by a cleric called Konrad (later 12th century),[55] the fragmentary Castilian *Roncesvalles* (13th century), and the Old Norse *Karlamagnús saga* (1230–50). Two assonanced decasyllabic versions in Occitan, the *Ronsasvals* and *Rollan a Saragossa*, are preserved in the same fourteenth-century manuscript. Both diverge significantly from the northern French tradition, and it is possible that the surviving texts represent an Occitan tradition of Roland dating back to the twelfth century.[56]

The Roland legend enjoyed great prestige in Italy, and several fourteenth-century Franco-Italian works—*L'Entrée d'Espagne*, *La Prise de Pampelune*,[57] and *Aquilon de Bavière*[58]—recount the hero's pre-Roncevaux exploits.[59] Subsequently the chivalric romances of the Italian Renaissance assured Roland's continued popularity throughout Europe into the eighteenth century. In the imagination of these later Italian poets, however, Roncevaux fades as the focal point of the hero's biography, and Roland's heroic fury is transformed. Boiardo's *Orlando Innamorato* (1483–95) presents the hero in the throes of passionate love, pursuing the elusive Angelica; in Ariosto's sequel, *Orlando Furioso* (1516–21), Orlando discovers that Angelica has given herself to the Saracen Medor. The hero descends temporarily into utter madness but is eventually cured and restored to his true vocation of service to God.[60]

Roland in the Modern Era

The "epic" Roland of the chansons de geste was resurrected in the nineteenth century.[61] Romantic poets were especially drawn to the stark grandeur of the landscape framing the hero's death. Alfred de Vigny's poem "Le Cor," published in 1826, depicts Roland's final hours at Roncevaux, evoking the towering mountains and the melancholy strains of Roland's horn.[62] This was also the era that witnessed the birth of an intense scholarly interest in the *Chanson de Roland* that continues to this day. Francisque Michel rediscovered the Oxford version at the Bodleian Library and published the text in 1837. Soon conscripted into the service of French national pride, Roland became an exemplar of devotion to country and God. The tale of heroic sacrifice in the face of devastating odds was especially evocative in the humiliating time of the Franco-Prussian War. In 1870, during the siege of Paris, the distinguished medievalist Gaston Paris delivered a lecture on the *Chanson de Roland* and "French nationality," in which he called upon his countrymen to recognize themselves as the descendants of those slain at Roncevaux as well as those who avenged them.[63]

Although the *Roland* (and the chanson de geste in general) has never generated the same appeal as the Arthurian legend in the realm of modern popular culture, there have been some innovative reworkings in recent decades. François Suard cites several musical and theatrical performances in the late twentieth and early twenty-first centuries that draw directly or indirectly upon the Roland tradition.[64] The rather obscure 1978 film *La Chanson de Roland*, directed by Frank Cassenti and starring Klaus Kinski, depicts a group of twelfth-century pilgrims engaged in a rendition of the Roncevaux tale; the film alternates between the two story levels and time frames. The text's potential for inculcating patriotic values is attested by numerous children's versions from 1911 to the present day.[65] On this side of the Atlantic, the Roland material inspired a 1999 comic book, *Roland: Days of Wrath*, whose authors rank Roland among the greatest superheroes of all time.[66]

Le Charroi de Nîmes and *La Prise d'Orange* (mid-12th century)

Le Charroi de Nîmes and *La Prise d'Orange* are presented here as a two-part segment in the poetic biography of Guillaume d'Orange, a framework that reflects the way in which the texts were regarded by medieval poets, compilers, and audiences. [67] Recounting the foundational conquests of Guillaume d'Orange in what is now southern France, the works are closely related in the cyclical manuscripts and may even have formed a single narrative in earlier versions. [68] The two songs represent complementary stages of the hero's development: each celebrates a major victory over the Saracens, achieved by a combination of brute force and wiliness. From these core narratives of the Guillaume cycle emerges the portrait of a distinctive epic protagonist, whom Jean Frappier aptly characterizes as "fiery, picturesque, truculent, hot-tempered and generous, independent and loyal, emotional and magnanimous, irascible and yet merry." [69]

Le Charroi de Nîmes

> "Baron," dist il, "envers moi entendez.
> Qui avroit ore mil tonneaus ancrenez
> Comme cil est que en cel char veez,
> Et fussent plain de chevaliers armez,
> Ses conduisist tot le chemin ferré
> Tot droit a Nymes, cele bone cité,
> Sifaitement porroit dedenz entrer." (vv. 939–45)

> ["Barons," he said, "listen to me. If someone had a thousand barrels with hoops, like the one you see in that cart, and if they were full of armed knights, and if he could lead them along the road straight to Nîmes, that good city, he would be able to enter inside."]

The *Charroi de Nîmes*, [70] containing 1,486 decasyllabic lines grouped in assonanced laisses, is the shortest poem of the Guillaume cycle. It survives in eight principal manuscripts, all of which place the work in its proper fictional chronology between the *Couronnement de Louis* and the *Prise d'Orange*. [71] The work's appeal among medieval and modern audiences may be attributed to its combination of dramatic intensity and humor, as well as its masterful deployment of epic technique. Edward A. Heinemann, who has examined the metrical art of the *Charroi* in painstaking detail, contends that the poem surpasses even the *Chanson de Roland* in the art of laisse structure and patterned repetition.[72]

Summary

In distributing fiefs to his barons, King Louis has neglected to provide for his most loyal and valiant knight, Guillaume d'Orange. Furious, Guillaume confronts Louis, reminding him of all the battles he has waged on the king's behalf. In particular, he recalls his duel with the emir Corsolt in the fields outside Rome, resulting in the injury that led to his surname "Guillelmes au cort nes" (v. 147) [Guillaume of the Short Nose]. Faced with the wrath of his most valued warrior, Louis offers him the lands of three recently deceased vassals; the knight rejects each of these proposals, citing the hereditary rights of the vassals' sons. The king eventually offers Guillaume a portion of his kingdom, but Guillaume proudly refuses, declaring that it would be shameful to deprive his lord of such revenue. Instead, prompted by a suggestion from his nephew Bertrand, Guillaume proposes that the king grant him the right to conquer a series of lands held by the Muslims, including the cities of Nîmes and Orange. Guillaume will hold these lands as Louis's vassal, and the king will reap the material benefits. When Louis consents, Guillaume persuades 30,000 poor young knights to follow him, promising lands and castles to those who will fight by his side.

Guillaume and his men make initial stops at the abbey-church of Brioude and the cathedral of Notre-Dame du Puy and then proceed to Nîmes, a city controlled by the Saracen king Otrant. As they approach enemy territory, they encounter a Saracen peasant driving a cart with a barrel full of salt. This inspires the crafty knight Garnier to devise a Trojan-horse-style strategy for invading Nîmes: after obtaining from the local peasantry a large number of carts and oxen, they load them with barrels in which they hide armed Christian knights. Guillaume d'Orange disguises himself as a merchant and leads the carts into the city of Nîmes. He invents an elaborate identity, claiming to have traveled far from his native Canterbury to buy and sell his wares. Thanks to his distinctive nose, however, he is soon recognized by the Saracen king. When Otrant's brother Harpin taunts him, mocking his humble attire and pulling his beard, Guillaume is goaded into revealing his true heroic identity. He kills Harpin and summons his own hidden troops, who leap out of their barrels and enter the fray. Guillaume and his men defeat the Saracens, defenestrate Otrant, and capture the city. The peasants recover their carts and oxen and receive compensation. King Louis rejoices at the news of Guillaume's victory.

History and Geography

Although historical antecedents have been established for Guillaume d'Orange and parts of his epic biography, the *Charroi de Nîmes* is not based upon an actual historical event.[73] The Muslims did occupy Nîmes twice (in 719 and 737), but Charles Martel reconquered the city in 738, and it endured no further incursions during the reigns of Charlemagne and Louis the Pious. Guillaume's imagined conquest is, however, situated in a narrative space marked by convincing references to external reality. Scholars have often noted that the itinerary followed by Guillaume and his men from Paris to Nîmes is remarkable for its geographical precision.[74] The route carefully mapped by the poet (vv. 782–841, 1032) corresponds to the Voie de Regordane used by medieval merchants and jongleurs, as well as pilgrims traveling to Saint-Gilles. For Joseph Bédier, the *Charroi's* pointed geographical references confirmed the notion that local legends preserved along pilgrimage routes inspired literate poets to compose the chansons de geste.[75] It is generally recognized today that such allusions are insufficient proof of a primary collaboration between poets and monasteries. Nonetheless, the *Charroi's* attention to toponyms and trajectories does suggest that the poet was intimately familiar with the region between Paris and Nîmes. More important, the geographical reference points contribute to a certain "reality effect" that distinguishes the *Charroi* from the *Chanson de Roland*, whose fictional space is largely symbolic. Though highly stylized and far from realistic, the *Charroi* intermittently mentions landmarks and familiar objects to create a fleeting illusion of reality.[76] At once inscribed in a transcendent journey and anchored in the recognizable space of contemporary travel, Guillaume's expedition to Nîmes evokes both mythical and earthly dimensions.

Royal Ingratitude

The first half of the narrative corresponds to a topos found in both epic and moralizing texts: the outraged vassal's invective against an ungrateful sovereign.[77] The *Charroi* poet represents the conflict quite vividly, in a fast-paced exchange between Guillaume and the ineffectual King Louis. In a series of (partially) parallel laisses, Guillaume vigorously asserts the role of memory in the lord-vassal relationship and, by extension, in the epic aesthetic (vv. 131–255). Recalling his exploits in the king's service, Guillaume punctuates his tirade with two related formulas: "Dont ne te menbre" (vv. 134, 183) [Do you not remember?] and "Rois, quar te menbre" (vv. 157, 203, 213) [King, do remember]. In reiterating the deeds narrated in the *Couronnement de Louis*, Guillaume functions as object and subject of the narration, as both warrior and jongleur. Within the fiction, his litany of reminders serves to reproach the ungrateful king; on the level of discourse, it serves to jog the listener's memory by situating the action of the *Charroi* in a chain of chivalric accomplishments.

Guillaume affirms his steadfast loyalty not only by citing feats of valor and constant sacrifice but also by emphasizing his own mindset, ever focused upon his vassalic obligations. He reminds his lord that when the haughty Acelin challenged Louis's right to the throne, not a single baron spoke up until Guillaume intervened: "Quant me menbra de naturel segnor. / Passai avant, tant fis plus que estot, / Si le tuai a un pel con felon"[78] (vv. 188–90) [When I remembered my true lord. I came forward, acting like a fool, and killed him with a pike]. Ideally, critical moments in the political sphere, such as challenges to royal power—or, implicitly, the distribution of fiefs—should trigger the memory of the lord-vassal bond.

A new series of parallel constructions emerges when Louis tries to appease Guillaume by offering him fiefs made available by recent deaths. These proposals are instantly rejected, prompting Louis to offer a quarter and then half of his kingdom. Here the repeated hemistich "Non ferai, sire" [I will not do it, lord] forms a rhythmical pattern of resistance, highlighting Guillaume's resolve in the face of royal inconstancy.[79] Of particular note is Guillaume's stance in favor of the hereditary nature of fiefs, which reflects an essential development in the history of feudalism between the ninth and the twelfth centuries. In the earlier feudal age, the exploitation of a fief did not extend beyond the lifetime of the vassal. By the time the *Charroi* was composed, fiefs typically reverted to the overlord only until the vassal's heirs were properly invested. The *Charroi*, like many chansons de geste, attests to the remembered and ongoing conflicts involved in feudal succession.

Guillaume's critique does not constitute a condemnation of royal power, but rather of Louis's negligence in the exercise of that power. Guillaume is not a rebel baron: though he is briefly tempted to cross the line, his nephew Bertrand placates him by intoning a feudal credo:

"Cuit li abatre la corone del chief:
Ge la li mis, si la vorrai oster!"
Dist Bertran: "Sire, ne dites pas que ber.
Vo droit segnor ne devez menacier,
Ainz le devez lever et essaucier,
Contre toz homes secorre et aïdier."
Et dit li quens: "Vos dites voir, beaus niés;
La loiauté doit l'en toz jorz amer.
Dex le conmande, qui tot a a jugier." (vv. 435–43)

["I think I'll knock the crown off his head: I put it there, and I want to
remove it!" Bertrand says, "Lord, you are not speaking like a valiant
knight. You should not threaten your rightful lord, but rather elevate
and exalt him, help and aid him against all men." And the count said:
"You speak truly, fair nephew; one should always love loyalty: God,
who judges all things, commands it so."]

Reconquest

Guillaume's proposal to wrest lands from Saracen domination is motivated
by multiple factors.[80] Forgotten by the king, constrained by his support of
hereditary fiefs, he finds himself without resources, unable to exercise lar-
gess or even provide for his horse (vv. 80–84). Though no longer youthful,
he is still "young" in the feudal sense, that is, unestablished, landless, and
thus unable to marry and accede to full adulthood in the feudal world.[81]
In addition to these socioeconomic considerations, Guillaume's conquest
takes on a spiritual dimension when he (rather belatedly) reveals that his
desire to liberate Nîmes and other occupied lands was inspired by an un-
fulfilled vow. During the feast of Saint Michael, when visiting a baron in
Saint-Gilles, he was led by his host's wife to an upstairs chamber, where she
fell at his feet. Instead of the seduction scenario he momentarily feared,
the gesture was intended to elicit his pity: the lady placed him before a
window, where he observed a panoramic view of Christian suffering:

"Tote la terre vi plainc d'aversiei,
Viles ardoir et violer mostiers,
Chapeles fondre et trebuchier clochiers,
Mameles tortre a cortoises moilliers,
Que en mon cuer m'en prist molt grant pitié,

Molt tendrement plorai des elz del chief.
La plevi ge le glorïeus del ciel,
Et a saint Gile, dont venoie proier,
Qu'en cele terre lor iroie aïdier." (vv. 570–78)

["I saw the entire land full of demons, cities being burned and churches
violated, chapels destroyed and steeples torn down, courtly women's
breasts twisted, so that my heart grew full of great pity, and I wept
most tenderly. Then and there I pledged to the glorious king of heaven,
and to Saint Giles, to whom I had come to pray, that I would go help
the people of that land."]

In contrast to the topographical precision that characterizes the poem as a
whole, this description evokes a conventional *locus horribilis*, an infernal
space of destruction and sexual violence commonly associated with Sara-
cen presence.[82] The lone female character in the *Charroi de Nîmes* does
not arouse the hero's love, as will Orable in the *Prise d'Orange*, but rather
Christian compassion and crusading zeal.[83]

The Comic Mode

In the Guillaume cycle, the high seriousness of feudal and military conflict
is often tempered with moments of humor. [84] Philip E. Bennett affirms
that the comic mode is integral to epic artistry as it was conceived by the
poets who reworked earlier songs into the surviving cyclical redactions.[85]
Indeed, characters such as Rainouart, and often Guillaume himself, are
often said to be cast in the heroicomic tradition. This mixing of epic and
comic modes is nowhere more pervasive than in the *Charroi de Nîmes*.
Guillaume's distinctive laugh, positioned at strategic intervals, emblema-
tizes the rapid changes of register that generate much of the work's energy.
The second-hemistich formula "s'en a un ris jeté" [he burst out laughing]
is found throughout the cycle, and in the *Charroi*, as elsewhere, the hero's
laughter is not a simple expression of merriment. In fact, Guillaume laughs
at critical junctures in the narrative pertaining to matters of grave conse-
quence: when he discovers the king has neglected him, when Bertrand
proposes the conquest of Saracen-occupied territory, when Louis offers
half his kingdom (vv. 44, 459, 478). Alain Corbellari characterizes these
outbursts as both a salutory reaction to adversity and a gesture of defiance
to those who would challenge him.[86]

Comic effects penetrate the epic framework from the beginning of the text. The dramatic tension of Guillaume's confrontation with Louis is twice interrupted by details that divert the hero's towering strength from the heroic to the mundane. Arriving at the king's palace, Guillaume stomps up the steps so forcefully that the laces of his leather shoes break, thus terrifying the barons in attendance (vv. 56–57). Later he leans on the bow he has brought back from the hunt, cracking the bow in two and sending the pieces flying until they fall beneath the king's nose (vv. 123–28). These parallel scenes of rupture humorously figure the breach in lord-vassal relations. In addition, as Bennett notes, the mishaps gently mock the epic model of brute force, as the hero's fabled strength paradoxically threatens to make him ridiculous.[87]

Guillaume's autobiographical tirade showcases his own body as a site of rupture—literal rupture and rupture with the heroic. Recalling the battle in which the Saracen Corsolt sliced off a piece of his nose, Guillaume embellishes, claiming that he had to readjust his nose with his own two hands; treated by an incompetent doctor, he was left with a truncated and humped nose that humiliates him in front of his peers (vv. 136–48). The anatomical details deflect attention from Guillaume's military victory to his signature deformity, casting the celebrated battle scar as an ordinary, unsightly injury. The new version of events also allows the poet to provide a lighthearted explanation for two conflicting traditions concerning the hero's nose: "cort" (short) and "corb" (crooked).[88]

In the first half of the poem, then, many of the *Charroi's* comic effects derive from the juxtaposition of heroic deeds and attributes with scenes of material fragility. Contrastive humor is also evident in the transitional laisses between Guillaume's appearance at court and his expedition to Nîmes. In three parallel laisses (vv. 765–81),[89] the narrator enumerates the equipment being loaded onto three hundred packhorses. The first two laisses furnish an inventory of liturgical objects—chalices, psalters, missals, crucifixes, rich cloths. The third laisse, however, shifts abruptly to a list of essential culinary equipment—pots, pans, cauldrons, tongs, andirons. The comic descent from spiritual to earthly concerns is underscored by patterns of repetition and variation. Each phase of the enumeration begins with a variation on the same intonation verse: "Bien vos sai dire que porte li premiers . . . Bien vos sai dire que reporte li autres . . . Bien vos sai dire que reporte li tierz" (vv. 765, 770, 775) [I can well tell you what the first group carried . . . I can well tell you what the second carried . . . I can well tell you what the third carried]. Similarly, each list concludes with a two-line explanation of the objects' purpose, casting kitchen paraphernalia in the same incantatory mold as devotional objects: "Quant il venront enz el regne essillié, / Serviront tuit Damedieu tot premier . . . Quant il venront enz el regne sauvage, / S'en serviront Jhesu l'esperitable . . . Quant il venront enz el regne essillié, / Que bien en puissent atorner a mengier" (vv. 768–69, 773–74, 778–79) [When they arrive in the devastated kingdom, they will all first serve God . . . When they arrive in the savage kingdom, they will serve Jesus, the celestial spirit . . . When they arrive in the devastated king-dom, they will be able to prepare food].

The second half of the *Charroi* is more consistently and overtly comic, beginning with the culture clash that marks the Christian knights' encoun-ter with a Saracen peasant. Communication between Guillaume and the peasant breaks down because of social rather than religious difference. When Guillaume demands information on the state of affairs in Nîmes ("des estres de la ville"), the peasant misconstrues both context and inten-tion, and informs his interlocutor about the price of bread (vv. 901–16). Subsequently, humor revolves principally around the disguises assumed by Guillaume and his knights. Epic gravity gives way to farce when Bertrand, unaccustomed to his peasant shoes and inexperienced in the conduct of oxen, lands his cart squarely in the mud (vv. 988–1014). Once again, for-mulaic style serves comic purposes, as the poet frames patently nonheroic material in the conventional language of epic warfare. The formula "qui le veïst" [if you had seen him], typically employed to conjure a scene of intense battle, evokes here a distinctly ignoble image: "Qui le veïst dedenz le fanc entrer / Et as espaules la roe sozlever, / A grant merveille le peüst resgarder" (vv. 1007–9) [If you had seen him step into the mud and lift the wheel with his shoulders, you could have looked upon him with great wonderment].

Guillaume's own lowly disguise, described in great detail (vv. 1036–46), paradoxically renders him both master and victim of a successful ruse. On the one hand, his merchant identity and tall tales provoke laughter at the gullible Saracens, who fail to perceive the inner layers of both attire and speech. When Guillaume engages in double talk, comedy of situation allies the audience with Guillaume against the uncomprehending King Otrant:

Et dit Guillelmes: "Beau sire, or vos soffrez;
Ge nen istrai huimés de la cité:
La vile est bone, g'i vorrai demorer.
Ja ne verroiz demain midi passer,
Vespre soner ne soleil resconser,
De mon avoir vos ferai tant doner,
Toz li plus forz i avra que porter." (vv. 1162–68)

[And Guillaume said, "Fair lord, now be patient; I will not leave the city today. It is a good city, and I wish to stay. Before you see midday pass tomorrow, or hear vespers ring or see the sun set, I will give you so much of my goods that even the strongest among you will have a heavy burden."]

On the other hand, Guillaume clearly bristles beneath his disguise, muttering under his breath and fairly bursting with the desire to expose his true identity. When Harpin tugs at his beard, Guillaume privately rages that the Saracen has failed to recognize him as Guillaume Fierebrace—when in fact it is precisely that lack of recognition that assured his entry into Nîmes.[90] In the Guillaume cycle, as François Suard notes, disguises are frequent but short-lived: once the mask has served its purpose, the hero is either recognized or provoked into revealing himself. Thus the disguise motif is both a comic strategy and a pretext for reflection upon the hero's identity.[91]

Bennett situates the Guillaume cycle's comic elements within the Bakhtinian model of the carnivalesque tradition. In medieval popular culture, certain feast days such as Mardi Gras and the Feast of Fools were occasions for subversive and irreverent behavior that allowed for bawdiness, disguise, and social inversions within limits circumscribed by official authority. Examining literary transpositions of this tradition in the Guillaume epics, Bennett finds that carnivalesque interludes are counterbalanced and redeemed by military victories and by Louis's continued presence on the throne.[92] The *Charroi de Nîmes* accords a privileged space to the carnivalesque without diminishing the hero's stature or chivalric potential. In the poem's final lines, Guillaume's victory and generosity reverberate throughout the land and confirm divine will:

Tres parmi France en vet la renomee.
Li quens Guillelmes a Nymes aquitee.

A Looÿs la parole est contee:
Li rois l'entent, grant joie en a menee,
Dieu en aore et Marie sa mere. (vv. 1482–86)

[Throughout France the news spreads: Count Guillaume has liber-
ated Nîmes. The news is told to Louis; when he hears it, he is over-
joyed; he gives thanks for it to God and Mary, his mother.]

La Prise d'Orange

> "Ne mengerai de pain fet de ferine
> Ne char salee, ne bevrai vin sor lie,
> S'avrai veü com Orenge est assise;
> Et si verrai icele tor marbrine
> Et dame Orable, la cortoise roïne." (vv. 284–88)
>
> ["I will eat neither bread made with flour nor salted meat, nor will I
> drink clear wine, until I have seen how Orange is situated; and I will
> see the marble tower, and Lady Orable, the noble queen."]

The *Prise d'Orange* follows the *Charroi de Nîmes* in the eight cyclical man-
uscripts that preserve the complete text.[93] Earlier scholars of the epic took
a dim view of the *Prise*, judging it to be a decadent work full of clichés
and contaminated by courtly romance and lyric.[94] Since the pioneering
work of Hans-Robert Jauss, notions of genre have become less norma-
tive, recognizing that textual traditions develop against the backdrop of
the audience's horizon of expectations.[95] The chanson de geste flourished
for centuries precisely because poets continued to test its possibilities and
expand its generic horizon. Recently the *Prise* has received a great deal
of critical attention by scholars interested in gender, genre, and medieval
orientalism.[96]

Summary

Having conquered Nîmes, Guillaume is overcome by boredom, since he
and his men have neither women nor war to occupy them. This situation
changes abruptly with the arrival of Gillebert, a Christian who recently
escaped from a Saracen prison in Orange, a city ruled by the fierce Aragon.
Gillebert sings the praises of both the city and its fair queen Orable, wife of
Aragon's father, the Saracen king Tibaut. Inflamed with desire, Guillaume
vows to capture Orange and Orable, but first he undertakes a reconnais-

sance mission with his nephew Guielin and the escaped prisoner Gillebert, who is now fluent in Saracen languages. The three men, unarmed, disguise themselves as Saracens by blackening their faces, and succeed in entering Orange, claiming to be interpreters in Tibaut's service. They inform Aragon that they came by way of the newly conquered Nîmes, where Guillaume Fierebrace briefly held them captive. Enraged, Aragon swears that he will kill Guillaume and scatter his remains to the winds. The Christians manage to secure a meeting with Orable, who resides in the tower of Gloriete, a site of exotic Oriental splendor. Orable asks for a description of the renowned Guillaume, and the disguised hero willingly obliges with a self-portrait that arouses the lady's interest.

Guillaume is soon recognized by a Saracen, and battle ensues. The Christians fight valiantly with clubs and drive the enemy from the tower of Gloriete. After Orable furnishes them with armor and weapons, the battle intensifies, but the Saracens enter the tower through an underground passage. Guillaume and his companions are captured, but Orable persuades Aragon to sequester the captives in her own prison until Tibaut returns. Messengers are dispatched to Tibaut, who assembles an army and sets out for Orange. Meanwhile Orable reveals to the prisoners a second underground passage, by which Gillebert returns to Nîmes for reinforcements. A Saracen spy has overheard their plan and informs Aragon, whereupon Orable, Guielin, and Guillaume are incarcerated together. When Guillaume despairs of their plight, he is mocked by his nephew Guielin, who taunts him about his lovelorn state. While Gillebert, Bertrand, and 15,000 troops make their way into Orange through the underground passage, Guillaume and Guielin begin to attack their Saracen captors. The Christian forces unite to decimate the Saracens, Bertrand slays Aragon, and Orange is conquered. Orable is baptized and receives the Christian name Guibourc, and she and Guillaume marry.

Orange and Orable

As was the case with the *Charroi de Nîmes*, the events related in the *Prise d'Orange* have little or no basis in fact. Although the city of Orange was indeed occupied by Muslims at the beginning of the eighth century, it was never conquered by Guillaume's historical prototype, Guillaume of Toulouse. The legend surrounding such a conquest, however, goes back at least as far as the 1125 *Vita sancti Wilhelmi*, whose author declares that Guillaume of Toulouse captured Orange from "Theobaldus" during the reign of Charlemagne. (Orable/Guibourc is not mentioned in this account.) The *Vita* is one of several sources that suggest an earlier, lost version of the *Prise d'Orange*. A number of chansons de geste, including the *Siège de Barbastre, Foucon de Candie,* and *Aliscans,* allude to Guillaume's conquest of Orange in ways that do not correspond to the extant version, including a siege of the city by Orable's husband Tibaut (merely adumbrated in the existing version) and the attribution of more conventional heroic exploits to Guillaume.[97]

In its surviving form, the *Prise* playfully reconfigures the epic conquest as both military and amorous venture. From the moment he hears Gillebert's description of Orange and Orable, Guillaume conceives a dual mission: "Ja ne quier mes lance n'escu porter / Se ge ne voi la dame et la cité" (vv. 264–65) [I will never again carry lance or shield if I can't see the lady and the city]. Proper names reflect the twinning of woman and city, both identified as precious commodities: the *or* (gold) in *Or*able and *Or*ange also echoes in the name of the queen's tower, Gl*or*iete. Onomastic play, evident throughout the poem, is especially significant with regard to the lady and her surroundings: *orable* in Old French means "worthy of adoration." Phonetically linked to her city and tower at the beginning of the narrative, Orable sheds her "pagan" name at baptism; as *Gui*bourc, she is henceforth identified with *Gui*llaume.[98]

Gillebert first describes Orange as an impregnable fortress guarded by 20,000 pagans armed with lances and 140 Turks bearing costly standards (vv. 195–96). Subsequent descriptions focus on the splendors of the palace, its vaults and mosaic borders, its painted flowers and sweet aroma of spices, its luxurious spaces closed to outside sun and heat (vv. 241–73, 458–62). Eastern palaces and gardens enjoyed great prestige in the medieval West, and the *Prise d'Orange* contains some of the most striking and detailed architectural descriptions found in French medieval texts.[99] Of particular note is the tower of Gloriete. Its name, derived from *gloire* (glory), is a common noun designating a richly decorated space, a small chamber, an arbor, or the highest room in the house.[100] Orable's tower incorporates these multiple meanings: Gloriete is an opulent decor with marble pillars, windows inlaid with silver, and a golden eagle. The interior chamber, replete with natural wonders, frames the portrait of the Saracen queen:

A une part de la chambre leanz,
Avoit un pin par tel esperiment
. . . .
Longue est la branche et la fueillë est grant;
La flor qu'en ist par est si avenant,
Blanche est et inde et si est vermeillant.
. . . .
Pitre et canele, garingal et encens
Flere soëf et ysope et piment.
La sist Orable, la dame d'Aufriquant;
Ele ot vestu un paile escarinant,
Estroit lacié par le cors qu'ele ot gent
De riche soie cousue par les flans;
Et Josiane, la niece Rubïant,
Le vent li fist a un platel d'argent.
Ele est plus blanche que la noif qui resplent
Et plus vermeille que la rose flerant. (vv. 650–66)

[On one side of the chamber within was a pine tree with magical properties. . . . Long are its branches and its leaves are large; the magnificent flower it bears is white, blue, and crimson. . . . Pyrethrum, cinnamon, galingale, and incense exhale sweet fragrances, along with hyssop and piment. There sits Orable, the lady from Africa,[101] clad in a sumptuous silk gown laced tightly around her noble body, sewn along the sides with rich silken ties. And Josiane, niece of Rubiant, fans her with a silver fan. She is whiter than glistening snow and more crimson than a fragrant rose.]

The description of Gloriete joins Oriental motifs to images from biblical and romance traditions. Presenting an exotic interior inhabited by women, the poet evokes the mystique of the seraglio without actually depicting one. Guillaume declares the site to be paradise (v. 675), and indeed the marvelous tree conjures images of Eden. Moreover, pine trees have special status in the chansons de geste as images of majesty: it is under a pine that Charlemagne receives the Saracen envoys and consults his barons in the *Chanson de Roland* (vv. 114, 168). The majestic tree in Charlemagne's garden traces a vertical axis linking the earth to the sky, symbolizing fertility and contact with the divine. By associating Orable with the monumental pine, the poet establishes her royal status before slipping into a sensual portrait that positions the queen as an object of desire.[102] Orable's classic crimson and white skin replicates the flowers growing on the tree, and the combination is again mirrored in the image of the damsel (niece of Rubiant) waving a silver fan. The crimson/white contrast, a staple of the romance portrait, appears somewhat overdetermined in the rendering of Orable's beauty, perhaps highlighting the importation of an "exotic" literary device into an epic description.[103]

Cultural Identity and the Saracen Queen Plot

To a certain extent, the *Prise d'Orange* projects an image of cultural identity as fluid and interchangeable.[104] Guillaume and his companions engage once again in a masquerade, a "conversion" (albeit a false and temporary one) that allows them to penetrate Orange disguised as Saracen interpreters. Crucial to this enterprise is Gillebert's fluency in exotic languages, namely Turkish, African, Bedouin, and Basque (vv. 326–27). A similar multilingualism is attributed to Guillaume in the *Chanson de Guillaume* and *Aliscans*, where the hero's fanciful linguistic repertory includes "sarrazinois," Greek, German, and Berber.[105] Indeed, the polyglot motif appears in a number of chansons de geste, frequently in conjunction with the hero-trickster in disguise. In these narratives, the poets draw attention to cross-cultural communication only to undercut its possibilities: like blackface or Saracen armor, the Western hero's clever code-switching allows him to change places just long enough to dominate the foreign adversary.[106] In the *Prise d'Orange*, the games of identity played by male characters also serve as a comic prelude to the more serious business of converting the Saracen Queen.

The marriage plot in the *Prise* is a variation on a micro-narrative common to a number of chansons de geste. This scenario features a Saracen Princess who becomes so enamored of a Christian knight that she renounces both family and religion.[107] The potentially subversive nature of her rebellion is effectively neutralized because it serves the ideological purposes of the Christian heroic ethos. Though framed by an exotic decor, the Saracen Princess corresponds to Western ideals of physical beauty, presenting the same luminous blond hair and fair skin as her Christian counterparts. At the same time, her beauty is inscribed more explicitly in the context of the material wealth admired and coveted by the Western male protagonist. She often demonstrates specialized knowledge in astrology, magic, or medicinal herbs. Intrepid and assertive, the Saracen heroine typically makes the first move, offering her love and assistance to the hero and his entourage. Her sensuality culminates in a conversion scene during which her nude body is plunged into the baptismal font under the gaze of the Christian knights.

Though she shares many traits with the Saracen Princess type, Orable is distinguished by her marital and royal status. She is dignified and discreet in her interactions with the Christian knights. Her ultimate union with Guillaume is first represented in a symbolic gesture, when she girds him with her husband's sword (vv. 948–52). She later promises to help Guillaume and his companions and convert to Christianity if Guillaume will marry her (vv. 1374–77). When Aragon's men imprison her with the Christian knights, she expresses concern for her spiritual well-being and her sexual reputation:

> "Diex," dist la dame, "beau pere esperitable,
> Que n'a baptesme receü ceste lasse?
> Gel cuidai prendre et estre en Deu creable.
> Sire Guillelmes, mar vi vostre barnage,
> Vostre gent cors et vostre vasselage,
> Quant por vos sui gitee en ceste chartre,
> A tele angoisse comme fust par putage." (vv. 1545–51)

["God," said the lady, "fair heavenly father, why has this poor wretch not received baptism? I hoped to be baptized and believe in God. Lord Guillaume, your bravery, your noble body, and your knightly valor have brought me harm, since I have been thrown into this prison because of you, with the same anguish as one accused of whoring."]

Although the *Chanson de Guillaume* alludes to Orable's magical powers, and the *Enfances Guillaume* relates the spells she cast over her Saracen husband Tibaut in order to avoid sexual contact with him, the queen is not associated with sorcery in the *Prise d'Orange*.[108] Her "Saracen" traits are thus somewhat attenuated in this text, where she appears as an exotic but easily convertible figure. Orable's baptism and marriage to Guillaume are recounted succinctly in the penultimate laisse (vv. 1861–78). These closing lines dwell on the multiple substitutions resulting from Guillaume's conquest: Orable changes her religion and her name, and the couple is married in a church that was formerly a mosque.

Narrative and Generic Structure

It has often been noted that the *Prise d'Orange* makes significant use of doubling to generate narrative events. Gillebert travels from Orange to Nîmes on two occasions; the Christian knights are twice captured, twice imprisoned, and twice liberated; two underground passages facilitate the journey in and out of Gloriete. Claude Lachet interprets these excessive narrative echoes as a comic device intended to poke fun at the artifices of adventure stories.[109] They might also be seen as a parody of the mirror episodes found in more "serious" epic, such as the dual horn scenes in the *Chanson de Roland*. As components of the larger narrative structure, however, the paired sequences reflect upon each other in the interest of dramatic progression. Gillebert's initial arrival in Nîmes triggers the expedition to Orange; his return for reinforcements prepares the Christians' victory. A first underground passage leads to the hero's captivity; a second ensures his definitive liberation.

The overarching structure of the *Prise* presents Guillaume at the height of his chivalric career. His dual conquest of Orable and Orange represents the culmination of a series of exploits celebrated in the *Couronnement de Louis* and the *Charroi de Nîmes*.[110] Within this epic trajectory, however, the poem engages in a great deal of generic play, pitting the ideals of the traditional chanson de geste against those of romance and lyric poetry, thereby generating parodic reversals of the heroic ethos.

When Guillaume resolves to capture Orange, his mission is framed by the thematics and language of courtly love lyric. Never having laid eyes on Orable, he is so struck by the descriptions of her beauty that he falls in love from afar like the desiring subjects of troubadour and trouvère lyric.[111] Suffering from acute lovesickness, he echoes the laments of lyric and romance lovers: "La seue amor me destraint et justise / Que nel porroie ne penser ne descrire / Se ge ne l'ai, par tens perdrai la vie" (vv. 289–91) [Her love torments and dominates me so much that I can neither imagine nor describe it. If I do not have her, I will soon lose my life].[112] Once in Orange, Guillaume oscillates between feats of extraordinary strength and episodes of fitful passivity. Trapped inside Gloriete, and then in Aragon's prison, he is frequently discouraged, wishing he were back in France or lamenting the absence of his mighty allies. On such occasions his nephew Guielin mockingly invites Guillaume to find solace in Orable's embrace, declaring that his uncle's sole motive for entering Orange was love (vv. 903–21, 1335–40, 1568–83). Guielin calls into question the entire heroic enterprise, predicting that Guillaume's reputation will henceforth be utterly transformed:

"Huimés dirai, ne me chaut qui le sache,
L'en soloit dire Guillelme Fierebrace,
Or dira l'en Guillelme l'Amïable:
En ceste vile par amistié entrastes." (vv. 1560–63)

["From now on I will say—and I don't care who knows it—people used to call you Guillaume of the Mighty Arms, but now they will call you Guillaume the Lover: you entered this city for love."]

This transformation reverberates throughout the narrative, defying audience expectations. Lachet has observed that Guillaume's heroic traits, though not entirely suppressed, are distributed among other characters.[113] Orable displays the courage and strategic ability usually associated with Guillaume Fierabrace; it is she who comes to the rescue of the hero in distress. Guillaume's habit of striking down an adversary with a single blow to the nape of the neck is transferred to Gillebert and Guielin. The love intrigue inflects conventional epic motifs as well: the Saracen prison, traditionally depicted as an infernal space teeming with serpents, appears here as a version of the courtly locus amoenus, where Guillaume enjoys a comfortable captivity in the presence of his beloved.[114]

The Prise d'Orange provides ample evidence of the elasticity of Old French epic even in the earlier period. Far from being "contaminated" by competing genres, the Guillaume cycle flourished precisely because of the ongoing process of generic innovation. Furthermore, the ironic perspective on Guillaume's trajectory does not undermine his heroic image. Rather, as Alain Corbellari argues, humor complements and supports the underlying seriousness of Guillaume's endeavors.[115]

Rewritings

Like the Guillaume cycle as a whole, the *Prise d'Orange* and the *Charroi de Nîmes* appealed to European audiences throughout the Middle Ages.[116] In the early thirteenth century, Wolfram von Eschenbach incorporated elements of the *Prise d'Orange* in his unfinished verse adaptation of the Guillaume material, titled *Willehalm*.[117] The anonymous fifteenth-century compilation known as the *Roman de Guillaume d'Orange* includes prose versions of both the *Charroi de Nîmes* and the *Prise d'Orange*.[118] While his star faded between the Renaissance and the mid-nineteenth century, Guillaume acquired status as a French national hero in the modern period. His legendary conquests particularly captured the imagination of playwrights and novelists during the period spanning the Franco-Prussian War and World War I. Of these works, Paul Tuffrau's *La Légende de Guillaume d'Orange* is perhaps the most widely known in France today.[119] Up through the 1990s, Guillaume's exploits in Nîmes and Orange continued to appear in popular novels and children's literature.[120]

Raoul de Cambrai (ca. 1200)

> Biax fu Raous et de gente faiture.
> S'en lui n'eüst un poi de desmesure
> mieudres vasals ne tint onqes droiture,
> mais de ce fu molt pesans l'aventure:
> hom desreez a molt grant painne dure. (vv. 319–23)

[Raoul was handsome and nobly built. If he had not had in him an immoderate streak, there could not have been a better vassal occupying his rightful place: but the outcome of this fault was to prove disastrous: an unbridled man has great difficulty in surviving.]

Raoul de Cambrai, the most celebrated of the "epics of revolt," depicts a world shattered by unrestrained impulse and rampant discord.[121] William Calin fittingly characterized the text as a "decomposing universe,"[122] and the notion of decomposition has been applied to the work's formal structure as well as its thematics of rupture and disintegration.[123] On the level of story, one observes three distinct narrative sections:[124]

(1) Raoul's struggle to take possession of the Vermandois and his death at the hands of Bernier ("Raoul");

(2) the wars of revenge waged by Raoul's nephew Gautier against Bernier and the subsequent rebellion of both parties against King Louis ("Gautier");

(3) the adventures of Bernier and his murder by Raoul's uncle, Guerri the Red ("Bernier").[125]

Although the "Raoul" section is privileged here as the historical and poetic core of the text, the following analysis takes into account the integral version of the poem as it was transmitted in surviving documents.

Summary

"Raoul" (vv. 1–3541)

Raoul is the son of Aalais, sister of King Louis,[126] and the deceased Raoul Taillefer, whom Louis invested with the fief of the Cambrésis. When Raoul is three years old, Louis is persuaded by advisers to give both the Cambrésis and Lady Aalais to Gibouin. Aalais refuses the marriage and, like Raoul's uncle Guerri the Red, is outraged by the king's actions. Raoul grows up to be a fine, strong young man and receives his chivalric education from Guerri. He is knighted by King Louis, who bestows upon him a sword second only to Durendal and the helmet of a Saracen slain by Roland. Raoul's closest companion is Bernier, the illegitimate son of Ybert of Ribemont. Bernier becomes Raoul's squire and receives his arms from Raoul.

When Raoul comes of age, he is prodded by Guerri to demand the restitution of the Cambrésis, which was to be held by Gibouin only until Raoul's majority. Raoul angrily confronts King Louis, who refuses to dispossess Gibouin but promises Raoul the next vacant fief. That fief proves to be the Vermandois, which was to be inherited by the four sons of Herbert of Vermandois—one of whom is Ybert, Bernier's father. The king reluctantly grants the fief to Raoul, who vows to take the land by force, haughtily rejecting pleas from Bernier and Aalais. So distraught is Aalais that she calls down a curse upon her son. Raoul and his forces march on Origny, attacking its inhabitants and setting fire to the church. All one hundred nuns are burned to death, including Bernier's mother Marsent, abbess of Origny. Bernier, who has witnessed his mother's horrible demise, bitterly reproaches Raoul, whom he has served loyally. Raoul responds by insulting Bernier and striking him. The dispute escalates, despite Raoul's offer of reparations and various attempts at peace. In a fierce battle against Bernier and Ernaut of Douai, Raoul is slain.

Guerri the Red retrieves Raoul's corpse as well as that of John of Ponthieu, a "giant" knight killed by Raoul in battle. Opening up both bodies, Guerri extracts the knights' hearts: John's is as small as a child's, while Raoul's is the size of an ox's.[127] Grief-stricken, Aalais turns to young Gautier as her only potential heir, and Gautier vows to avenge Raoul's death. Heloise, Raoul's fiancée, laments bitterly and swears that she will never marry.

"Gautier" (vv. 3542–5363)

Gautier is knighted and, along with Guerri the Red, pursues war against Bernier and the rest of the Vermandois clan. Two judicial duels between Gautier and Bernier fail to resolve the issue of Bernier's guilt in Raoul's death; Gautier and Guerri insist that Raoul was treacherously murdered, while Bernier maintains that he defied Raoul properly.[128] Aalais arrives at King Louis's court and lashes out at both the king and Bernier. Declaring

Louis unfit to rule, she also attempts to kill Bernier with a crowbar. The Cambrésiens and the Vermandois arrive at a truce and join forces against Louis, blaming him for the entire conflict. In the fighting that ensues, Bernier wounds the king in the thigh, and the rebellious barons set fire to the city of Paris.

"Bernier" (vv. 5364–8542)

Beatrice, daughter of Guerri the Red, hears of Bernier's chivalric exploits and becomes enamored of the knight without ever having seen him. She proposes to marry Bernier to preserve the peace between their two families, and both families eventually agree. King Louis interrupts the marriage celebration and takes Beatrice prisoner. He insists that she marry Erchambaut of Ponthieu, but Beatrice resists and is rescued by Bernier. Some two years later, when Beatrice is pregnant with their first child, Bernier repents of his history of violence and the couple set out on a pilgrimage to Saint-Gilles. En route, Bernier and his newborn son Julian are captured by different groups of Saracens. Acting on a false rumor of Bernier's death, Louis gives Beatrice in marriage to Erchambaut of Ponthieu, but Beatrice obtains an herb that protects her chastity by rendering Erchambaut impotent. By agreeing to fight on behalf of his Saracen captor Corsuble against another Saracen army, Bernier earns his freedom and recovers Beatrice. They have a second son, Henry, before Bernier sets out to find their long-lost elder son Julian. Agreeing once again to serve as Corsuble's champion, Bernier unwittingly engages in battle with his own son, but the strong family resemblance leads to recognition. The family is joyfully reunited. Ignoring advice from Beatrice, Bernier agrees to accompany Guerri the Red on a pilgrimage to Santiago de Compostela. As they pass Origny, Bernier utters a sigh, recalling Raoul's death. Guerri, his rage rekindled, murders Bernier treacherously by splitting his skull. Bernier piously forgives his killer before expiring, but his death provokes renewed conflict. Julian kills Gautier, but Guerri escapes and is never heard from again. Henry eventually becomes lord of Artois, and Julian Count of Saint-Gilles.

Textual Layering

As it has come down to us in the most complete surviving manuscript, BnF fr. 2493, *Raoul* bears the marks of a series of rewritings.[129] The tripartite narrative structure described above does not coincide with formal junctures: on the level of versification, the text divides into two parts, signaled by a shift from rhyme to assonance at the beginning of laisse 251 (v. 5374). Although assonance is usually associated with earlier epic compositional practice, the assonanced section of *Raoul de Cambrai* is in fact a more recent addition to this multilayered text. Drawing upon historical, textual, and codicological evidence, scholars have concluded that *Raoul de Cambrai* in its present form contains traces of at least three stages of composition:[130]

- a hypothetical early twelfth-century assonanced version of the song's core, "Raoul";
- a late twelfth-century reworking of "Raoul" in rhymed laisses, with the addition of the "Gautier" sequel;
- an early thirteenth-century continuation, "Bernier," composed in assonanced laisses to give the poem an archaic tone.[131]

History and Legend

Much of the early scholarship on the poem was devoted to its relationship with historical events and personages, since the central conflict in "Raoul," the rivalry over the Vermandois, has its origins in Carolingian and post-Carolingian history. The conflict between Cambrai and the Vermandois dates back to the 843 Treaty of Verdun, which gave Cambrai to Lotharingia and the Vermandois to Charles the Bald; Cambrai changed hands at least six times over the course of the following century.[132] The eponymous hero seems to be a composite of at least four historical Raouls. His story is perhaps most closely associated with that of Raoul, son of Raoul of Gouy, who perished in battle in 943 after invading the territory of Herbert of Vermandois; according to the annals of Flodoard, this Raoul's death greatly saddened King Louis IV "d'Outremer."[133] Another possible prototype is Raoul, son of the Count of Flanders, who engaged in territorial disputes with Herbert of Vermandois, set fire to the abbey of Saint-Quentin in 896, and was eventually killed by Herbert. King Louis is also an amalgam, inspired by Louis, son of Charlemagne, as well as Louis IV. In terms of contemporary concerns, the poem is clearly a response to tensions between the high aristocracy and the monarchy in the late twelfth century. Philip II Augustus (r. 1180–1223), in his ambition to strengthen the crown, did not hesitate to provoke strategic disputes among the nobility, and his maneuvers over the succession of the Vermandois were a notable example of this policy.[134]

The Poetics of *Démesure*

It is impossible to overstate the powerful sense of dissolution, violence, and alienation that characterizes "Raoul." The text is fraught with anticipatory passages that create an atmosphere of impending doom, attributing the crisis to multiple factors: the decisions of a weak and unjust monarch, Guerri's bellicose advice, Aalais's curse, Raoul's own temperament, and even the friendship between Raoul and Bernier.[135] As Reto Bezzola has written, *Raoul de Cambrai* lacks the moral center as well as the social and human ideals of the *Song of Roland* or the Guillaume cycle.[136] Nonetheless, the narrator-jongleur assures his audience in the opening lines that the song of Raoul is the best of all its kind, a song of "joie" [exuberance] and "baudor" [celebration]. *Raoul de Cambrai* thus presents a dystopian world infused with the terrible grandeur born of "démesure," a fatal excess of audacity and prowess.

Unlike Roland, whose putative tragic flaw is never confirmed by the poem's narrator, Raoul is deemed outrageous by his own allies as well as the narrator, particularly when he orders his men to desecrate the church of Origny.[137] He is guilty not only of cruelty and gratuitous violence but also of sacrilege. To the horror of his men, he commands that his tent be pitched inside the church: "devant l'autel faites aparillier / un riche lit ou me volrai couchier; / au crucefis me volrai apuier / et les nonnains prendront mi esquier" (vv. 1062–65) [Prepare a magnificent bed for me to sleep on in front of the altar; I will use the crucifix as a back rest and my squires can make free with the nuns]. His knights disobey the order, just as the seneschal will refuse to produce the sumptuous meal of peacock and swan that Raoul demands after the destruction of Origny: in the flush of victory, he has forgotten Lent.[138] Later, when engaged in single combat with Ernaut of Douai, Raoul blasphemes, declaring that God and the saints are incapable of saving his adversary. This utterance is marked as the culmination of his moral depravity: "Li quens Raous ot tout le sens changié. / Cele parole l'a forment empirié / q'a celui mot ot il Dieu renoié" (vv. 2842–44) [Count Raoul was like a man possessed. This speech has done him untold harm, for with these words he has denied God].

Some earlier scholars interpreted Raoul's character as evidence of a growing force of "individualism" in medieval society at the dawn of the twelfth century.[139] Dominique Boutet, however, warns us not to confuse the developing consciousness of the self, which does emerge during this period, with the more anachronistic notion of an autonomous individual. Boutet rightly observes that Raoul is far from being an individual struggling for order within himself; rather, he is caught up at the problematic intersection between judicial rights and interpersonal relationships.[140] In fact, Raoul is perhaps best understood as he functions within those relationships, each of which undergoes a process of degradation.[141] The ties of kinship, vassalage, and friendship that ought to have provided a foundation for chivalric self-realization instead propel Raoul into a downward spiral, casting him alternately as victim and aggressor.

Fatherless since birth, the young hero had a potential safety net in the form of two substitute fathers, King Louis and Guerri the Red.[142] Rather than providing protection and guidance, however, both paternal figures bear some responsibility for Raoul's later manifestations of *démesure*.[143] As Raoul's maternal uncle and lord, Louis fails miserably in his duty toward the child, as the jongleur pointedly notes: "Rois Loeys fist le jor grant folaige / qe son neveu toli son eritaige" (vv. 135–36) [King Louis committed an act of great folly that day, for he deprived his nephew of his inheritance].[144] Louis does eventually assume his proper role, providing his nephew with arms and warhorse and making him seneschal of his kingdom, but his initial misdeed proves irreparable. When he later promises the next available fief, granting forty hostages to secure his pledge, the narrator paradoxically condemns the king for offering the land while maintaining Raoul's right to claim it: "Raous ot droit, tres bien le vos dison, / mais l'empereres ot trop le quer felon / qi de tel terre fist a son neveu don / dont maint baron widierent puis arçon" (vv. 602–5) [Raoul was in the right, we tell you truly, but the emperor acted most perfidiously in giving away to his nephew such land as would cause numberless barons to quit the saddle].[145]

Raoul's paternal uncle, Guerri the Red, occupies a similarly equivocal place in the hero's trajectory. He is responsible for Raoul's chivalric education and consistently defends his nephew's interests and those of the clan. It is Guerri's influence, however, that fuels Raoul's violent tendencies. The jongleur explicitly blames Guerri for the war between Cambrésiens and Vermandois: "Par le concel au riche sor Gueri / commença puis tel noise et tel hustin / dont maint baron furent mort et traï" (vv. 360–62) [On the advice of the powerful lord Guerri he later unleashed such strife and turmoil as left many barons killed or betrayed]. Impulsive and belligerent, Guerri regularly employs language as a weapon, and his wrath is fatally contagious. This is most striking when Louis refuses Guerri's demand that the Cambrésis be restored to Raoul. Guerri storms into the hall where his nephew is blissfully engaged in a game of chess:

> "Fil a putain," le clama—si menti—
> "malvais lechieres, por qoi joes tu ci?
> N'as tant de terre, par verté le te di,
> ou tu peüses conreer un ronci."
> Raous l'oï, desor ces piés sailli—
> si haut parole qe le palais fremi,
> que par la sale l'a mains frans hon oï.
> "Qi la me tout? trop le taing a hardi!"
> Gueris respont, "ja te sera gehi:
> li rois meïsmes—bien te tient a honi—
> dont devons estre tensé et garanti."
> Raous l'oï, toz li sans li fremi. (vv. 486–97)

["Son of a whore," he called him—quite without foundation—"cowardly brute, why are you here playing games? I tell you truly, you haven't enough land to rub down an old nag on!" Raoul heard him; leaping to his feet, he speaks so loudly that the great hall shakes and many noble men all down the hall could hear him: "Who is taking it from me? I think him very foolhardy!" Guerri replies: "I'll tell you now: it's the king himself—how he must regard you as disgraced!— who should be upholding and protecting us." Hearing this, Raoul's blood boiled.]

The effect of Guerri's verbal aggression is underscored by the play of rhyme and repetition, which links the booming utterance ("si haut parole ... qe le palais fremi") with Raoul's visceral response ("oï ... toz li sans le fremi").

To be sure, Guerri is not always given to violent outbursts.[146] At one point, he even encourages Raoul to accept a peace proposal and to leave the Vermandois in the hands of Herbert's sons (vv. 1987–94). However, Guerri's moment of moderation proves to be short-lived, and just as inflammatory as his deliberate provocations. Raoul, who had initially been inclined to accept the accord, flies into a rage, calling his uncle a coward; Guerri angrily puts aside all thoughts of peace, and the war is rekindled (vv. 2000–2014). Thus the flawed relationship between uncle and nephew both duplicates and perpetuates the internecine strife leading to Raoul's death.

The protagonist's exchanges with his mother are no less combative. Before Raoul's incursion into the Vermandois, Aalais offers her own counsel, begging her son instead to enlist the Vermandois clan in reclaiming the land that is rightfully his (vv. 796–36). Her appeal, which includes valuable strategic recommendations, is framed by references to the bond between mother and child. Raoul haughtily spurns her advice, replacing the imagery of the maternal body with visions of carnage:

"Biax fix Raous," dist Aalais la bele,
"je te norri del lait de ma mamele.
Por qoi me fais dolor soz ma forcele?"
. . . .
Raous tenoit sa main a sa maissele,
et jure Dieu qi fu nez de pucele
q'il nel lairoit por tout l'or de Tudele.
Ains q'il nel lait en iert traite boele
et de maint chief espandue cervele. (vv. 826–41)

["Raoul, my son," said the lovely Alice, "I fed you with milk from my own breast. Why do you strike pain deep in my heart?" . . . Jutting his jaw in his hand, Raoul swears by God who was born of a virgin that he would not leave off for all the gold of Tudela. He would rather see people disemboweled, and the brains dashed from many heads, than give up.]

Once again, the sequence of rhymes is revealing, as the nurturing milk of mother's breast ("mamele" and "forcele") gives way to the spilling of entrails ("boele" and "cervele").

When reasoning proves fruitless, Aalais resorts to prophecy, a function often attributed to female characters in the Old French epic. She angrily predicts that Raoul will die at Bernier's hands, provoking a misogynistic tirade from her son and further strengthening his resolve to attack (vv. 911–31). Finally, she utters the curse that seals Raoul's fate: "'cil Damerdiex qi tout a a jugier / ne t'en remaint sain ne sauf ne entier!'" / Par cel maldit ot il tel destorbier, / con vos orez, de la teste trenchier!" (vv. 956–59) ["Let God who judges everything not bring you back safe and sound and in one piece!" Disaster overtook him as a result of this curse, as you shall hear— he had his head cut off!].

Alain Labbé situates the strident exchange between Raoul and Aalais within a broader crisis of communication in the poem. Afflicted with a "troubled virility" linked to his youth and lack of social well-being, Raoul is incapable of true dialogue.[147] Just as his fury toward Guerri magnifies the standard tensions between younger and older males, his knee-jerk response to Aalais reflects feudal society's most extreme attitudes toward women: offended by her speech and her very presence, he seeks to relegate her to a confined space and silence her.[148] A similar reflex is evident in his reaction to Bernier's mother Marsent, when she implores him to spare the Origny convent. This laisse, characterized by a remarkable formal virtuosity, opens with the abbess's entreaty ("proiere"), marked at the rhyme. Far from having its desired effect, her speech generates a torrent of insults from Raoul, whose response surely deploys every possible word for "whore" rhyming with "proiere." He denounces Marsent as a "putain chamberiere . . . maailliere . . . garsoniere . . . soldoiere . . . maistriere" (vv. 1152–62). Though he has a sudden change of heart in the following laisse, agreeing to a truce for love of Marsent ("por vostre amor qe m'en volez proier," v. 1183), he violates the verbal agreement within hours (vv. 1278, 1296).[149]

Of all the relationships depicted in *Raoul de Cambrai*, perhaps none is more unstable and catastrophic than the association between Raoul and Bernier. It is tempting to read this famed pair in terms of simple binary oppositions. Indeed, in the struggle for the Vermandois, the headstrong overlord Raoul is driven primarily by the impulse to war, while the aggrieved vassal Bernier is more amenable to a politics of reconciliation. Critics have even questioned whether Raoul or Bernier is the "true" protagonist, given Bernier's vital role in the narrative as well as evidence of a lost "song of Bernier" that may have constituted the original kernel of *Raoul de Cambrai*.[150] Like Raoul, however, Bernier exhibits a degree of complexity that defies easy categorization. From his first appearance in the poem, Bernier is an ambiguous figure. Raised in Aalais's household and cherished by Raoul, Bernier is admired for his good looks, skill in combat, wisdom, and judicious speech; nonetheless, he is stigmatized as a bastard, and the narrator deems him a "strange companion" whom Raoul should have decapitated early on (vv. 272–84, 415–18). Yet when Bernier strikes the fatal blow against Raoul, it is Bernier who is said to have God and righteousness on his side (v. 2922). Torn between conflicting duties to lord and lineage, Bernier maintains fealty to Raoul even after the latter's initial invasion of the Vermandois, explaining ruefully to Marsent that Raoul remains his lord, though he is as treacherous as Judas (vv. 1203–8). After the burning of Origny, however, Bernier alternately pursues vengeful and peaceful solutions. Haunted by the image of his mother perishing in flames, he repeatedly cites the list of Raoul's offenses, insisting that he has been poorly rewarded for his faithful service (vv. 1456–73, 1517–19, 1673–84). When Raoul finally offers public reparation, proposing to carry Bernier's saddle on his head for fifteen leagues,[151] Bernier refuses and calls for revenge. However, he subsequently renews his efforts at reconciliation, both before and after Raoul's death, and his discourse vacillates between guilt and self-defense for the remainder of the narrative. Thus Bernier's judicious assessment of Raoul's character applies equally to his own profound duality: "Raous, biaus sire, molt faites a proisier / et d'autre chose fais molt a blastengier" (vv. 1460–61) [Raoul, dear lord, you are very worthy of praise, and then in other ways you are very deserving of blame].[152]

Origny and the Power of Place

While all chansons de geste are concerned to some degree with the appropriation and retention of land, *Raoul de Cambrai* intensifies the subjective relationship of humans to space.[153] Much like the *Charroi de Nîmes*, *Raoul de Cambrai* begins with the problematic distribution of insufficient fiefs, but the two narratives propose radically different exit strategies. In the *Charroi de Nîmes*, the scarcity of land is a point of departure for the successful conquest of external territory; in *Raoul de Cambrai*, however, a similar shortage of available fiefs leads to internecine rivalry, generating a sense of confinement and an obsessive attachment to disputed spaces. As the focal point of this attachment, Origny is saturated with meaning and subject to multiple and conflicting interpretations, exemplifying the power of "place" that Molly Robinson Kelly examines in *The Hero's Place: Medieval Literary Traditions of Space and Belonging*, a study of the Roland, Alexis, and Tristan traditions.[154] Whereas "spatiality" refers to the physical spaces depicted in literature—their location, parameters, or geographic features—"place" is a construct that represents space as it is experienced subjectively and emotionally by characters. In *Raoul de Cambrai*, the narrator artfully interweaves descriptions of Origny's topography with allusions to its highly charged affective pull: "En Origni le borc grant et plaingnier /—li fil Herbert orent le liu molt chier— / clos a palis q'entor fisent fichier, / mais por desfendre ne valoit un denier" (vv. 1211–14) [The large and spacious town of Origny—Herbert's sons cared deeply for the place— had a dense palisade which they had erected around it, but it was worthless for purposes of defense]. The passage goes on to depict a meadow used for jousting and a ford beside which the nuns pastured their oxen: it is here that Raoul has his massive tent pitched, encompassing and appropriating the idyllic space that he has marked for annihilation and saying: "Alomes tost Origni pesoier!'" (v. 1114) ["Let's go quickly and break Origny into little pieces!"]. Indeed, Raoul's desire to destroy Origny is driven precisely by his adversaries' attachment to the place: "Je vuel le liu destruire et essillier, / por ce le fas li fil Herbert l'ont chier" (vv. 1066–67) [I want to destroy the place utterly, because it is well loved by Herbert's sons]. This metonymic displacement foreshadows Raoul's own demise: toppled from his horse, he strikes a final blow that misses its human target and plunges into the land at Origny (vv. 2936–51).[155]

Bernier's relationship to Origny is a tortured one. Though he values the site as a hereditary fief to be claimed by his male relatives, Bernier cherishes Origny primarily as the sacred dwelling place of his mother, the proper name conjuring his origins (*orine* or *origne* in Old French). After Marsent's death, the blazing abbey is foremost in his recurring litany of Raoul's transgressions: "Ma mère arcistes en Origni mostier" (v. 2092) [You burned my mother in the church at Origny].[156] Once Bernier has avenged this offense in the meadows of Origny, however, he comes to associate the place with Raoul, whose spectral image triggers the final events of the poem:

Si con il vinrent es prés sos Origni
en celle place ou Raous fu ocis
li cuens Berniers fist un pesant sospir;
. . . .

"Il me remembre de Raooil le marchis
qui desor lui avoit tel orguel pris
qu'a .iiii. contes vaut lor terre tolirr.
Vees ci le leu tot droit ou je l'ocis." (vv. 8188–8201)

[As they reached the meadows below Origny, Bernier heaved a great
sigh by the spot where Raoul was killed. . . . "I am reminded of Mar-
quis Raoul who was consumed with such pride that he resolved to
take the land of four counts for himself. This is the very place where
I killed him."]

The visual memory provokes Guerri's fatal blow, and the text explicitly
associates Bernier's brutal end with the land. In a scene highly reminiscent
of Raoul's death, Bernier's brains are dashed out on the ground ("enmi
la place," v. 8233) and he receives communion in extremis in the form of
three blades of grass (vv. 8257–58). Origny is thus finally the site of a tragic
reenactment uniting Marsent, Raoul, and Bernier in violent death.[157]

The Craft of Continuation

Since the "Gautier" and "Bernier" sections clearly reflect later additions to
the core narrative of Raoul's struggle to possess the Vermandois, they were
long dismissed as second-rate sequels, easily detachable from the whole.
More recent scholarship, however, has approached the work as a progres-
sive composition with its own coherent structure, an authentic text that
was received as such by a thirteenth-century public.[158]

The "Gautier" section prolongs the conflict between Cambrésiens and
Vermandois much as the Lorraine cycle recycles its narrative material,
by extending the feud to a new generation. Gautier functions largely as
a double of Raoul, reiterating his predecessor's relationships with Bernier
and Guerri. The "Bernier" section represents a more significant formal and
thematic departure, for it exhibits the characteristics of later epic compo-
sition or *chanson d'aventures*. Whereas "Raoul" deploys the incantatory
patterns common to early chansons de geste, including similar laisses
that halt the flow of action to render the thickness of events, "Bernier"
privileges narrative progression and proliferation. The poet introduces
Christian-Saracen conflict and incorporates stock motifs from the "family
romance": separations, peregrinations, and hidden identities culminate in
a father-son encounter that seems to drift far from the original subject

matter. Love and marriage often drive the action, prodded by the feisty and resourceful Beatrice.

Despite these changes in tonality and plot structure, continuity is maintained by the presence of key characters such as Bernier, Guerri, and Louis, as well as the cyclical resurfacing of the old Cambrésis-Vermandois conflict.[159] Furthermore, the continuators did preserve the fundamental conception of human agency and political change found in the core narrative. François Suard aptly describes this tragic vision in which history escapes those who wish to control it, and social interactions manifest an ineluctable drive toward rupture.[160] The poem's conclusion, far from resolving the chronic discord between the two lineages, contains the seeds of another (unrealized) continuation: Bernier's sons survive, and the narrator cannot confirm Guerri the Red's putative withdrawal from society: "mais on ne sait, certes, que il devint; / hermites fu, ainsis con j'ai oït" (vv. 8534–35) [But it is not known what became of him; I have heard that he became a hermit].[161] Each attempt at closure proves futile, confirming Emmanuèle Baumgartner's characterization of *Raoul de Cambrai* as a cycle unto itself.[162]

Reception

The latent affinity between *Raoul de Cambrai* and the Lorraine cycle was eventually exploited by the mid-thirteenth-century poet who composed *La Vengeance Fromondin*.[163] This text incorporates the burning of Origny into the Lorraine-Bordelais conflict, aligning Raoul with the Lorraine camp and Bernier with the treacherous Bordelais clan. The rewriting substantially modifies key aspects of the narrative as we know it, though we cannot be sure what version of *Raoul de Cambrai* served as the poet's source. *La Vengeance Fromondin* attenuates Raoul's *démesure* and recasts Bernier as an intrinsically flawed member of an unworthy lineage. King Louis is replaced by a rather benign Pepin the Short, who assists Raoul in defending Cambrai and seizing the Vermandois. While one might object that it is "unfaithful" to the spirit of the surviving *Raoul de Cambrai* poem, *La Vengeance Fromondin* demonstrates the vitality and flexibility of the Raoul narrative.[164]

Like many chansons de geste, *Raoul de Cambrai* was largely forgotten between the end of the Middle Ages and nineteenth-century medievalism.

Victor Hugo was inspired by Raoul's relentless pursuit of Ernaut of Douai in "L'aigle du casque" (*La Légende des Siècles*): "Alors commença l'âpre et sauvage poursuite, / Et vous ne lirez plus ceci qu'en frémissant" [Then began the bitter and savage pursuit, and you will read no further without shuddering].[165]

Ami et Amile (ca. 1200)

> Il s'entresamblent de venir et d'aler
> Et de la bouche et dou vis et dou nés,
> Dou chevauchier et des armes porter,
> Que nus plus biax ne puet on deviser.
>   Dex les fist par miracle. (vv. 39–43)

[They resembled each other in their manner of coming and going, and had the same mouth, face, and nose; they rode alike, bore their arms alike, such that no one could imagine finer men. God worked a miracle in making them.]

Composed in decasyllabic, assonanced laisses ending in hexasyllabic *vers orphelins*, *Ami et Amile* is situated formally in the Old French epic tradition.[166] It appears in a single manuscript, BnF fr. 860, in the company of four other chansons de geste of the Charlemagne cycle; it is preceded by *Roland* and *Gaydon* and followed by *Jourdain de Blaye* and *Auberi le Bourguignon*. *Ami et Amile* includes familiar motifs from the epic intertext, such as the lineage of traitors and the *judicium Dei*, but it is more concerned with individual concerns than community and devotes less textual space to battle than most Old French epics. The poet adapts the framework of the chanson de geste to a narrative grounded in folklore and oriented toward spiritual fulfillment. William C. Calin has aptly defined the text as a "song of deeds in arms and a poem of moral and religious experience."[167]

Summary

Conceived in the same hour and baptized on the same day, Ami and Amile are destined for an exceptional friendship. Pope Ysoré is godfather to both boys, and he bestows upon each one an identical goblet. They grow up separately, Ami in Auvergne and Amile in Berry. At the age of fifteen, each having been received into knighthood, they set out in search of each other. When they finally meet, they recognize each other instantly and unite in friendship. Ami and Amile make their way to Charlemagne's court, where they distinguish themselves in battle and incur the hatred of the treacherous Hardré. When Hardré's plot against them fails, peace is established by virtue of a marriage between Ami and Lubias, Hardré's niece. The couple moves to Blaye, and the perfidious Lubias vows to undermine her husband's friendship with Amile.

Charlemagne's daughter Belissant becomes enamored of Amile, who refuses her advances. When she slips into his bed in the dead of night, Amile lets himself be seduced, believing the lady to be a chambermaid. Hardré overhears the encounter and denounces Amile to Charlemagne. Called upon to defend himself in judicial combat, Amile secures as hostages the queen and her two children, but he knows that his guilt will mean certain defeat. Ever loyal, Ami changes places with his friend and poses as Amile at Charlemagne's court. Meanwhile Amile takes on Ami's identity in Blaye, taking care to avoid sexual contact with Lubias by feigning illness and placing a sword between himself and his friend's wife in bed. Ami defeats and kills Hardré in judicial combat, thus establishing Amile's innocence. Charlemagne offers Belissant in marriage to the victor, and Ami accepts, even though an angel warns that he will be struck with leprosy as punishment for his fraudulent promise. The two friends resume their true identities and their separate lives. Ami eventually becomes a leper. Though aided by his young son Girard, he is shunned by Lubias, who turns him out of the castle. Ami undertakes a long journey, accompanied by two faithful serfs, and is finally reunited with Amile thanks to the twin goblet that allows Amile to recognize his ailing and deformed friend.

An angel informs Ami that he may be cured only if Amile sacrifices his own sons and bathes Ami in their blood. Amile obliges, Ami is healed, and Amile's sons are miraculously restored to life. Ami returns home and forgives Lubias. The two friends undertake a pilgrimage to Jerusalem, where they worship the Holy Cross. During the return voyage, Ami and Amile fall ill and die in Mortara, where pilgrims still visit their tomb.

The Narrative Tradition

Ami et Amile is part of a network of medieval texts devoted to the same basic legend.[168] The earliest extant version is a late eleventh-century Latin verse epistle by Radulfus Tortarius (Raoul le Tourtier), a monk from the abbey of Fleury. Radulfus claims that this tale of true and faithful friendship, reminiscent of classical bonds such as that between Damon and Pythias, was well known not only in Gaul but also in the far-flung land of the Saxons.[169] Following MacEdward Leach, most scholars divide the versions into two principal groups: secular (or "romantic") versions and hagiographic narratives.[170] Secular versions emphasize the extraordinary friendship between the protagonists and the trials they must undergo, while hagiographic versions elaborate upon the heroes' Christian virtues, the miracles wrought on their behalf, and their martyrdom. Among the works in the secular category are Radulfus's epistle, the Anglo-Norman octosyllabic *Amis e Amilun* (ca. 1200), the Middle English verse romance *Amis and Amiloun*,[171] and a fifteenth-century French miracle play.[172] The hagiographic tradition may be traced back to the anonymous twelfth-century Latin prose *Vita Sanctorum Amici et Amelii*, which appears to be the "immediate or ultimate source" of subsequent hagiographic versions.[173] The chanson de geste rendering has generally been classified among the secular versions, but given its strong emphasis on divine will and Christian typology, it would be more accurate to situate the work at the intersection between secular and hagiographic.

The legend's origins are difficult to ascertain and—as the reader will by now anticipate—have given rise to considerable scholarly controversy.[174] One school of thought attributes ancient, folkloric origins to the tale. Leach argues that *Ami et Amile* bears a significant "source relation" to two principal folktales, the Two Brothers and the Faithful Servant (or Faithful John).[175] Citing the lack of concrete evidence for this traditionalist position, Bédier integrates the tale into his individualist narrative of origins. Drawing on a pair of tombs in Mortara, one of which bears the name Amelius, he posits the existence of a local legend that attracted French pilgrims making their way to Rome on the Via Francigena.[176] Others trace the legend to the celebrated friendship between two historical figures from the early eleventh century, Guillaume V, Duke of Aquitaine, and Guillaume II "Taillefer" of Angoulême.[177] These source studies, though speculative and often conflicting, reveal the rich intertextual web linking *Ami et Amile* to tales of male friendship from classical mythology, folklore, and history.

Male Friendship as a Transcendent Ideal

In this chanson de geste, service to the emperor and questions of feudal justice are subordinated to the overarching theme of friendship, which is embedded in the names of the eponymous heroes. Simon Gaunt reminds us that manuscripts of this period do not use capital letters to distinguish proper names from other nouns; hence, when Amile is designated as the "amis" of the character named "amis," the two characters merge into each other and into the notion of "friend" itself.[178] It is important to note, however, that "friendship" is not a universal concept but has different meanings in different historical and cultural contexts.[179] Although the Old French words *ami*, *amistiet* (*amitié*), and *compaing/compaingnon* look familiar to readers of modern French, their semantic range is far from identical. In early French medieval texts, the word *amistiet* primarily designates military, judicial, and lineal alliances; the bond of *compagnonnage* implies a freely chosen engagement with reciprocal duties, or a less formal comradeship in arms; both of these relationships could involve some degree of affection, but emotional attachment was secondary.[180] During the time *Ami et Amile* was composed, *compagnonnage* in particular was beginning to include aspects of modern *amitié*, that is, a close bond independent of social structures.[181] The homosocial bond between Ami and Amile encompasses a range of spiritual, military, and affective ties. Their union is divinely ordained rather than freely chosen: "Ansoiz qu'Amiles et Amis fussent né, / Si ot uns angres de par Deu devisé / La compaingnie par moult grant loiauté" (vv. 19–21) [Before Ami and Amile were born, an angel sent by God had told of their great friendship and loyalty]. However, when they finally meet as adults, Ami and Amile take an oath of "compaingnie nouvelle" (v. 200) [new friendship/companionship]. Initially played out in a military context, their *compaingnie* is put to a series of tests, which reveal that the bond between Ami and Amile transcends all other human relationships.

The *vers orphelins* concluding the first two and the last two laisses bracket the narrative by asserting the friends' exemplary unity, from their miraculous origins to the end of time:

"Par lor grant compaingnie" (v. 18)
"Dex les fist par miracle" (v. 43)
"Li dui baron ensamble" (v. 3490)
"Jusqu'en la fin dou monde" (v. 3504)

[Through their great companionship . . . God worked a miracle in making them . . . The two barons together . . . Until the end of the world]

The poet returns insistently to the motif of the friends' uncanny resemblance in a pattern of disjunctive echoes that punctuate the narrative (vv. 39–43 [the epigraph above], 1048–53, 1958–61, 3103–6, 3342–44). The resemblance encompasses facial features, movement, and chivalric disposition. Their extraordinary likeness is affirmed by both narrator and characters (Ami, Belissant, Ami's vassal Gautier) and is mirrored in the twin goblets that grace their baptism and effect their final reunion. Virtually indistinguishable to all who behold them, Ami and Amile display a physical unity that reflects their mystical companionship. According to A. H. Krappe, the heroes were twins in the original legend, participating in a network of "twin legends in hagiographic garb" inspired by the Dioscuri cult.[182] Finn Sinclair reads this twinning as the "focus for a narrative play between difference and sameness" in which the identity of the male body is idealized. According to this perspective, the narrative follows an arc from initial harmony and identity to rupture and difference, figured by Ami's leprosy; the miraculous cure at the end of poem restores unity and wholeness as the two friends regain their physical sameness.[183]

The poem's narrative structure foregrounds twinship on other levels as well. Danon and Rosenberg divide the tale into five parts, each of which culminates in a reunion of the two friends: (1) birth, baptism, and quest; (2) life at Charlemagne's court; (3) judicial combat; (4) Ami's leprosy; (5) Ami's cure.[184] Parallel episodes abound:[185] the companions serve Charlemagne against two armies, the Bretons and the forces of Gombaut of Lorraine (vv. 208–25, 283–382); Hardré persecutes the two friends through guile ("par sa losenge," v. 238) as his niece Lubias later persecutes Ami "de ses losenges" (v. 2074); the two bedroom scenes involve concealed identity (vv. 685–91, 1158–60). In addition, minor characters often appear in pairs and function as spectral figures: Ami and Amile twice take two prisoners in battle (vv. 224, 381); the traitor Hardré beheads two dead knights and carries the heads back to court as evidence of prowess, thus prefiguring Amile's two beheaded sons (vv. 387–403); the ailing Ami is served by two faithful serfs who compensate for the neglect of the hero's two brothers (2411–21, 2512–71).

This pattern of doubling, more insistent than that found in any other chanson de geste, serves as a structural backdrop for an exclusive friendship that supersedes all other social relationships as well as feudal and moral codes.[186] The homosocial bond is clearly privileged over hetero-

sexual relationships. It is true that the narrator solemnly intones the in-
dissolubility of the marital bond: "Maris et fame ce est toute une chars /
Ne faillir ne se doivent" (vv. 2117–18) [Husband and wife are one flesh and
must never fail each other]. However, this pronouncement comes in the
context of Lubias's cruelty toward her leprous husband: conjugal unity is
valorized in the context of female treachery but easily sacrificed elsewhere
for the sake of male *compaingnie*. Also sacrificed are fundamental prin-
ciples of fealty and justice. As Gaunt puts it, "the ethical framework of the
text becomes extremely fluid in order to accommodate their actions."[187]
When Amile is denounced by Hardré for his sexual encounter with Belis-
sant, he openly recognizes his guilt, knowing that the royal hostages will
pay for his sin. His acknowledgment is placed prominently at the end of
two similar laisses: "Hom qui tort a combatre ne se doit. / Par pechié les
ai mortes. . . . Hom qui tort a combatre ne se seit. Or voldroie mors iestre"
(vv. 994–95, 1016–17) [A guilty man should not fight. By my sin I have
killed them. . . . A guilty man cannot fight. I wish I were dead.] Ami, citing
their physical resemblance and undying loyalty, does not hesitate to offer
himself as a surrogate (vv. 1041–92). Though he deceives Charlemagne and
his court, Ami is nonetheless rewarded with victory in judicial combat.

This morally problematic outcome may be explained in various ways.
In a general sense, Ami and Amile are vindicated because the text's moral
universe aligns the audience exclusively with the heroes.[188] Indeed, Belis-
sant believes that Amile can be exonerated owing to Hardré's fundamental
status as a traitor (v. 722).[189] There are other extenuating circumstances,
since Amile was not entirely aware of Belissant's identity—though he en-
tertained the possibility that his nocturnal visitor might be Charlemagne's
daughter (v. 677). Moreover, Ami's ambiguous oath, like that of Iseut in
Béroul's *Tristan*, is formally true: Ami accurately states that Belissant's na-
ked flesh has never touched his own (vv. 1425–28).[190] The outcome thus
appears to privilege the letter of the oath rather than its spirit, pointing up
the inadequacies of judicial combat. Emanuel Mickel, however, attributes
Hardré's defeat more specifically to the traitor's renunciation of God on
the second day of battle:[191] "Ier fiz bataille el non dou Criator, / Hui la ferai
el non a cel seignor / Qui envers Deu nen ot onques amor. / Ahi, diables!
com ancui seraz prouz" (vv. 1660–63) [Yesterday I did battle in the name
of the Creator. Today I will fight in the name of that lord who never loved
God. Ah, Devil, how glorious you will be today!] It is only after this blas-

phemous declaration that Ami is able to strike a decisive blow. Thus, in Mickel's view, immanent justice prevails, for an omniscient and omnipotent God "can reconcile the letter and the spirit of the law."[192]

In the final analysis, the poet goes to great lengths to pose a moral dilemma whose resolution is predicated upon the heroes' friendship. Amile's transgression and Ami's deception are overlaid with mitigating circumstances and ultimately justified after an appeal to God's mercy in the context of *compaingnie*. Ami's triumph over Hardré is immediately preceded by a *prière du plus grand péril* that links the plea for victory to a desired reunion with Amile:

"Dex," dist il, "Peres qui formas tout le mont,

. . . .

Et Daniel garis en las fosse au lyon,

Si com c'est voirs et noz bien le creons,

Me doingniéz voz ocirre cel glouton,

Qu'encor revoie le mien chier compaingnon

Qui est a Blaivies en ma meillor maison." (vv. 1667, 1670–74)

["God," he said, "Father who created the whole world . . . who saved Daniel from the lions' den—as is true and as we believe—allow me to slay that scoundrel, so that I may once again see my dear companion, who is in Blaye in my best dwelling."]

Ami's second transgression proves more serious. His bigamous vow is preceded by another prayer, this time for God's counsel. He once again evokes Daniel and adds Saint Susanna, whom God protected from false witness (vv. 1762–74). However, Ami does not wait for divine counsel but rather preempts it by resolving to pledge his troth to Belissant in Amile's stead, accepting his fate in the name of friendship (vv. 1771–73). Even when an angel apprises him of the dire consequences of his vow, he surrenders his body to God's will (vv. 1821–23).[193] Disobeying the laws of God leads to great suffering, but expiation is accomplished through a final test of friendship. Amile swears by God, who raised Lazarus from the dead, that he would forsake his wife and sons as well as all material possessions to bring about Ami's cure (vv. 2836–42, 2878–91): "Car au besoing puet li hom esprouver / Qui est amis ne qui le weult amer" (vv. 2856–57) [For in a time of need a man can determine who is his friend and who loves him].

Ami et Amile thus presents a radically exclusive version of the epic homosocial bond, or as Gaunt describes it, a "fantasy solution to the problem of potential enmity between companions."[194] Unlike Raoul and Bernier in *Raoul de Cambrai*, Ami and Amile are of equal social status; unlike Roland and Oliver in the *Chanson de Roland*, they enjoy a perpetually harmonious relationship.[195] Their attachment is not without a certain erotic charge: in the text, the word *compaingnie* is also used to depict sexual relations, and there are strong suggestions of a homoerotic rivalry between Hardré and Ami for the affection of Amile.[196] When Hardré begs Amile to be his *compaing*, Amile asserts exclusivity: "Mon compaingnon le plevi ge l'autrier / Qu'a compaingnie n'avrai home soz ciel" (vv. 598–99) [I promised my companion the other day that I would never have such a friendship with another man in this world]. Like the love between Tristan and Iseut, the *compaingnie* between Ami and Amile clashes with the demands of social interactions. Requiring duplicitous behavior and horrific sacrifice, this friendship appears as an ideal only in the context of divine will and spiritual abnegation.[197]

Lubias and Belissant

In *Ami et Amile*, male companionship not only transcends heterosexual unions but also leads to an explicit and troubling devalorization of women.[198] In an important essay on the exclusion of women in this text, Sarah Kay analyzes the juxtaposition of two principal models of medieval misogyny: the feudal model, which posits women as objects that serve to facilitate transactions between men, and the clerical model, which attributes "malign agency" to women and their sexuality.[199] Both models are evident in the initial presentation of Lubias, whose character is already tainted by her origins in the lineage of traitors. When an act of treachery threatens to destroy him, Hardré offers his niece to Ami/Amile as a form of appeasement and compensation: "Je voz donrai de mon avoir mil onces, / Et Lubias, la cortoise, la blonde. / L'un de voz ferai riche" (vv. 467–69) [I will give you a thousand ounces of my fortune, as well as the courtly, blonde Lubias. I will make one of you rich and powerful]. Amile demurs (which may partially explain Lubias's future attempts to discredit him), but Ami willingly accepts. Once the marriage has taken place, Lubias is immediately cast as a threat to the heroes' friendship: "S'elle onques puet, el le cunchiera, / Les amistiés d'Amile li toldra" (vv. 493–94) [If ever she

can, she will cover him with shame and deprive him of Amile's friendship].
She reveals herself at once to be an inherently evil woman ("male fame," v.
500), falsely claiming on two occasions that Amile sought her favors (vv.
501–5, 1206–15).
Both Ami and Amile give voice to the commonplaces of medieval mi-
sogynistic discourse. Warning Amile of the potential danger lurking in
Belissant's sexuality, Ami admonishes his friend:

"La fille Charle ne voz chaut a amer
Ne embracier ses flans ne ses costéz,
Car puis que fame fait home acuverter,
Et pere et mere li fait entr'oublier,
Couzins et freres et ses amis charnéz." (vv. 566–70)

["Beware of Charles's daughter; don't love her and don't take her in
your arms. For once a woman has subjugated a man, she makes him
forget father and mother, cousins and brothers and all his friends
and family."]

In one sense, Ami correctly predicts that Amile will suffer from the lady's
embrace. Ironically, however, Belissant will later prove to be quite accom-
modating, endorsing even the sacrifice of her sons. What Ami describes
here corresponds more closely to the exclusive relationship that binds him
to Amile. Paradoxically, then, Ami's antiwoman tirade calls into question
the very essence of his friendship with Amile. Amile, for his part, invokes
the stereotype of women's untrustworthiness in a somewhat more plau-
sible context, when he has taken Ami's place and must endure Lubias's
treachery. Believing that she is addressing Ami, Lubias falsely accuses
Amile of trying to seduce her. "'Dex,' dist Amiles, 'qui haut siés et loinz
vois, / Esperitables iestez, . . . / Tant par est fox qui mainte fame croit / Et
qui li dist noient de son consoil'" (vv. 1216–19) ["God," said Amile, "you
who sit on high and see all, you who are pure spirit, . . . a man must be mad
to believe any woman or to tell her any of his secrets."] Lubias's false, pride-
ful discourse is also punished with physical violence when Amile, follow-
ing Ami's advance instructions, strikes Lubias in the face (vv. 1068–69,
1032–33).
    Whereas Lubias is guilty of deceitful speech, Belissant deceives by si-
lence. Resolved to seduce Amile, who has resisted her previous advances,

she slips into his room under cover of night and refuses to identify herself (v. 686). Belissant explicitly flouts social and paternal rules: "Il ne m'en chaut, se li siecles m'esgarde / Ne se mes pere m'en fait chascun jor batre, / Car trop i a bel home" (vv. 659–61) [I don't care if the whole world sees me or if my father has me beaten for it daily. For Amile is such a handsome man!] In this respect Belissant is analogous to the assertive Saracen Princess type, whose unruliness is justified by her alignment with the protagonist against his enemy.[200] She also recalls the heroines of certain *chansons de toile* or weaving songs, who actively pursue their objects of desire (often mercenaries like Amile) against parental wishes.[201] Belissant's guileful seduction temporarily incurs Amile's wrath and sets in motion a chain of events threatening the lives of both heroes. In the end, however, the seduction plot realizes its potential as a male wish-fulfillment fantasy common to many medieval narratives: Amile is rewarded with a bride, a fief, and an enhanced social position as Charlemagne's son-in-law.[202] Belissant's scheme proves to be, as she says, a "bel engien" (v. 698), that is, a fine trick. After her marriage, the lady is fully absorbed into the value system of male prerogatives and male bonds. In stark contrast to Lubias, she welcomes the ailing Ami with open arms, kissing and embracing him in the name of Amile's friendship (vv. 2753–63). When she learns of the gruesome miracle that saved Ami's life, she is unwavering in her loyalty: "Se je cuidasse huimain a l'ajorner / Que volsissiéz mes anfans decoler, / Remese fuisse, gel voz di sans fausser, / Por recevoir d'unne part le sanc cler" (vv. 3229–32) [If I had known this morning at daybreak that you were going to behead my children, I tell you truly that I would have stayed behind to help you collect their brightly colored blood].

Thus Belissant ceases to occupy the forbidden place between Ami and Amile. Lubias's unsuccessful attempt to occupy that space is emblematized in the oft-noted bedroom scene, in which Amile, posing as Ami, positions a sword between himself and Lubias in the conjugal bed—again, in keeping with specific instructions from Ami. Overcome with fear, Lubias threatens to mobilize her male relatives and the bishop in order to sever "compaignie" with her husband (vv. 1169–76). Amile claims that he is following doctor's orders, his condition requiring him to abstain from sexual contact with women ("habitacion / Ne compaingnie," vv. 1198–99) for thirty days. The obvious intertextual link to Béroul's romance of *Tristan* has been widely commented.[203] In the romance, King Mark comes upon the lovers in the forest as they lie sleeping, separated by Tristan's sword. Misreading the sign, he inaccurately concludes that their relationship is chaste and substitutes his own sword for Tristan's. When they awaken, the lovers misread Mark's gesture and flee, frightened for their lives.[204] In both the romance and epic scenes, the sword functions as an ambivalent sign of separation, authority, and latent violence. As a conventional phallic symbol, it also figures the absent member of an erotic triangle: just as Mark's sword inserts him between the two lovers, Amile's sword stands in for the *compaingnie* of Ami. Ami's return to the conjugal bed will prove short-lived. When his health begins to decline, Lubias—the "male damme" (v. 2063)—shrinks from physical contact, first lying beside him fully dressed, and then banishing him entirely from the castle. Ami finds true refuge only when he is reunited with Amile and welcomed by Belissant, who declares: "Voz et mes sires estiiéz compaignon, / Ne gerréz mais en lit s'avec noz non" (vv. 2761–62) [You and my husband were companions; you will never again lie in a bed except with us].[205]

Leprosy, Infanticide, and Pilgrimage

Ami et Amile has been said to offer a more realistic image of leprosy than its counterparts in romance.[206] Though the poet does not provide a detailed clinical description of the disease, its progression is manifest in brief allusions to Ami's symptoms and appearance.[207] Initially, his nose becomes sunken and painful, and he has trouble breathing (vv. 2059–60); he is soon too feeble to walk or ride a horse (vv. 2077–78); his nose and lips swell (v. 2150); his body burns like fire (v. 2174); eventually, few dare to approach him because of his foul breath (vv. 2297–98). The poem also evokes the very real fear of contagion and the dilemma faced by victims' healthy spouses, as well as the plight of lepers doomed to a life of begging.[208] However, Ami's leprosy functions less as the reflection of a physiological and social reality than as the marker of spiritual disposition.[209] In the Middle Ages, leprosy was subject to two contradictory interpretations. The disease was often regarded as an outward sign of moral turpitude, thus authorizing the leper's status as an object of contempt and derision. Alternatively, leprosy could be read more positively as a test sent by God to prove faith, allowing the victim to achieve salvation through suffering.[210] *Ami et Amile* explicitly links the disease to Ami's bigamous oath, but, as we have seen, his sin is mitigated by generous intentions and faith in divine providence.

Leprosy is the external sign of Ami's sin ("pechié," v. 2197) but also a mirror that reveals the moral failings of those who scorn and injure him.

By the standards of "reality," one might sympathize with Lubias's desire to avoid contact with a leprous husband. Her request for an annulment is consistent with some medieval customs.[211] She is supported by the nobles and merchants in her community, who defend her right to separate from their lord: "Droit a ma damme, que mal est mariee" (v. 2152) [My lady is in the right, for she is unhappily married]. While the *malmariée* might be sympathetic in some contexts, however, we have seen that the text supports the ecclesiastical imperatives of marital indissolubility and attributes Lubias's motives to sheer wickedness. Lubias is analogous to the werewolf's wife in Marie de France's "Bisclavret": both wives recoil from their husbands' monstrosity, failing to penetrate outward appearances and becoming monstrous themselves by their disloyalty. Lubias reneges on her agreement to provide shelter for Ami and beats her son Girart for helping to nurse his father (vv. 2311–13). On the other hand, Girart, like Belissant, proves to be a model of Christian charity, denying the revulsion provoked in others by his father's body: "Li vostre chars ne m'iert ja en vilté, / Ansoiz m'est douce et moult bonne et soéz" (vv. 2300–2301) [Your body will never disgust me; on the contrary, to me, it is sweet and very good and pleasing].

Similarly, Ami's cure, which strikes the modern reader as barbaric, is inscribed in a tradition of Christian suffering and faith. The power of children's blood in the healing of leprosy may be traced to ancient Hebrew legends and came to represent the redemptive blood of Christ in medieval lore.[212] Like Abraham, whose sacrifice is mentioned earlier in the text (vv. 1278–79), Amile agonizes over the prospect of infanticide but places his faith in God (vv. 2917–45). His eldest son willingly gives himself up to death, promising to pray for his father's redemption (vv. 3000–3011). Sinclair reads the episode as the ultimate expression of idealized twinship: "the doubled father produces sons who in their turn produce the father's rebirth, the body fragments and is then restored, a perspective that turns around sameness, substitution, and the return of the same."[213]

When Ami and Amile take up the cross in the final laisses, their departure represents a definitive detachment from feudal and familial ties. Ami entrusts his lands to his son Girard, and Amile places his domains in Belissant's care, charging her with the raising of the young sons he will never see again (vv. 3460–68). Unlike crusading epic heroes, Ami and Amile do not engage in holy war with the Saracens but undertake a purely spiritual journey. Whereas their previous voyages involved separation and reunion, necessitating two complementary narrative threads, the pilgrimage merges the heroes' trajectories and culminates their earthly wanderings. Buried on the pilgrimage route, Ami and Amile are jointly commemorated by their fellow pilgrims and the song that celebrates their deeds:[214]

> Li pelerin qui vont parmi l'estree,
> Cil sevent bien ou lor tombe est posee.
> Ici sera la chansons definee
> Des douz barons qui a esté chantee.
> Ce est d'Amile a la chiere membree,
> D'Ami le conte, qui ot tel renommee
> Que touz jors mais noz sera ramembree. (vv. 3497–3503)

[Pilgrims who follow the route know well where their tomb is located. Here ends the song sung of the two barons. It tells of Amile, whose beauty was legendary, and of Count Ami, whose fame was such that we will remember it always.][215]

Posterity

The continuation *Jourdain de Blaye*, a *chanson d'aventures* composed in the early thirteenth century, immediately follows *Ami et Amile* in the manuscript. It opens with a brief account of Ami's son Girard, who is slain by Hardré's nephew Fromont and deprived of his hereditary fief of Blaye. The remainder of the story is devoted to Girard's son Jourdain, who kills Charlemagne's nephew and marries the princess Oriabel. After numerous adventures, Jourdain kills Fromont and becomes king of Marcasile. *Ami et Amile* and *Jourdain de Blaye* are often said to constitute the "little cycle" of Blaye.

Both poems were later reworked into alexandrine verse. The fifteenth-century reworking of *Ami et Amile* fills in the gaps between the two works, and the late fourteenth-century alexandrine *Jourdain de Blaye* continues Jourdain's tale up until his death.[216] *Ami et Amile* and *Jourdain de Blaye* were adapted into prose in the fifteenth century. The prose version of *Ami et Amile* passed into print editions in the sixteenth century under the title *Milles et Amys*; this is also the title of Alfred Delvau's nineteenth-century adaptation.[217]

Huon de Bordeaux (second half 13th century)

"Auberon sus per droit nom appellés;
Droit a Monmur, certe, la fu ge neif.
Julez Sezaire me norit moult souueff,
....
Morge la fee, qui tant ot de biauté,
Ce fu ma mere, se me puist Dix sauver;
....
Moult ayme droit et foid et loialteit,
Pour ceu ai ge Huon en teilt charteit.
Il est proudom, car bien l'ai esprouvér." (vv. 10688–93, 10717–19)

["I am called Auberon, and I was born in Monmur. Julius Caesar
raised me tenderly; . . . the beautiful Morgan le Fay was my mother,
so help me God. . . . I prize righteousness, faithfulness, and loyalty,
and for this reason I cherish Huon: I know that he is a worthy man,
for I have put him to the test."]

Huon de Bordeaux [218] exemplifies the *chanson d'aventures*, a hybrid form
of epic production that emerged in the thirteenth century.[219] The story
takes the form of a triptych, with the first and third sections anchored in
more conventional epic schemas and a lengthy middle section devoted to
the hero's marvelous adventures in the Orient. Though initially situated
within the tradition of revolt epic, *Huon* expands the narrative horizon by
reframing the protagonist's banishment as a quest, with motifs drawn from
folklore and adventure romance. Unlike earlier epic heroes, Huon under-
goes a process of initiation, a rite of passage from adolescence to mature
knighthood that tests both his prowess and his moral fiber. Crucial to this
process is the fairy king Auberon, whose otherworldly intervention allows
Huon to triumph in feudal confrontations as well as exotic adventures.

Summary

This summary omits a number of secondary characters and encapsulates
the hero's numerous adventures.

Treachery at Charlemagne's Court (vv. 1–2521)

Huon and Gerard, the youthful sons of the deceased Seguin of Bordeaux,
are the victims of a plot devised by the traitor Amaury. Enlisting the help

of Charlot, Charlemagne's unworthy son and heir to the throne, Amaury contrives to ambush the brothers during their journey to Charlemagne's court. Huon kills Charlot in self-defense, unaware of his adversary's identity until he reaches the court, where Amaury falsely accuses him of murder. Charlemagne, grief-stricken, wishes to kill Huon on the spot, but he is persuaded to let the matter be decided by a judicial combat between Huon and Amaury. Charlemagne does, however, impose an unusual condition: if the defeated knight dies before confessing his guilt, the victor will not be considered innocent but instead will lose his lands. Huon defeats and kills Amaury without extracting a confession, and Charlemagne banishes the young hero from court.

When the barons object to the harsh sentence, Charlemagne offers Huon the possibility of a pardon, but the terms are daunting: Huon must undertake an expedition to the court of the emir Gaudisse of Babylon (here understood as Cairo). Upon arriving, he is to kill the first Saracen he sees, kiss the emir's daughter, tear out Gaudisse's mustache and four molars, and bring them back to Charlemagne. Huon is enjoined to complete these tasks without help from any Christian, though he may be accompanied until he arrives at the Red Sea. Huon takes his leave, and Gerard returns to Bordeaux, where he eventually reveals his true nature as an evildoer.

Huon's Adventures (vv. 2522–8982)

Huon, accompanied by a small group of knights, first visits his uncle the pope, who absolves him of his role in Charlot's death. After a brief sojourn in the Holy Land, Huon sets out for the Red Sea, traveling first through strange and marvelous lands. He passes through the forest of the fairy king Auberon, a diminutive creature of great beauty who befriends him and gives him a magic goblet from which only the pure of heart may drink, as well as a horn that will allow him to summon Auberon whenever he is in danger. The hero first avails himself of the horn in Tormont, where he is attacked by his renegade uncle Dudon. Auberon saves Huon but forbids him to proceed to Dunostre, the home of the giant l'Orgueilleux. Undaunted, Huon makes his way to the giant's castle, which is guarded by two fearsome automatons. With the help of a Christian captive named Sebille (who happens to be Huon's cousin), he gains access to the castle, appropriates the giant's magic hauberk, and slays him.

Huon crosses the Red Sea on the back of Malabron, a sea monster sent by Auberon. In Babylon, he confronts numerous dangers but manages to fulfill the obligations imposed by Charlemagne, aided once again by Auberon. He also accepts the love of the emir's daughter Esclarmonde but agrees to Auberon's stipulation that the couple not consummate their relationship before they can be married in Rome. During their sea voyage, however, Huon willfully disregards Auberon's command and forces himself upon Esclarmonde, whereupon the ship is caught in a violent storm. Huon and Esclarmonde are washed up onto an island, where pirates kidnap Esclarmonde and bring her to Aufalerne, kingdom of the Saracen Galafre. She is forced to marry Galafre, but he promises to respect her virginity for three years. Meanwhile Malabron rescues Huon, who enters the service of a minstrel, joins a Saracen army besieging Aufalerne, and eventually reunites with Esclarmonde and his Christian companions.

Huon's Return (vv. 8983–10797)

Once Esclarmonde is baptized in Rome, she and Huon marry. At the abbey of Saint-Maurice-es-Prés they fall into a trap prepared by Huon's brother Gerard, who seizes the material evidence of Huon's exploits in Babylon—the emir's mustache and four molars—and imprisons him in Bordeaux. Gerard proceeds to steal the treasures Huon has brought back from the Orient and distributes the ill-gotten riches at Charlemagne's court. The scoundrel then claims that his brother has not fulfilled his promises to Charlemagne, and Huon's case is submitted to the judgment of the peers. At the trial, held in Bordeaux, Duke Naimes is Huon's only advocate. Charlemagne vows that he will not take another meal until Huon is executed and orders his table prepared. The hero seems doomed, but Auberon suddenly appears, equipped with his talismans, his enchanted table towering over that of the emperor. Auberon subjects those present to the test of the magic goblet: while Huon and Esclarmonde succeed, Charlemagne's secret sin makes him unable to drink from the vessel. Auberon forces Gerard to confess his crimes, reproduces the stolen treasure, has Gerard and his men hanged, and reconciles Huon with Charlemagne. Huon recovers the fief of Bordeaux and will inherit Auberon's kingdom of Monmur in three years, when the fairy king enters heaven.

Sources

Huon de Bordeaux draws its narrative material from diverse sources.[220] The first part of the poem contains a lengthy summary of the *Chevalerie Ogier de Danemarche*, in which Charlemagne's son Charlot kills the son of Ogier, thus provoking a fierce and lengthy war. There are links to other chansons de geste as well, notably revolt epics such as *Renaut de Montauban*, and the Lorraine cycle, where a character named Huon de Bordeaux appears for the first time. The section devoted to Huon's adventures is a veritable mosaic of motifs drawn from epic, folklore, and romance. The horn given by Auberon to Huon is a clear allusion to the celebrated horn of Roland. As in the *Chanson de Roland*, the hero debates with his companion before sounding the horn with great fury, and the sound carries over a tremendous distance.[221]

> "Je cornerait, qui qu'i en doit peser."
> Il prant le cor de blanc yvoire cler,
> Met l'a sa bouche, s'ait tantit et sonnez
> Per teilt vertut et per si grant fierteit
> Que de la bouche en volle li sang cler. (vv. 4521–25)

["I will sound the horn, no matter what anyone thinks." He takes up the horn of shining white ivory, puts it to his mouth, and blows it with such strength and such force that blood spurts from his mouth.]

Scholars have long debated the origins of Auberon himself: some locate his antecedents in Germanic myth, while others argue for Celtic sources.[222] Indeed, many episodes display ties to international folklore, but most of these motifs had already been mobilized by French literary works by the time of *Huon*'s composition. Manifestations of the marvelous associated with Auberon recall well-known romance ingredients: the magic goblet has been linked to the Grail for its inexhaustibility and power to distinguish good from evil, and a storm conjured by Auberon recalls the tempest of the fountain in Chrétien de Troyes's *Chevalier au lion*.[223] *Huon de Bordeaux* does not appear to be the product of an ancient legend, but rather an imaginative conjuncture of elements drawn primarily from recent literary sources.[224]

Problems of Law and Justice

The conflict between Huon and Charlemagne addresses vital issues of feudal law, including notions of guilt and innocence as well as the regulation of conflict. Having struck the blow that killed his overlord's son, Huon must defend himself against a charge of murder that also implies a breach of his feudal tie to Charlemagne. The event is carefully constructed to disculpate the hero on both counts by adducing two extenuating circumstances: the jongleur makes it clear that Huon killed Charlot in self-defense and that he was unaware of his adversary's identity.[225] The text gives particular attention to the excuse of ignorance, which Huon cites in a series of disjunctive echoes that form a prominent internal motif.[226] The paradigm appears in its fullest form in this passage:

"Je ne dit mie que Charlot n'aie ocis,
Maix, per Celui qui en la croix fuit mis,
Quant ju antrait en la cit de Paris
Que je ne soz queil homme j'oi ocis,
Que fuit son perre, ne qui l'angenuït,
Ne je ne soz que se fuit Charlon filz." (vv. 1672–77)

["I never said I didn't kill Charlot, but in the name of the One who was put on the cross, when I entered the city of Paris, I did not know whom I had killed, nor who his father was; I did not know he was Charlemagne's son."]

Although criminal intent was not taken into account in archaic judicial procedures, intentionality was becoming a greater factor in the determination of guilt or innocence by the thirteenth century, just as sin was increasingly defined as a voluntary act.[227] Because Huon is morally innocent, he fully expects the judicial duel to exonerate him. However, Charlemagne's unwarranted intervention in the procedural rules of the *judicium Dei* calls into question not only the king's integrity but also the intrinsic value of trial by combat. Owing to the extraordinary clause calling for the guilty party's confession, the judicial duel fails to bring closure. Faced with diabolical treachery and the breakdown of royal justice, Huon can be vindicated only by proving himself worthy of assistance from another sort of king altogether.

Clearly, the unflattering portrait of Charlemagne that emerges in *Huon de Bordeaux* is a far cry from the idealized warrior-king depicted in the *Chanson de Roland*. Marguerite Rossi has convincingly argued that *Huon de Bordeaux* is a response to the perceived failings of Louis IX, whose dealings with the high nobility scandalized many of his contemporaries.[228] In fact, the *Huon* poet may have targeted a specific instance of royal intransigence—the trial of Enguerrand IV, Lord of Coucy, in 1259. This high-ranking noble, who had put to death three young Flemish aristocrats for alleged poaching, was incarcerated in the Louvre before his trial and denied the right to a judicial duel. The trial itself bears many similarities to the events recounted in *Huon de Bordeaux*, as does the sentence: among Enguerrand's numerous punishments was the imposition of a pilgrimage to the Holy Land (which he managed to avoid by paying a hefty fine).[229] The thirteenth-century public may well have discerned the parallels between Enguerrand and Huon, though the latter is a morally sanitized version of his historical prototype. In portraying a similarly highborn nobleman as an innocent victim of royal injustice, the *Huon* poet offers a severe critique of Louis IX's inflexibility.

This critique is voiced primarily by the venerable Duke Naimes, whose image as Charlemagne's wise councilor remains untarnished in *Huon de Bordeaux*. When the king names the outrageous terms of the judicial duel, Naimes tries in vain to dissuade his lord:

—"Per foid," dit Nayme, "oncque maix n'oiit tel!
Saichiez, frans roy, que vous le sormenés,
Que tort li faite, pour Dieu de maiesteit."
—"Certe," dit Charle, "je n'an ferait or el;
Ainsi ert il, qui qu'an doie pezer." (vv. 1748–52)

["By my faith," said Naimes, "I have never heard of such a thing! Know, noble king, that you are abusing your power: you do him great wrong, by God in his Majesty!"—"I will not budge," said Charles. "It will be as I say, no matter who objects."]

Similarly, when Charlemagne summarily banishes Huon, Naimes warns that disinheriting a prominent noble has grave consequences:

"Que diront dont li hault homme gentis?
Vous jugement n'iert maix en France oii;

Tout diront mais, li grant et li petit,
Qu'an vous viellesse estes tous rasottis.
Encor vous prie je, amperrere gentis,
De lui vous prengne et menade et mercis." (vv. 2274–79)

["What then will the powerful nobles say? Your judgments will no
longer be listened to in France. Great and small alike will declare that
you are senile in your old age. I beg you again, noble emperor: be
compassionate, and have mercy on him."]

Unmoved, Charlemagne retorts that he would not change his mind even if
all the men in the world were to speak up in Huon's defense (vv. 2282–85).
Throughout the opening section of the poem, the king's vengeful obsti-
nacy stands in stark contrast to Naimes's discourse of reason and mercy.
Whether Huon's predicament alludes specifically to the Enguerrand de
Coucy affair or to Louis IX's stance with regard to the upper nobility in
general, the initial episode of *Huon de Bordeaux* is clearly an indictment
of the misuse of royal power.

Huon's Journey

Like the quests of Arthurian romance, Huon's journey unfolds as a se-
quence of adventures that form a meaningful trajectory in time and space.
Yet despite the introduction of romance motifs and strategies, the nar-
rative does not undergo a full-blown generic shift to courtly romance.
Rather, the *Huon* poet adapts the resources of romance to the exigencies
of epic, situating Huon's quest within the framework of Christian-Saracen
confrontation. The first stage, in accordance with the traditional epic pil-
grimage, involves expiation and spiritual obligation. In Rome, after Huon
devoutly forgives Charlemagne and all those who sought to harm him,
the pope declares him cleansed of his sins (vv. 2593–2610) and the hero is
poised to succeed in Auberon's later test of purity. In Jerusalem, he pros-
trates himself at the Holy Sepulchre and pronounces a conventional epic
prayer (vv. 2879–98). His itinerary then takes him through a transitional
space, a series of exotic lands punctuating the route to the Red Sea. This
stage of Huon's journey exemplifies the profoundly ambiguous representa-
tion of the Orient in Western medieval texts. Among the "savage lands" (v.
2922) he traverses are the stereotypically horrible countries of Femmenie,
where the sun never shines and women cannot bear children, and Cou-

mant, where the red-eyed, large-eared, furry populace feasts on raw meat (vv. 2923–35). Huon quickly abandons these infernal spaces and proceeds to the land of "Foid" or Faith, where loyalty and faithfulness reign supreme and virtue is tested by the ability to bake delicate cakes in silken cloths (vv. 2939–45). The depiction of spaces in and beyond the Holy Land thus encapsulates the alternation between topophilia and topophobia in Western constructions of the Oriental world.[230]

The hero's first encounter with Auberon, while also vaguely situated on the route to the Red Sea, occurs in an otherworldly realm more closely associated with the marvelous forests of Celtic-based romance. Auberon himself has the power to transcend the boundaries of human space, and his portrait places him at the intersection of multiple traditions: classical antiquity (his father was Julius Caesar), Arthurian legend (Morgan le Fay was his mother), and Christianity. Indeed, although his powers derive from gifts bestowed by fairies at his birth, Auberon also participates in the divine: he will occupy a throne prepared beside God when he chooses to leave the world here below (vv. 3561–62). His luminous beauty is attributed both to Jesus (v. 3166) and to one of the fairies presiding over his birth, who, having spitefully determined that Auberon would be a hunchbacked dwarf, compensated for this deformity by granting him beauty second only to God's (vv. 3500–3511). Auberon functions as a benefactor, a surrogate father, and a measure of Huon's moral and chivalric progress.[231] Huon accomplishes a great deal through his own prowess and ingenuity, but Auberon's interventions are vital to the hero's success.[232] In Tormont and Babylon, Auberon and his army effectively annihilate the Saracen forces: a powerful fairy thus replaces Charlemagne as the exemplary crusading king.[233]

During his quest, Huon benefits not only from magic auxiliary figures such as Auberon and the shapeshifting Malabron but also from resourceful female characters. These heroines do not resemble the healers or love objects of conventional courtly romance, but rather the intrepid women of epic in the tradition of Guibourc in the Guillaume cycle and Beatrice in Raoul de Cambrai. Huon's cousin Sebille helps him defeat the giant l'Orgueilleux by striking the hulk between the legs with a large club, causing him to fall to the ground and succumb to Huon's sword (vv. 5294–5304).[234] Gaudisse's daughter Esclarmonde is instrumental in freeing Huon and his companions from prison in Babylon. It is important to note that although the fair Esclarmonde emerges as one of the prizes of the hero's quest, Huon's journey is not motivated by love. It is the sensual and assertive princess who takes the initiative in the relationship. After Huon fulfills his promise to Charlemagne by kissing Esclarmonde three times in front of Gaudisse's entire court, the princess faints from the sweetness of the embrace: "Sa doulce allainne m'ait si mon corpz navrez, / Se je ne l'ai enneut a mon costeit, / G'istrait du sance ains qu'i soit ajornez" (vv. 5847–49) [His sweet breath has so wounded me that if I don't have him by my side tonight, I shall go mad before daybreak]. When she offers her love and assistance, however, Huon initially rejects her on the basis of religion. It is only when he begins to fear starvation that he agrees to accept her help and promises to bring her to France after his escape. Esclarmonde is a classic Saracen Princess, a projection of Western male desire who renounces religion, homeland, and family to assist a beloved Christian knight:

"Aidier vous vuelz que serez delivrez,
Et li mien pere ne puis ge plus amer.
Car il ne croit fors Mahom le dervé;
Por çou le ha ge, si me puist Dix salver.
Mais, s'il vausist Damedieu aourer,
Ja ne fesisse envers lui fauseté." (vv. 6452–57)

["I want to help you so that you will be freed, and I can no longer love my father, for he believes only in crazy Mohammed: for this I hate him, may God save me. But if he agreed to worship God, I would never betray him."]

In a structural move reminiscent of Chrétien de Troyes's romances, the hero's quest appears to be moving toward closure when he makes a grave error. Huon's sexual transgression reveals that he has not yet achieved the personal growth necessary for true chivalric and moral excellence. Like Chrétien's fallen hero Yvain, Huon is stripped of the trappings of knighthood and wanders naked through the countryside. Before his reintegration, he undergoes a transitional phase initiated by the colorful and aptly named Estrument,[235] an elderly Muslim minstrel who first reacts with terror at the sight of the wild man ("saulvaiges hons," v. 7468). Here the poet injects the thematics of identity, fusing the romance tradition of chivalric incognito with the epic tradition of disguise associated with Guillaume d'Orange.[236] By claiming to be a Muslim merchant, Huon ingratiates himself with the minstrel, acquires clothing and sustenance, and begins his path toward redemption and reunion with Esclarmonde.

The Estrument episode is one of many comic interludes in *Huon de Bordeaux*.[237] Here the humor derives in large part from irony: witness the self-conscious glorification of the minstrel's art:

> Que li veÿst sa vieelle atramper!
> A .xxx. corde fait sa herpe sonner,
> Tout li pallais commance a retinteir.
> . . . .
> Dïent paien: "Ve ci boin menestrez.
> Il lou covient moult richement luier." (vv. 7647–53)

[If only you had seen him tune his vielle and pluck the thirty strings of his harp! The whole palace began to resonate. . . . The pagans said: "This is a good minstrel: it is right to compensate him quite richly."]

Reduced to serving Estrument, Huon must endure not only a significant loss of social status but also the minstrel's repeated condemnation of a certain scoundrel named Huon who is responsible for the death of Gaudisse. This slippage from serious to comic is typical of the adventure section of the poem, as the perils of Huon's situation are frequently mitigated by various forms of humor. William Calin has identified numerous comic techniques deployed by the poet, from traditional epic motifs such as anticlerical humor and exaggeration to the more nuanced comedy of character.[238] Most of the humorous passages are concentrated in the episodes depicting Huon's interactions with Auberon, which fluctuate between rapture and rage. As Calin notes, "Auberon and Huon, each a comic character in his own right, interact to form a perfect comic pair."[239] Thus Huon's journey is punctuated by modulations of style and register that profoundly alter the horizon of expectations associated with the chanson de geste.

Formal Characteristics

Huon de Bordeaux illustrates many of the formal innovations associated with the *chanson d'aventures*. Though it retains the assonanced decasyllabic laisse,[240] the assonance verges on rhyme, particularly the frequent assonance in *e*. The average number of lines per laisse is high: 116 in manuscript M, 118 in P.[241] (By way of comparison, the *Song of Roland* averages

13.7 lines per laisse.) In most cases, the laisse's primary function is narrative, hence the relatively infrequent use of parallel laisses. The incantatory rhythms and traditional motifs of earlier epic still provide the stylistic framework for the story, but they are adapted to suit a wider variety of narrative situations. The narrator retains the formulas of oral composition and delivery, admonishing the audience to be quiet and listen to his worthy song (vv. 1–2, 44–45). However, it is generally assumed that *Huon* is the work of a single learned poet, rather than the product of a long oral tradition.

Rewritings and Spin-offs

Huon de Bordeaux is one of relatively few chansons de geste that have retained their popularity almost without interruption from the Middle Ages to the present. The adventure component likely accounts for the story's broad appeal through the ages. By the early fourteenth century, *Huon* had become the nucleus of a small cycle, with a prequel (the *Roman d'Auberon*) as well as a number of sequels devoted to Huon's later adventures and those of his descendants (*Esclarmonde, Clarisse et Florent, Yde et Olive, Croissant*, and *La Chanson de Godin*). In the fifteenth century, *Huon* was rewritten in rhymed alexandrine verse and also translated into prose.[242] Printed in 1513, the prose version was edited eleven times in the course of the sixteenth century. Abridged versions were widely circulated as part of the seventeenth-century Bibliothèque Bleue collection. In the eighteenth century, the Count of Tressan adapted the story for the Bibliothèque Universelle des Romans, and Alfred Delvau produced his own adaptation in the nineteenth-century Nouvelle Bibliothèque Bleue.[243] *Huon de Bordeaux* was also the subject of numerous theatrical productions from the sixteenth through the twentieth century.[244] The story continues to find favor with French audiences today, including young people: approximately twenty adaptations for children have been published since 1898.[245]

Huon was known and translated outside of France, including two versions in Middle Dutch and a 1533 English translation by John Bourchier, Lord Berners. It is possible that Shakespeare knew Bourchier's adaptation and modeled the celebrated figure of Oberon in *A Midsummer Night's Dream* after the fairy king Auberon.

Epilogue

The Legacy of the Chansons de Geste

… furent en sa court tant de cy puissant et vaillant chevalier, comme le mest plusieur istoire, que ce fut chose merveilleuze, telz comme Rolland, son nepveu, Olivier, Ogier le Danoys, le duc Name de Bavier, Regnault de Montabant et ces frères, l'airchevesque Turpin, Richair de Normendie, et plusieur aultre, qui tous furent moult vaillant aus airme. Entre lesquelle celluy Rolland, en son tampts, fut cy très preu et fist tant de vaillant fait digne de mémoire que plusieurs biaulx livre en sont fait. Et fut sa mort la plus plainte des crestiens que jamaix fut de chevalier; parquoy, encore aujourd'huy, quant on plaint la mort d'aulcun, voulluntier ung aultre dirait que "ce n'est pas la mort Rolland."

[In his (Charlemagne's) court there were so many strong and valiant knights, as many (hi)stories relate, that it was a marvelous thing: his nephew Roland, Oliver, Ogier the Dane, Duke Naimes of Bavaria, Renaut of Montauban and his brothers, the archbishop Turpin, Richard of Normandy, and others, all of whom were most valiant in war. Among them, Roland was in his time very brave, and accomplished so many deeds worthy of memory that many fine books tell of them. And Christians lamented his death more than that of any other knight; this is why, even today, when someone mourns a death, another person will readily say, "It's not like the death of Roland!"]

LA CHRONIQUE DE PHILIPPE DE VIGNEULLES

Thus Philippe de Vigneulles, merchant and chronicler of early sixteenth-century Metz, attests to the cultural legacy of the chansons de geste. Preserved in beautiful books as well as popular parlance, the heroic tales were disseminated throughout Europe and across the centuries and were adapted to diverse aesthetic and social contexts. This brief overview of the Old French epic's posterity in the later Middle Ages and beyond will consider three principal phenomena: the wave of French prose reworkings or *mises en prose* at the end of the medieval period; translations and adaptations into other languages during the Middle Ages; and aspects of modern medievalism.[1] Each of these topics could easily fill several volumes; this epilogue aims merely to convey a broad outline of the French epic's influence, with particular attention to the chansons de geste discussed in the present study.[2]

The *Mises en Prose*

The thirteenth century heralded the emergence of prose as a vehicle for French vernacular historiography and romance.[3] While it did not replace verse, prose came to be regarded as a more truthful and authoritative signifying practice. Verse was said to distort the truth, partly because it was founded upon an oral tradition now deemed less reliable, and partly because the constraints of versification obliged authors to sacrifice veracity.[4] Unlike romance and chronicles, the Old French epic remained solidly attached to verse composition until the end of the fourteenth century.[5] However, the chansons de geste formed an integral part of the wave of Middle French prose translations that swept the literary landscape in the fifteenth century. By the end of the Middle Ages, nearly half of the extant Old French epics had been reworked or "translated" into prose.

The translators' prologues reveal a great deal about the changing tastes of late medieval audiences. These prologues still critique the metrical constraints of verse and praise the truthfulness of prose, but they also justify prosification in terms of textual economy, enhanced comprehension, and aesthetic values. Jean Wauquelin in the prologue to his prose *Belle Hélène de Constantinople* (1448) claims to have reworked a rhymed version into prose "pour retrenchier et sincoper les prolongacions et motz inutiles qui souvent sont mis et boutez en telles rimes" [in order to cut and reduce the lengthiness and unnecessary words that are often placed in such rhymes].[6] Philippe de Vigneulles, who translated the Lorraine cycle into prose in 1515, also mentions the preference for brevity and adds that the public no longer understands the language of the old poems; for Philippe, linguistic updating was an important part of the prosifier's task.[7] The anonymous translator of the prose *Guillaume d'Orange* cites the greater appeal of prose for contemporary audiences: "plus volentiers s'i esbat l'en maintenant qu'on ne souloit, et plus est le laingage plaisant prose que rime" [people enjoy prose more now than before, and the language of prose is more pleasing than verse].[8] Prologues also speak to the suitability of epic material, deemed worthy for its exemplary treatment of chivalry and its potential for moral edification.[9]

Modern scholars long dismissed these works as derivative and mediocre, devoid of epic grandeur.[10] Happily, recent scholarship has recognized the historical and cultural value of the *mises en prose*, which must be appreciated as literary artifacts in their own right.[11] The translations exhibit diverse compositional techniques but share some general features: content is typically rearranged into chapters, which are introduced by rubrics; the prose is characterized by an emphatic, "diffuse" style that privileges subordinate clauses and a heavy-handed use of synonymic doubling.[12] The prosifiers tend to eliminate the repetitions characteristic of verse epic but amplify other passages according to their own intentions or those of their patrons. The radical modification of epic style and tone may be observed in the following comparison between the twelfth-century verse epic *Garin le Lorrain* and the fifteenth-century prose translation copied by David Aubert for Philip the Good of Burgundy.[13] The episode in question is the death of Thierry of Maurienne, father of the future queen Blanchefleur. In the verse, Thierry's deathbed scene occurs in the middle of a laisse:

Or chanterom del riche roi Tierri
qui fu navrez. Dex! quel domage ot ci!
Confés se fist a moines beneïz,
de ses pechiez fu molt bien repentiz.
Ses barons fet de devant lui venir. (vv. 1894–98)

[Now we will sing of the powerful King Thierry, who was wounded. God, what a shame this was! He made his confession to the holy monks; he repented sincerely of his sins. He summoned his barons before him.][14]

The narrator-jongleur speaks or "sings" in the first person and participates in the event by lamenting the imminent death of the king. The passage contains thirty-four words and, after the second line, privileges a paratactic compositional style: the text proceeds by the accretion of independent clauses, each contained within the framework of the decasyllabic line.

The prose translation shifts the event to the beginning of a chapter, where it is preceded by the rubric "Comment le roy Thierry de Morienne donna sa fille en mariage au duc Guerin de Loheraine a tout son royaulme par le consentement des barons de ses paiis" [How King Thierry of Maurienne gave his daughter in marriage to Duke Garin of Lorraine, along with his entire kingdom, with the consent of the barons of his land]:

> L'istoire racompte que le roy Thierry de Morienne estant en son lit malade et navré a mort en plusieurs lieux, comme les mires et medecins le rapporterent et certiffierent par les sciences qu'ilz avoient acquises, considerant en l'estat mondain que une foiz convenoit morir et prendre fin, pensant a plusieurs choses, que d'heure en heure il affoiblissoit, il appella ses gardes et conseilliers.

> [The story relates that King Thierry of Maurienne, being confined to bed, sick and mortally wounded in several places, as the doctors and physicians reported and certified by the knowledge they had acquired, considering that the time had come to die and take leave of this world, thinking about several things, as he became weaker by the hour, he called his guards and advisers.][15]

In the *mise en prose*, the narrator removes himself from the affective pull of the diegetic world, eliminating the expression of regret over the king's demise. The passage contains sixty-three words, nearly twice as many as the verse, and is hypotactic, incorporating the content into a single complex sentence through the use of participles and subordinating conjunctions. The translator amplifies the original by the use of synonymic doublets ("mires et medecins"; "morir et prendre fin") and by a nod to the physicians' expertise. Prose reworkings mark another stage in the blurring of boundaries between chanson de geste and romance, which already exhibited significant generic overlap on the level of content by the late thirteenth century. With the disappearance of formal markers such as laisse structure, and the substitution of the translator's voice for that of the narrator-jongleur, the prose successors to the chansons de geste—often called *romans*—merge to some extent with their romance counterparts.

Admittedly, the sinuosities of Middle French prose have found few admirers in the modern era, even among enthusiasts of the chansons de geste. Nonetheless, prose adaptations of epic (as well as romance) enjoyed tremendous favor in their day and can tell us much about the aesthetic and moral values that shaped late medieval literary production. Most of the *mises en prose* were commissioned by noble patrons. The dukes of Burgundy were particularly avid consumers of the prose epics, appropriating the chivalric narratives in the interest of their political and cultural ambitions. Philip the Good, Duke of Burgundy from 1419 to 1467, ordered a number of epic reworkings, including the *Histoire de Charles Martel*, a compilation that includes a prose version of the Lorraine cycle (quoted above), as well as *Girart de Roussillon* and *La Belle Hélène de Constantinople*, both translated by Jean Wauquelin.[16] Wauquelin, who bestows lavish praise upon his patron in dedicatory prologues, appears to have exercised multiple functions at the ducal court, including the purchase, restoration, and binding of books.[17] However, not all translators and patrons were associated with aristocratic circles. Philippe de Vigneulles, a successful cloth merchant from Metz, produced his own translation of the Lorraine epics as a monument of civic pride, undertaken in the honor of God and his beloved city.[18] Patrons and audiences were not exclusively male: Marie de Clèves, widow of Charles d'Orléans, commissioned a prose version of the *Geste du Chevalier au cygne*.[19] Jean Wauquelin's prologue to the *Belle Hélène de Constantinople* explicitly refers to a public of both men and women ("pour homme et pour femme").[20]

The Charlemagne, Guillaume, and Crusade cycles were all reworked into prose.[21] Curiously, the *Chanson de Roland*, today considered the quintessential Old French epic, did not pass directly into the *mises en prose*, with the exception of the episode of Aude's death.[22] As François Suard notes, the smaller cycles are particularly well represented in the corpus of *mises en prose*, notably *Renaut de Montauban* (also known as the *Quatre Fils Aymon*) and *Huon de Bordeaux*, along with their continuations.[23] The prose reworkings served as the basis for incunabula (early print editions), beginning with *Fierabras* in 1478 and continuing through the sixteenth century. These editions often attest to the existence of chansons de geste that have not survived in verse form. The enormously popular *Valentin et Orson*, which appeared in over a dozen early print editions in Lyon and Paris, is the prose version of a lost verse epic. Like many late chansons de geste, it weaves together diverse folklore motifs, notably the Wild Man of the Woods and the Persecuted Wife, with heroic exploits against the Saracens.[24] *Valentin et Orson, Huon de Bordeaux,* the *Quatre Fils Aymon,* and the *Belle Hélène de Constantinople* are among the prose epics that continued to circulate in the form of chapbooks—mass-produced, inexpensive volumes sold by itinerant peddlers in the countryside. Most prominent among these popular versions was the Bibliothèque Bleue series from Troyes, so named for the books' blue paper covers; prose epics were disseminated in this fashion from the seventeenth to the nineteenth century. Beginning in the eighteenth century, adaptations for a more cultivated public appeared in such series as the Bibliothèque Universelle des Romans; the Count of Tressan produced sixteen volumes in this series, haughtily distinguishing his work from the less refined volumes in the Bibliothèque Bleue.[25]

The Chansons de Geste Outside France

Old French epic material was widely disseminated throughout Europe and found its most fertile ground in Italy. There is evidence from sculptures and proper names that chansons de geste were circulating in northern Italy as early as the twelfth century; written allusions to oral performances are attested from the late thirteenth century.[26] The poems also entered Italy in written form, transmitted in French manuscripts purchased by the seigneurial courts of Liguria, Lombardy, and Venice, which also commissioned Italian copies of chansons de geste.[27] A significant corpus of "Franco-Italian" or "Franco-Venetian" epic manuscripts dates from the mid-thirteenth to the early fifteenth century. These texts were composed in an artificial, hybrid language combining French and Italian linguistic features. The term "Franco-Italian" covers a wide range of linguistic possibilities: as Leslie Zarker Morgan explains, "there is a gradation between extremely deliberate mixture or editing . . . and attempts at writing in French."[28] The complex corpus may be divided into three principal categories: (1) those representing Italianized copies of French originals, with varying degrees of linguistic hybridity; (2) adaptations of Old French epics, with varying degrees of elaboration; (3) original works composed in the literary language of Franco-Italian.[29] Notable texts in the first category include seven manuscripts containing the *Aspremont* (set in Italy) and two Franco-Italian versions of the *Chanson de Roland,* the manuscripts known as V4 and V7. In the second category, manuscript V13 contains the largest number of Franco-Italian reworkings of French epic poems, gathered in a compilation known as the *Geste Francor*; this collection includes works devoted to Bovo (Beuve de Hantone), Berta da li pe grant (Berte as grans piés), Uggieri il Danese (Ogier le Danois), Orlandino (young Roland), and Karleto (young Charlemagne).[30] Also represented in the Franco-Italian corpus are *Aliscans* and *Renaut de Montauban*. In the third category, Charlemagne's Spanish campaigns are the subject of a fourteenth-century original composition from Padua, the *Entrée d'Espagne*, which Jane Everson describes as "a landmark not only in the transmission and development of Carolingian epic in Italy, but of Italian literature as a whole."[31] In this prequel to Roncevaux, the relationship between Charlemagne and Roland is characterized by discord, and Roland's early exploits extend from Spain to the East, as the fiery young hero journeys into the "tere alïenor."[32] Also of note is the fourteenth-century *Ugo d'Alvernia* (*Huon d'Auvergne*). As yet unedited, this tale relates the hero's dispute with Charles Martel and a lengthy series of exotic adventures, including a descent into hell.[33]

These Franco-Italian works composed in northeastern Italy preserved the structure of the traditional epic laisse. In Tuscany, however, ottava rima (composition in eight-line stanzas) became the dominant form of narrative poetry during the fourteenth and fifteenth centuries and served as an important vehicle of Carolingian epic material. Italian verse narratives in ottava rima include works on Roland's exploits in the Spanish campaigns (*Spagna in rima*), the *Aspremont* tradition (*Cantari di Aspromonte*), and versions of the stories devoted to Beuve de Hantone, Fierabras, Ogier le Danois, and Renaut de Montauban.[34] At the same time, the French epic tradition was also transmitted in Italian prose works, most notably *Aquilon de Bavière* and the chivalric texts of the fifteenth-century Florentine author Andrea da Barberino. Andrea produced prose adaptations of Charlemagne material in *I Reali di Francia* and *Aspramonte*, as well as a prose *Ugo d'Alvernia*; his prose rendering of the Guillaume cycle (*Storie Nerbonesi*) is the only Italian version of the Guillaume d'Orange material from this period.[35] The French epic tradition would continue to thrive in Italy throughout the Renaissance in the chivalric romances, in ottava rima, of renowned authors such as Pulci (*Morgante maggiore*, 1481), Boiardo (*Orlando innamorato*, 1486), and Ariosto (*Orlando furioso*, 1516).[36]

By contrast, remnants of the chanson de geste tradition in the Iberian

Peninsula are scarce and fragmentary.[37] The thirteenth-century Castilian *Roncesvalles*, preserved in a 100-line fragment, is based on a French version that postdates the Oxford and rhymed redactions and shares traits with the *Pseudo-Turpin*; it depicts the scene in which Charlemagne and his surviving barons discover the bodies of the knights slain at Roncevaux.[38] There is, in addition, indirect evidence of lost Spanish versions of Old French epic material.[39] The *Nota Emilianense*, dated between 1065 and 1075, is a Latin summary of what is believed to be a lost *Cantar de Rodlane* (*Chanson de Roland*).[40] Later chronicles provide further testimony of lost *cantares*, including one or more songs devoted to the hero Bernardo del Carpio. Nephew of Alfonso II the Chaste, Bernardo features in an alternative, anti-French version of the Roncevaux battle, in which he leads Spanish forces to a victory against Charlemagne's rear guard.[41] The French epic tradition is also discernible in Spanish prose romances such as the fourteenth-century *Hystoria de la reyna Sebilla* and a 1521 translation of Jehan Bagnyon's prose *Fierabras* titled *Historia del Emperador Carlo Magno y de los doce pares de Francia*.[42]

The chansons de geste had considerable success in northern Europe. A series of Old Norse prose translations of French epics form part of the genre called *riddarasögur* (tales of knights). They were produced in the thirteenth century during the reign of Hákon, king of Norway from 1217 to 1263, who is also credited with having commisioned a number of the translations. The majority of the texts are gathered in the *Karlamagnús saga*, a collection of independent translations that appears in cyclical manuscripts. The first branch appears to be a translation of a French compilation that contained summaries of various chansons de geste. Other branches contain versions of the *Enfances Ogier, Aspremont, Saisnes, Otinel*, the *Voyage de Charlemagne*, and the *Roland*.[43]

Chansons de geste from several different cycles were adapted into Middle High German.[44] The *Rolandslied*, composed by the cleric-poet Konrad around 1170, was likely commissioned by Henry the Lion, whose campaigns against the Slavs unleashed a wave of crusading fervor.[45] Though its source was a model close to the Oxford *Roland*, the 9,000-odd-line *Rolandslied* is more than twice as long as the Oxford version. It was reworked in the early thirteenth century by Der Stricker in *Karl der Grosse*, a work probably composed for the Holy Roman emperor Frederick II, who sought to place himself in Charlemagne's imperial suc-

cession. Der Stricker added material about Charlemagne's youth and fo-
cused on his identity as emperor.[46] Carolingian material is also elaborated
in the mid-fourteenth-century *Karlmeinet*, a verse compilation including a
branch devoted to Charlemagne's youth (*Meinet*).[47] The cycle of Guillaume
d'Orange inspired Wolfram von Eschenbach's unfinished verse *Willehalm*,
which incorporates material from *Aliscans* and the *Prise d'Orange*. The
cycle of rebellious barons also made its way into Middle High German,
with prose versions of *Girart de Roussillon*, *Renaut de Montauban*, and
Ogier le Danois.[48] Finally, in the mid-fifteenth century, Countess Elisa-
beth of Nassau-Saarbrücken produced adaptations of four chansons de
geste: *Herzog Herpin* (*Lion de Bourges*), *Huge Scheppel* (*Hugues Capet*),
Die Könige Sebille (*Reine Sebile*), and *Loher und Maller* (*Lohier et Malart*).
Locating spaces in the heroic material for the foregrounding of women's
political roles and speech, Elisabeth modified her source texts to enhance
and valorize female rulers.[49]

The Low Countries proved to be a particularly significant point of re-
ception and diffusion, beginning as early as the twelfth century.[50] There are
approximately twenty-seven Middle Dutch romances derived from Old
French epic material: all but one are fragments, and all are composed in
rhyming couplets rather than laisses. Bart Besamusca divides the corpus
into three categories based on the relationship between Dutch texts and
French sources (when the latter may be determined).[51] A first group con-
tains more or less faithful Middle Dutch renditions of French sources. The
oldest text in this category is the Limburg *Aiol* (ca. 1200), followed by the
first part of the *Roman der Lorreinen* (mid-13th century), which contains
translations of *Garin le Lorrain* and *Gerbert de Metz*; there is also a 97-
line fragment of a Dutch *Aspremont* (ca. 1300). The second and largest
category encompasses adaptations of Old French texts, of which only a
few will be mentioned here.[52] A version of the *Chanson de Roland*, the
Roelantslied, dates from the twelfth century; the fragment contains ap-
proximately 2,000 extant verses limited to the defeat of the rear guard
at Roncevaux.[53] The Guillaume cycle is represented by *Willem van Orin-
gen* (mid-13th century), based on the *Moniage Guillaume*; codicological
evidence suggests that the full text was originally accompanied by other
works in the same cycle.[54] *Huge van Bordeus*, an adaptation of *Huon de
Bordeaux*, dates from the fourteenth century and contains episodes that
originally featured in the *Huon* continuations. *Renout van Montalbaen*, a

Middle Dutch version of *Renaut de Montauban* from the early thirteenth century, is among the works that Dutch scholars believe to be based on oral rather than written sources: the adaptation deviates so significantly from extant French versions that the poet may well have reconstructed his tale based on recollections from recitations.[55] In the third group of texts are original compositions in Middle Dutch, notably a continuation of the *Roman der Lorreinen* known as *Lorreinen II* that does not correspond to the extant French continuations of the Lorraine cycle. The indigenous Dutch rendition grafts elements from the Charlemagne cycle onto the feud between Lorrains and Bordelais: Pepin the Short has been succeeded by Charlemagne, and Gelloen (Ganelon) assumes leadership of the treacherous Bordelais clan.[56]

There is abundant evidence of an early and extensive dissemination of chansons de geste in England. Anglo-Norman manuscripts preserve versions of some of the oldest and most illustrious French epics, such as the Oxford version of the *Chanson de Roland* and the *Chanson de Guillaume*. At least two Anglo-Norman compositions, *Beuve de Hantone* (early 13th century) and *Horn* (ca. 1170), are thought to be indigenous works.[57] These two texts were adapted into Middle English, as was the Anglo-Norman version of *Ami et Amile*.[58] Middle English adaptations of the Charlemagne cycle include a fragmentary version of the *Roland* and multiple versions of *Fierabras*. A fourteenth-century compilation in Welsh gathers several poems from the Charlemagne cycle, including the *Roland* and the *Voyage de Charlemagne*.[59] *Huon de Bordeaux* was particularly appreciated in England: the prose version was adapted by John Bourchier, Lord Berners, in 1533, and printed several times. A theatrical version, *Hewen of Burdoche*, was staged in 1593. One or both of these adaptations may have inspired the character Oberon in Shakespeare's *Midsummer Night's Dream*.[60]

Recent scholarship has sought to expand the field of inquiry by moving beyond a purely linguistic or stylistic comparison between source text and translation.[61] Like the *mises en prose*, rewritings of the Old French epic on "foreign" soil are revealing zones of contact between received material and the preoccupations of individual translators, patrons, and audiences. As Sif Rikhardsdottir affirms, "By reading vernacular translations in connection with and through the intellectual history that sustained them, they gain value as cultural and theoretical evidence of medieval reading practices."[62]

Modern Medievalisms

Although some French epic material continued to be transmitted almost without interruption from the Middle Ages on, for instance in the Bibliothèque Bleue,[63] the prestige of the chansons de geste in France began to pale in comparison with that of classical heroic literature beginning in the Renaissance. During the Romantic period, however, both scholars and poets sought to promote indigenous heroic models. The early medievalist Paulin Paris challenged readers to find a "pagan" epic that might rival the moving episode of Begon's death in *Garin le Lorrain*; in his voluminous study of the chansons de geste, Léon Gautier proclaimed that the *Chanson de Roland* contained passages worthy of the *Iliad*.[64] Philological projects evince a deep engagement with the epic ethos. Paulin Paris described the work of translation as a "hand-to-hand combat" with the monuments of French national poetry; by translating these works into modern French, he hoped to "conquer" the contemporary reading public.[65] As we have seen, the chansons de geste, and the *Chanson de Roland* in particular, were instrumental in nineteenth-century constructions of nationhood.[66] Harry Redman Jr. traces the multiple transformations undergone by Roland during this period. A "hero for all seasons," Roland was portrayed by Alfred de Vigny as a "doomed idealist," while Victor Hugo painted him as a swashbuckling man of action. In the wake of France's humiliating defeat in the Franco-Prussian War, the memory of Roncevaux inspired hope of eventual retaliation against the Germans.[67]

The celebrated philologist and academician Joseph Bédier (1864–1938) was perhaps the most influential mediator between medieval Francophone literature and the modern reading public. We have already discussed his "individualist" position in the debate over the origins of the chansons de geste.[68] Bédier was a prolific editor, commentator, and translator, with a particular attachment to the Oxford *Roland*. Michelle R. Warren has fruitfully examined his career in the context of the colonial experience: Bédier spent most of his formative years on the island of Réunion before pursuing university studies in Paris, and his construction of medieval literary history is informed by what Warren terms "creole medievalism."[69] Warren demonstrates the ways in which Bédier's translation of the *Roland* supports notions of French cultural purity by homogenizing the culturally diverse Frankish army and buttressing the oppositions between Franks and

Saracens.[70] Bédier was also a fervent admirer of the Guillaume d'Orange tradition, to which he devoted the first volume of his *Légendes épiques*. He composed two plays adapted from the Guillaume material: a three-act *Légende des Aliscamps*, never performed, and a shorter one-act version titled *Chevalerie*, performed in 1915 at the Comédie Française.[71] Fashioned as an instrument of nationalistic fervor, *Chevalerie* stages Vivien's courageous vow never to retreat in the face of the enemy, thus serving as a model for young Frenchmen bound for the battlefields of World War I.[72]

In fact, over the centuries, Old French epic narratives have lent themselves to diverse types of performance, reintroducing the immediacy of the performer's voice and corporeal presence. *Huon de Bordeaux* was the subject not only of theatrical presentations but of operas and pantomime ballets.[73] A late twentieth-century rendition of the *Roland* illustrates the epic's potential for cultural preservation and renewal. *La Chanson de Roland*, a production of the Compagnie Picrokole presented in France and abroad between 1990 and 1996, featured a single narrator-performer, Jacques Gouin, using figurines to represent the characters. Élisabeth Gentet-Ravasco, who adapted the chanson de geste for this production, presented the work in the context of modern preoccupations. Against the backdrop of the fledgling European Union, the troupe was drawn to a work that had been disseminated in diverse languages across the continent; in light of persistent religious intolerance and warfare, the *Chanson de Roland* could serve as a reminder of the consequences of sectarianism.[74]

With few exceptions, such the relatively obscure 1977 Cassenti film *La Chanson de Roland*, the chansons de geste have not given rise to cinematic versions.[75] They have, however, been embraced by other forms of popular culture, especially children's literature.[76] From the beginning of the twentieth century, adaptations for children and young adults have exploited the didactic, moral, and imaginative potential of epic narratives, principally the *Roland*, the Guillaume cycle, the *Quatre Fils Amyon*, and *Huon de Bordeaux*. In addition to the tales' obvious usefulness for instilling patriotism, they have served as entertaining history and vocabulary lessons (often presenting a highly stereotyped image of the Middle Ages), vehicles of moral instruction (promoting self-sacrifice and loyalty), and sources of visual pleasure (through accompanying illustrations).

❖

The chansons de geste gave rise to a vast and complex intertextual network spanning ten centuries and multiple language traditions. Each adaptation bears the marks of aesthetic, linguistic, and cultural engagement with source material in a specific temporal and geopolitical context. The Old French epics and their avatars occupy a vital place in Western literary history and criticism. As poetic responses to the ideals and deficiencies of the feudal world, the chansons de geste elucidate medieval perspectives on power and the proper functioning of society; as tales of heroism, friendship, and faith, they participate in a broader meditation on the human experience.

CHANSONS DE GESTE—DATES AND VERSIFICATION

The following list is not a complete catalog of chansons de geste, but rather a reference source for works listed in chapter 2. Dates are approximate and reflect the most recent and credible dates proposed by the texts' editors and commentators. Versification is based on the manuscripts used in the critical editions cited in the Select Bibliography. Where the Select Bibliography lists multiple editions, a specific editor is noted.

Aliscans. Late twelfth century; 8,304 rhymed decasyllables.

Ami et Amile. Ca. 1200; 3,504 decasyllables with a 6-syllable *vers orphelin* at the end of each laisse.

Anseïs de Carthage. Thirteenth century; 11,607 rhymed decasyllables.

Anseÿs de Metz (de Gascogne). Mid-thirteenth century; 14,597 assonanced decasyllables in Green's partial edition, but approximately 25,000 lines in total.

Aspremont. Late twelfth century; 11,172 assonanced decasyllables.

Auberi le Bourguignon (Auberi le Bourgoin). Ca. 1250; approximately 26,000 rhymed decasyllables.[1]

Aye d'Avignon. Early thirteenth century; 4,132 rhymed alexandrines.

Aymeri de Narbonne. Early thirteenth century; 4,586–4,697 rhymed decasyllables with a 6-syllable *vers orphelin* at the end of each laisse.

Bataille Loquifer. Thirteenth century; 4,222 rhymed decasyllables.

Bâtard de Bouillon. Mid-fourteenth century; 6,546 rhymed alexandrines.

Baudouin de Sebourc. Fourteenth century; 25,778 rhymed alexandrines.

Belle Hélène de Constantinople. Mid-fourteenth century; 15,538 rhymed alexandrines.

Berte as grans piés. Late thirteenth century; 3,486 rhymed alexandrines.

Beuve de Hantone. First half thirteenth century; 10,614 rhymed decasyllables.

Canso d'Antioca. Late twelfth century; 714-line fragment of rhymed alexandrines with a 6-syllable *vers orphelin* at the end of each laisse.

Canso de la Crozada. Eleventh century (1212–19); 9,582 rhymed alexandrines with a 6-syllable *vers orphelin* at the end of each laisse.

Chanson d'Antioche (ed. Nelson). Late twelfth century; 11,407 rhymed alexandrines.

Chanson de Bertrand du Guesclin. Twelfth century (1380–85); 24,346 rhymed alexandrines.

Chanson de Guillaume. Mid-twelfth century; 3,554 assonanced decasyllables, with intermittent refrains.

Chanson de Jérusalem. Late twelfth century; 9,891 rhymed alexandrines.

Chanson de Roland (Oxford version). Late eleventh or early twelfth century; 4,002 assonanced decasyllables.

Chanson des Saisnes. Late twelfth century; 7,838 rhymed alexandrines.

Charroi de Nîmes. Mid-twelfth century; 1,486 assonanced decasyllables.

Chétifs. Twelfth century; 4,101 rhymed alexandrines.

Chevalerie Ogier de Danemarche. Early thirteenth century; 12,346 assonanced decasyllables.

Chevalerie Vivien. Late twelfth or early thirteenth century; 1,906 lines, mixture of decasyllables and alexandrines; 6-syllable *vers orphelin* in the C redaction.

Chevalier au cygne. Late twelfth century; 4,571 rhymed alexandrines.

Chrétienté Corbaran. Thirteenth century; 1,464 rhymed alexandrines.

Couronnement de Louis. Mid-twelfth century; 2,695 assonanced decasyllables.

Daurel et Beton. Late twelfth century; 2,188 rhymed decasyllables.

Doon de Mayence. Later thirteenth century; 11,505 rhymed alexandrines.

Doon de Nanteuil. Late twelfth or early thirteenth century; 220-line fragment of rhymed alexandrines with a 6-syllable *vers orphelin* at the end of each laisse.

Enfances Renier. Thirteenth century; 20,065 rhymed decasyllables.

Enfances Vivien. Thirteenth century; 3,095 assonanced decasyllables.

Fierabras. Late twelfth century; 6,408 rhymed decasyllables.

Fin d'Elias. Early thirteenth century; 2,432 rhymed alexandrines.

Florence de Rome. Early thirteenth century; 6,410 assonanced alexandrines.

Foucon de Candie. Thirteenth century; 9,882 rhymed decasyllables, 5036 rhymed alexandrines.

Galien le Restoré. Fifteenth-century reworking; 4,911 rhymed alexandrines.

Garin le Lorrain. Second half twelfth century; 18,650 assonanced decasyllables.

Gaufrey. Later thirteenth century; 10,731 rhymed alexandrines.

Gaydon. Early thirteenth century; 10,896 rhymed decasyllables.

Gerbert de Metz. Late twelfth century; 14,795 assonanced decasyllables in Taylor's edition, of which the first 2,470 are part of *Garin le Lorrain.*

Girart de Roussillon. Late twelfth century; 10,001 rhymed decasyllables.

Girart de Vienne. Late twelfth century; 6,934 rhymed decasyllables with a 6-syllable *vers orphelin* at the end of each laisse.

Gormont et Isembart. Late eleventh or early twelfth century; 661 assonanced octosyllables, with frequent 4-line refrain at the end of the laisse.

Gui de Bourgogne. Early thirteenth century; 4,304 rhymed alexandrines.

Gui de Nanteuil. Late twelfth or early thirteenth century; 2,913 rhymed alexandrines.

Guibert d'Andrenas. Early thirteenth century; 2,387 rhymed decasyllables with a 6-syllable *vers orphelin* at the end of each laisse.

Hervis de Metz. Early thirteenth century; 10,521 assonanced lines, mostly decasyllabic; the Senlis Tournament episode contains 564 alexandrines.

Horn. Late twelfth century; 5,240 rhymed alexandrines.

Huon de Bordeaux (ed. Kibler and Suard). Second half thirteenth century; 10,797 assonanced lines, mostly decasyllabic, but vv. 1–79 alexandrines.

Istoire le Roy Charlemaine. Late thirteenth century; 23,348 rhymed alexandrines.

Jourdain de Blaye. Early thirteenth century; 4,345 assonanced decasyllables, with a 6-syllable *vers orphelin* at the end of each laisse.

Lion de Bourges. Mid-fourteenth century; 34,298 rhymed alexandrines.

Mainet. Late twelfth century; approximately 800-line fragment, partly assonanced, partly rhymed alexandrines.

Maugis d'Aigremont. Thirteenth century; 9,078 rhymed alexandrines.

Moniage Guillaume (long version). Second half twelfth century; 6,862 assonanced decasyllables.

Moniage Rainouart (I). Early thirteenth century; 7,531 rhymed decasyllables with a 6-syllable *vers orphelin* at the end of each laisse.

Mort Aymeri de Narbonne. Late twelfth century; 4,011 assonanced decasyllables with a 6-syllable *vers orphelin* at the end of each laisse.

Naissance du Chevalier au cygne. Late twelfth century; "Elioxe" version 3,499 rhymed alexandrines; "Beatrix" version 3,196 rhymed alexandrines.

Narbonnais. Early thirteenth century; 8,054 rhymed decasyllables with a 6-syllable *vers orphelin* at the end of each laisse.

Otinel. Late twelfth century; 2,133 rhymed decasyllables.

Parise la Duchesse. Thirteenth century; 3,106 assonanced alexandrines.

Prise d'Acre; Mort Godefroi; Chanson des Rois Baudouin (continuous narrative, second branch of the Jerusalem Continuations). Thirteenth century; 6,778 rhymed alexandrines.

Prise de Cordres et de Sebille. Thirteenth century; 2,948 assonanced decasyllables with a 6-syllable *vers orphelin* at the end of each laisse.

Prise d'Orange. Mid-twelfth century; 1,887 assonanced decasyllables.

Quatre Fils Aymon. Alternative title of *Renaut de Montauban*, q.v.

Raoul de Cambrai. Ca. 1200; 8,542 decasyllabic lines, rhymed until v. 5373, then assonanced.

Renaut de Montauban (ed. Thomas). Early thirteenth century; 14,310 rhymed alexandrines.

Retour de Cornumaran. Thirteenth century; 1,503 rhymed alexandrines.

Rollan a Saragossa. Thirteenth century; 1,409 assonanced decasyllables.

Ronsasvals. Thirteenth century; 1,802 assonanced decasyllables.

Siège de Barbastre. Early thirteenth century; 7,692 rhymed alexandrines with a 6-syllable *vers orphelin* at the end of each laisse.

Tristan de Nanteuil. Mid-fourteenth century; 22,361 rhymed alexandrines.

Vengeance Fromondin. Second half thirteenth century; 6,672 rhymed decasyllables.

Vivien de Monbranc. Thirteenth century; 1,102 rhymed alexandrines.

Voyage (Pèlerinage) de Charlemagne à Jérusalem et à Constantinople. Twelfth century; 870 assonanced alexandrines.

NOTES

Chapter 1. The Historical and Poetic Context

Translation of the epigraph from *Otinel*, vv. 1–5, is my own.

1. A thirteenth-century play by Adam de la Halle, *Le Jeu de Robin et Marion*, does contain a musical line that is purportedly from *Audigier*, a parody of the chansons de geste. While there is no proof of its authenticity, the melody is consistent with the simple, monotonous chant characteristic of oral epic. See Rychner, *La chanson de geste*, 17–18.

2. The chansons de geste thus follow the ancient tradition of epic as a lofty work rooted in song: cf. Virgil's "Arma virumque cano."

3. Translation from Duggan, *Romances of Chrétien de Troyes*, 188–89. Quotations of primary sources refer to the editions listed in the bibliography. In the case of multiple editions, notes will specify the editor's name.

4. On the relationship of chanson de geste and epic in its broader sense, see Poirion, "Chanson de geste ou épopée?"; Suard, *Guide de la chanson de geste*, 30–32; Calin, *A Muse for Heroes*, 5–9.

5. Paris's theory is elaborated in his *Histoire poétique de Charlemagne*.

6. See Bédier, *Les légendes épiques* and *"La Chanson de Roland" commentée*.

7. Bédier, *"La Chanson de Roland" commentée*, 30.

8. On French nationalism and the role of the epic in the late nineteenth and early twentieth centuries, see Duggan, "Franco-German Conflict."

9. See Menéndez Pidal, *"La Chanson de Roland" et la tradition épique des Francs*.

10. The oldest and most celebrated version of *The Song of Roland* is preserved in Oxford, Bodleian Library, Digby 23. The manuscript dates from the second half of the twelfth century, but it preserves a text dating from the late eleventh or early twelfth century. On the names Roland and Olivier see Lejeune, "La naissance du couple littéraire."

11. See Lord, *The Singer of Tales*. Lord pursued the work of his teacher, Milman Parry, who died unexpectedly before publishing a full account of his research. The 2000 edition of Lord's book includes a CD with audio recordings of South Slavic oral poets.

12. See esp. Duggan, *"The Song of Roland": Formulaic Style;* Heinemann, *L'art métrique.*

13. See the series of four essays by Calin and Duggan gathered under the title "Un débat sur l'épopée vivante."

14. Le Gentil, "Les chansons de geste: le problème des origines."

15. Boutet, *La Chanson de geste* and "The Chanson de geste and orality."

16. See, for example, the prologues of *Doon de Mayence* and *Berte as grans piés.* Such passages must not necessarily be taken at face value, and may well be rhetorical devices used to lend authenticity. Boutet maintains that a "great number" of chansons de geste present themselves in this way ("The Chanson de geste and orality," 361), but this is not the case for the earlier epic texts.

17. Johannes de Grocheio, "On Secular Music," 22–23.

18. William of Malmesbury, *Gesta regum Anglorum,* 1: 454–55.

19. *Robert the Monk's History of the First Crusade,* 62–63, 80.

20. *Le Roman de Flamenca,* v. 695.

21. Jean Renart, *Roman de la Rose,* vv. 1328–68.

22. *Raoul de Cambrai,* ed. and trans. Kay, vv. 2265–70.

23. For a review of the research, see Leverage, *Reception and Memory,* 28–50.

24. See Busby, *Codex and Context,* vol. 2, chap. 7; for a summary of Busby, see Leverage, *Reception and Memory,* 96–99.

25. *Huon de Bordeaux,* ed. Ruelle, my translation.

26. Rychner, *La chanson de geste,* 49–54. He proposes sittings of 1,000–2,000 lines.

27. See in particular Taylor, "Was There a Song of Roland?"; Busby, *Codex and Context;* Leverage, *Reception and Memory,* chap. 2. See also, in this volume, 64.

28. Busby, *Codex and Context,* 1: 152–63.

29. For a reconsideration of the orality/literacy dichotomy, see Coleman, *Public Reading and the Reading Public.* Though she does not specifically consider the chansons de geste, Coleman makes a convincing case for the widespread practice of "aurality" (the reading aloud of written texts) in fourteenth- and fifteenth-century England and France.

30. See Lejeune, *Recherches sur le thème.*

31. See, for example, *La Bataille Loquifer,* vv. 3623–3962.

32. Kay, *Chansons de Geste in the Age of Romance*, 5.

33. See Grisward, *Archéologie de l'épopée médiévale*.

34. See Maddox, "The 'Archaeology' of Medieval Epic," for a critique of Grisward's study. See also Suard, *Guide de la chanson de geste*, 52.

35. In particular, Grisward analyzes the first part of the *Narbonnais*, in which Aymeri of Narbonne sends his sons into the world; their destinies appear to be structured by the trifunctional pattern. See also Bennett, *Carnaval héroïque*.

36. The fragmentary *Gormont et Isembart*, one of the oldest epics, is in assonanced octosyllabic verse.

37. *Garin le Loherenc*, ed. Iker-Gittleman, my translation. All subsequent quotations of *Garin le Lorrain* are from this edition.

38. See *Chanson de Roland*, ed. Short, note to line 77.

39. See, in this volume, 34.

40. Suard, *Guide de la chanson de geste*, 73–76.

41. Both of these works may be consulted for a more thorough and technical analysis of formulaic style.

42. Heinemann, *L'art métrique*, 143, my translation.

43. Rychner, *La chanson de geste*, 71–72.

44. *Moniage Guillaume*, v. 591, my translation.

45. *Ami et Amile*, ed. Dembowski, v. 2253, my translation.

46. *Chanson de Roland*, ed. Short; *Song of Roland*, trans. Burgess, v. 814. All subsequent quotations of the *Chanson de Roland* are from the Short edition and Burgess translation.

47. Rychner, *La chanson de geste*, 72–74.

48. *Garin le Loherenc*, v. 4995.

49. *Garin le Loherenc*, v. 9834.

50. *Chanson de Roland*, v. 179.

51. Rychner, *La chanson de geste*, 74–107.

52. *Hervis de Mes*, my translation.

53. The verb is in the preterite. The *-ait* ending in the third-person singular preterite is a Lorraine dialectal feature. See Herbin's introduction in *Hervis de Mes*, liii.

54. Laisses 83–85. See, in this volume, 67–71, for a more detailed discussion of the similar laisse sequences in the *Chanson de Roland*.

55. Rychner, *La chanson de geste*, 124–25.

56. Boutet, *La chanson de geste*, 77–86; Heinemann, *L'art métrique*, 137–220; Jones, *The Noble Merchant*, 97–121; Rossi, "Huon de Bordeaux," 131–59.

57. Heinemann, *L'art métrique*, 238–81.

58. Leverage, *Reception and Memory*, 188–200.

59. In his rigorous and detailed study *Les motifs dans la chanson de geste*, Jean-Pierre Martin distinguishes "narrative motifs" (conventional episodes rendered in the same fashion) from "rhetorical motifs" (figures of expression used for the most characteristic moments of epic narrative).

60. See Rychner, *La chanson de geste*, 141; Duggan, *"The Song of Roland": Formulaic Style*, 138–48.

61. Parry, "Epic Technique of Oral Verse-Making," 80.

62. This definition follows Duggan, *"The Song of Roland": Formulaic Style*, 10–15. See also Kay, "The Epic Formula"; Windelberg and Miller, "How (Not) to Define the Epic Formula."

63. Duggan, *"The Song of Roland": Formulaic Style*, 139.

64. Ibid., 147–48.

65. *Ami et Amile*, ed. Dembowski, vv. 421–22, my translation.

66. Duggan, *"The Song of Roland": Formulaic Style*, 105.

67. *Gerbert de Mez*, my translation.

68. Boutet, *La chanson de geste*, 33.

69. *Vivien de Monbranc*, my translation.

70. On the epic prologue, see Martin, "Sur les prologues."

71. Zumthor, *La lettre et la voix*, 19–21, 38–39.

72. Jauss, *Toward an Aesthetic of Reception*, 84.

73. See Calin, *Old French Epic of Revolt*.

74. On French medieval law and literature, see Bloch, *Medieval French Literature and Law*; Ribémont, *Crimes et châtiments*, esp. "La chanson de geste, une 'machine judiciaire'?"

75. Ribémont, "La chanson de geste, une 'machine judiciaire'?" viii.

76. See, in this volume, 41–45.

77. Ribémont, "Épopée médiévale et questions de droit," 253.

78. Bloch, *Medieval French Literature and Law*, 21.

79. On Saracens in the Old French epic, see Bancourt, *Les Musulmans*; Daniel, *Heroes and Saracens*; Ramey, *Christian, Saracen and Genre*; Akbari, *Idols in the East*.

80. Picherit, "Les Sarrasins dans *Tristan de Nanteuil*"; Vallecalle, "*Aquilon de Bavière*," 165–66.

81. See Jones, "Les chansons de geste et l'Orient."

82. Calin, "Rapports entre chanson de geste et roman," 410–11. The Saracen Princess will be discussed in greater detail in chapter 3.

83. Brault, "Le portrait des Sarrasins."

84. Kay, "La représentation de la féminité," 225, my translation.

85. Kay, *Chansons de Geste in the Age of Romance*, 52–63.

86. *Raoul de Cambrai*, vv. 1166–99; *Hervis de Mes*, vv. 2914–3098.

87. *Chanson de Guillaume*, vv. 1239, 1278–85, 2235–48. On Guibourc see Black, "Gendered World."

88. For a more detailed description of Old French epic cycles, see, in this volume, 26–49. See also Bloch, *Etymologies and Genealogies*, 92–109, for a nuanced study of the "significant conjunction of narrative poetry, early medieval linguistics, and the economics of the lineal family" (108).

89. See, in this volume, 32–35.

90. See Farnsworth, *Uncle and Nephew*, esp. 225–33; Goody, *Development of the Family*, 225–26. For a review of the literature on uncles and nephews, see Kay, *Chansons de Geste in the Age of Romance*, 82n15; Harney, *Kinship and Polity*, 33–36.

91. *Aye d'Avignon*, v. 2676, my translation.

92. See Jauss, *Toward an Aesthetic of Reception*, 83–87; Jones, *The Noble Merchant*, 40–46; Vance, *Reading "The Song of Roland*,*"* 11.

93. Kibler, "La chanson d'aventures."

94. On *Huon de Bordeaux*, see Rossi, *"Huon de Bordeaux" et l'évolution du genre épique*; on *Aye d'Avignon*, see Woods, *"Aye d'Avignon": A Study of Genre and Society*; on *Hervis de Metz*, see Jones, *The Noble Merchant*.

95. Gaunt, *Gender and Genre*, 8.

96. See, for example, Baldwin, *Aristocratic Life*, xi.

97. See Kay, *Chansons de Geste in the Age of Romance*, for a provocative discussion of the two textualities. Kay analyzes epic and romance as alternative responses to the political context, each illuminating the political unconscious of the other.

98. See, in this volume, 53–56, 136–40.

Chapter 2. The Texts

For this chapter in particular, François Suard's monumental *Guide de la chanson de geste*, which offers a systematic and encyclopedic study of the entire corpus, was indispensable.

Translations of the epigraph from Bertrand's *Girart de Vienne*, vv. 11–16, 21–23, 46–47, 53–54, and 56, and of the other epigraphs in this chapter, are my own.

1. An example is BnF fr. 19160, a cyclical manuscript containing three branches of the Lorraine cycle. The prequel *Hervis de Metz* ends with an epi-

logue that links it to the beginning of the core text, *Garin le Lorrain*. However, no attempt was made to resolve certain inconsistencies, such as the name and cultural identity of Hervis's wife (Aelis of Cologne or "Terrascone" in *Garin*, Beatrice of Tyre in *Hervis*).

2. See Sunderland, *Old French Narrative Cycles*, 4–11.

3. Suard, *Guide de la chanson de geste*, 122.

4. *Hervis de Mes*, vv. 626–30.

5. See Corbellari, *Guillaume d'Orange*, 20–23.

6. All quotations of the *Chanson de Roland* are from Ian Short's edition. English renderings follow *The Song of Roland* in Glyn Burgess's translation.

7. See Suard, *Guide de la chanson de geste*, 184.

8. Jehan Bodel, *Chanson des Saisnes*, my translation.

9. See Métraux, "Le *Charlemagne* de Girart d'Amiens."

10. See the epilogue, 141–42.

11. On the Guillaume cycle, see Frappier, *Cycle de Guillaume d'Orange*.

12. Scholars have proposed other historical prototypes as well. See Corbellari, *Guillaume d'Orange*, 59–92, for an overview. This Guillaume d'Orange is not to be confused with the sixteenth-century William, Prince of Orange, who led a Dutch revolt against the Spanish crown.

13. See Ferrante's introduction in *Guillaume d'Orange*, 1–2.

14. On the manuscript tradition of the Guillaume cycle, see Sunderland, *Old French Narrative Cycles*, ix–x, chap. 1; Tyssens, *La Geste de Guillaume*.

15. A *charroi* is a convoy of carts used to transport merchandise.

16. In the *Couronnement* and succeeding songs in the cyclical manuscripts, Guillaume is said to have a short nose ("cort nes"); however, the *Fragment de la Haye* and the *Chanson de Guillaume* describe the appendage as a crooked nose ("corb nes"). See Corbellari, *Guillaume d'Orange*, 113–19.

17. See, in *Chanson de Guillaume*, Bennett's introduction, 9–12.

18. On the thirteenth-century development of the cycle, see Guidot, *Recherches*.

19. Calin, *Old French Epic of Revolt*, 227.

20. Suard, *Guide de la chanson de geste*, 243. On historical antecedents, see Lejeune, *Recherches sur le thème*, 45–195.

21. Montpellier Méd. H 247. See Busby, *Codex and Context*, 1: 399–400.

22. See Boutet, "Au carrefour des cycles épiques."

23. See Jones, "Of Giants and Griffons."

24. Suard, *La chanson de geste*, 99.

25. See, in *Renaut de Montauban*, Thomas's introduction, 9.

26. Suard, *Guide de la chanson de geste*, 219–22.

27. *Renaut de Montauban*, ed. Verelst.

28. Suard, "*Renaut de Montauban*: Enjeux et problèmes," 17.

29. See the epilogue, 140–41, 147.

30. *Girart de Roussillon*, 3: 475–76.

31. Kay, *Chansons de Geste in the Age of Romance*, 53–54.

32. In "Le contexte idéologique de *Girart de Roussillon*," Dorothea Kullmann convincingly demonstrates that the ending of *Girart* reflects specific clerical debates with regard to heretical movements in the first half of the twelfth century.

33. Ibid., 272.

34. Kay, *Chansons de Geste in the Age of Romance*, 216.

35. Bibliothèque Royale de Belgique, II.181.

36. *Gormont et Isembart*, vi–viii. Bayot points out (vii) that this form is found in only two other early Romance works, the *Roman d'Alexandre* by Albéric and the Occitan *Chanson de Sainte Foi*; the latter, however, is rhymed rather than assonanced.

37. *Gormont et Isembart*, xiii.

38. For a recent overview of the manuscript tradition and composition of the Lorraine cycle, see Herbin, "Variations."

39. See for example Calin, *A Muse for Heroes*, 43. Like Charles Martel in *Girart de Roussillon*, Pepin takes his vassal's fiancée for himself: Queen Blanchefleur was originally promised to Garin.

40. The two poems are so closely joined that editors have not always agreed on the division between *Garin* and *Gerbert*. It is now generally accepted that the first 2,470 lines of Taylor's edition of *Gerbert* constitute the end of *Garin*; this is reflected in Iker-Gittleman's 1996 edition of *Garin le Loherenc*.

41. See Jones, *The Noble Merchant*.

42. A similar plot line is found in the *Enfances Vivien*.

43. See Herbin, "*Anseÿs de Gascogne* et la Flandre."

44. See Jones, "Recasting *Raoul de Cambrai*," and, in this volume, 110.

45. See Jones, "'Se je fusse hons.'"

46. Herbin, "Variations," esp. 158–59.

47. Ibid., 158. See also Herbin, "*Yonnet de Metz*."

48. See, for example, Parmly, *Geographical References*; Guidot, "L'extension cyclique," 106–7.

49. On the death of Begon, see Herbin, "Variations," 151–54; Jones, "Death of Bégon."

50. Gittleman, *Le style épique*, 16–17.

51. "Berte au grant pié, Betris, Alis": *Testament*, v. 347, in Villon, *Poems*.

Villon does not mention Queen Blanchefleur, whose vigorous and faithful defense of the Lorraine heroes stands in stark contrast to the cowardice and inconstancy of King Pepin.

52. My translation. See variants in *Garin le Loherenc*, 3: 726. This is the reading given in manuscripts DEGPQX.

53. See Cook, "*Chanson d'Antioche*," 1–8. For a historical perspective, see Riley-Smith, *The Crusades: A History*.

54. Cook, "*Chanson d'Antioche*," 9, 13. Beginning in the 1970s, a wave of critical editions has made the cycle accessible. See especially Mickel and Nelson, *Old French Crusade Cycle*; *La Chanson d'Antioche*, ed. and trans. Guidot; *Baudouin de Sebourc*, ed. Crist and Cook; *Le Bâtard de Bouillon*, ed. Cook; *Saladin*, ed. Crist.

55. See Cook, "Les épopées de la Croisade," for a detailed description of the works and their manuscript tradition. Cook proposes here to abandon the notion of a "first" and "second" Crusade cycle (97).

56. All quotations of the *Chanson d'Antioche* are from the Nelson edition.

57. See Cook, "*Chanson d'Antioche*," 40–45.

58. *Chanson d'Antioche*, ed. Guidot, 10, my translation.

59. Sweetenham, "How History Became Epic," 439–44.

60. See Guidot, "Le crime, les hommes et Dieu."

61. Daniel, *Heroes and Saracens*, 112.

62. *Chanson de Jérusalem*, vv. 5261–5330.

63. On the Swan Knight legend, see Lecouteux, *Mélusine et le Chevalier au cygne*, 109–58. Lecouteux also examines the close structural relationship between the Swan Knight and Mélusine legends.

64. Jean d'Arras composed his prose *Mélusine* in 1393 for his patrons Marie, Duchess of Bar, and her brother Jean, Duke of Berry.

65. See Lecouteux, *Mélusine et le Chevalier au cygne*, 11–13.

66. Cook, "Les épopées de la Croisade," 97.

67. See *Baudouin de Sebourc*, xxxiv–xlviii.

68. See *Le Bâtard de Bouillon*, xliv–liii.

69. Cook, "Les épopées de la Croisade," 95–97.

70. See *Saladin: Suite et fin du deuxième Cycle de la croisade*.

71. *Ami and Amile*, 1.

72. See Weill, "Auberi, un Bourguignon exilé," 168; Herbin, "Auberi le Bourguignon." There is at the present time no complete, satisfactory critical edition of the text.

73. Weill, "Auberi, un Bourguignon exilé," 176.

74. Others are *Berte as grans piés*, *Parise la Duchesse*, *La Belle Hélène de Constantinople*, *La Reine Sebile*, and *Florence de Rome*.

75. Kay, *Chansons de Geste in the Age of Romance*, 190.

76. On the "family romance" narrative, see Fenster, "The Family Romance of *Aye d'Avignon*," 11; on epic conflict and romance resolution, see Woods, "*Aye d'Avignon*": *A Study of Genre and Society*.

77. See Suard, *Guide de la chanson de geste*, 228–29.

78. *Aye d'Avignon*, 7.

79. The five volumes of *Der festländische Bueve de Hantone*, edited by Albert Stimming, contain the Continental version. Jean-Pierre Martin's edition of the Anglo-Norman version is in press.

80. See Martin, "*Beuves de Hantone* entre roman et chanson de geste"; Weiss, "The Courteous Warrior."

81. *Horn* is a hybrid text, generally designated in English as a "romance" or in French as a *roman*. Suard contests the "romance" label and classifies *Horn* as a *chanson d'aventures*: see *Guide de la chanson de geste*, 251.

82. See Kay, *Chansons de geste in the Age of Romance*, 219–31.

83. Weiss, "The Courteous Warrior," 150–55.

84. For an account of these reworkings, see Hogetoorn, "Bevis of Hampton," 63–64.

85. See Cook, "Unity and Esthetics"; Suard, "L'épopée française tardive."

86. Cook, "Unity and Esthetics," 106, 111–14.

87. Claude Roussel examines the intricate network of epic and folktale components in *Conter de geste au XIVe siècle*.

88. Ibid., 23–24, following the pattern described by Aarne and Thompson.

89. Ibid., 7; on the Bibliothèque Bleue, see, in this volume, 141.

90. Cuvelier, *Chanson de Bertrand du Guesclin*, my translation.

91. *Lion de Bourges*, lvii–lxii.

92. Ibid., ix–x. Both *Tristan de Nanteuil* and the *Chanson de Bertrand du Guesclin* allude to *Lion de Bourges*.

93. See *The "Canso d'Antioca*," 136–38; Suard, *Guide de la chanson de geste*, 45–47; Colby-Hall, "Lost Epics."

94. *The "Canso d'Antioca*," 136.

95. For a thorough consideration of the French and Occitan versions of the Antioch material, see *The "Canso d'Antioca*," 63–71.

96. *Daurel et Beton*, 122–24 and vv. 208–15.

97. See Michel Zink's introduction to Guillaume de Tudèle and Anonymous, *Chanson de la Croisade Albigeoise*, 18–23.

98. Ibid., 21–22. Others, including the poem's first editor, Eugène Martin-Chabot, have proposed a later date, because the poet refers to the death of Guy of Montfort, which occurred in 1228. Zink attributes this to an interpolation.

Chapter 3. Selected Works

1. The oldest extant version of the *Chanson de Roland*, dating from the late eleventh or early twelfth century, is found in an Anglo-Norman manuscript from the second half of the twelfth century at Oxford University, Bodleian Library, Digby 23, and is commonly referred to as "Oxford" or "O." Unless otherwise indicated, my analysis of the poem refers to this version. All quotations of the *Chanson de Roland* are from Ian Short's edition. English renderings follow *The Song of Roland* in Glyn Burgess's translation.

2. The work survives in seven subtantial manuscripts and three fragments. By privileging the Oxford version, I do not wish to minimize the importance and interest of the later redactions, all of which play an important role in the Roland tradition. For a complete edition of the French texts, see *La Chanson de Roland/The Song of Roland: The French Corpus*, edited by Joseph J. Duggan. On the history of *The Song of Roland* in the nineteenth century, see Duggan's general introduction to that edition; Duggan, "Franco-German Conflict"; Taylor, "Was There a Song of Roland?"

3. See Short's and Moignet's introductions to their respective editions of the *Chanson de Roland*; Kibler, "Rencesvals."

4. *Chanson de Roland*, ed. Moignet, Documents, 290.

5. See, in this volume, 3–6.

6. Wace, *Roman de Rou*, vv. 8013–18, and *History of the Norman People*, 181.

7. Burgess favors this identification because of Thorold's political experience and possible ties to the monastery of Mont-Saint-Michel, referred to in line 1428. See *The Song of Roland*, 14.

8. Taylor, "Was There a Song of Roland?," 64–65.

9. Farnham, "Romanesque Design."

10. For a review of the various structural descriptions, see Brault, "Structure et sens," 1–4.

11. The episode does not appear in the Lyon manuscript, the Latin legends, or the fragmentary texts. On the authenticity debate, see Duggan, *"The Song of Roland": Formulaic Style*, 63–104; Schenck, "The Baligant Episode."

12. See esp. Brault, "Structure et sens," 5–8.

13. See Leverage, *Reception and Memory*, esp. chap. 7, "Repetition Effects."

14. On the Saracens' names, see Bédier, *"La Chanson de Roland" commentée*, 299–300.

15. On the Saracens' false promises, see Cook, *Sense*, 59–61, 77.

16. Kinoshita, *Medieval Boundaries*, 15–45.

17. Ibid., 33–34.

18. Robert Francis Cook's *The Sense of the "Song of Roland"* is a model of close reading informed by a deep understanding of the feudal ethos. My interpretation of the *Roland* owes much to this reading and commentary. For other commentaries, see Bédier, *"La Chanson de Roland" commentée*; Vance, *Reading "The Song of Roland."*

19. Among the proponents of the *démesure* theory are Burger in *Turold, poète de la fidélité* and Calin in *A Muse for Heroes*. For challenges to this conventional reading, see Brault, "Sapientia," and Cook, *Sense*.

20. Cook, *Sense*, 15.

21. Calin, *A Muse for Heroes*, 19.

22. Cook systematically and convincingly debunks this interpretation throughout *The Sense of "The Song of Roland."*

23. See Cook, *Sense*, x, note 3, for a review of the scholarship.

24. See, for example, Burger, *Turold, poète de la fidélité*, 111. Burger attributes the defeat of the rear guard to Roland's sin of pride, claiming that Roland arrogantly believes he can achieve victory. For Burger, the poem is primarily a story of transgression and expiation.

25. See Cook, *Sense*, 70–71; Brault, "Sapientia"; Jones, "Roland versus Oliver," 204–5.

26. Cook, *Sense*, esp. 46–47.

27. See, for example, Burger, *Turold, poète de la fidélité*, 140–41.

28. Cook, *Sense*, 93.

29. Payen, *Le motif du repentir*, 109–17.

30. Kay, "Life of the Dead Body," 94–97.

31. See Haidu's analysis of this passage in *The Subject of Violence*, 29–30.

32. On the history and representation of Charlemagne, see McKitterick, *Charlemagne: The Formation of a European Identity*; Durand-Le Guern and Ribémont, *Charlemagne: Empereur et mythe d'Occident*.

33. On the question of Charlemagne's authority in decision-making, see Cook, *Sense*, 17–27, 115.

34. See Durand-Le Guern and Ribémont, *Charlemagne: Empereur et mythe d'Occident*, 119.

35. Joshua 10.12–14.

36. The account first appears in the thirteenth-century *Karlamagnús saga* but may have originated as early as the tenth century. See Suard, *Roland ou Les avatars d'une folie héroïque*, 42–43.

37. See *Chanson de Roland*, ed. Moignet, 45.

38. Ruggieri, *Il processo di Gano*.

39. Mickel, *Ganelon, Treason*. Mickel also offers a useful summary of Ruggieri's arguments. Cook vehemently refutes claims that Ganelon's defense has any legitimacy whatsoever: see *Sense*, 112–24.

40. Schenck, "If There Wasn't 'a' Song of Roland, Was There a 'Trial' of Ganelon?" Schenck is reluctant to speak of a "trial," referring instead to Ganelon's "punishment" (144).

41. Ibid., 149; Mickel, *Ganelon, Treason*, 42.

42. Kinoshita, *Medieval Boundaries*, 34–44, esp. 41.

43. Following Sarah Kay, I use "counternarrative" here in the sense of alternative narratives that serve to critique the epic text from within. See her *Chansons de Geste in the Age of Romance*, esp. 5, 229–30.

44. See *Songs of the Troubadours and Trouvères*, 186–87.

45. Kinoshita, *Medieval Boundaries*, 42–43.

46. See Kinoshita, *Medieval Boundaries*, 43.

47. Kinoshita notes that Bramimonde cannot "be recuperated as a feminist subject. . . . For Bramimonde, conversion means submitting both to a Christian God and to a discursive regime that demands women's silent acquiescence" (43).

48. These are the versions known as Venice 4, Paris, Cambridge, Lyon, Châteauroux, and Venice 7. See *La Chanson de Roland/The Song of Roland: The French Corpus*.

49. See Palumbo's review of the literature in "Le 'Roman de la Belle Aude,'" 340.

50. Duggan, "L'épisode d'Aude," 276–77.

51. Palumbo, "Le 'Roman de la Belle Aude,'" 349.

52. Edited by H. M. Smyser under the title *The Pseudo-Turpin*.

53. See "De tradicione Guenonis," 210.

54. Ibid., 220.

55. Translated under the title *Priest Konrad's "Song of Roland"* by J. W. Thomas.

56. In *Le Roland Occitan*. For a review of the Roland tradition in Occitan, see *The "Canso d'Antioca*," 165–74. On the putative Occitan roots of the Roland tradition, see Lafont, *La Geste de Roland*.

57. By Niccolò da Verona; under the title *Continuazione all' "Entrée d'Espagne"* in Niccolò, *Opere*.

58. By Raffaele da Verona.

59. See, in this volume, 141–42.

60. On the pan-European reception of the Roland material, see Suard, *Roland ou Les avatars d'une folie héroïque*.

61. On the reception of Roland during this period, see Redman, *The Roland Legend in Nineteenth-Century French Literature*.

62. Vigny, *Œuvres complètes*, 1: 135–37.

63. See Taylor, "Was There a Song of Roland?," 35.

64. Suard, *Roland ou Les avatars d'une folie héroïque*, 355–84.

65. Castellani, "Le félon, l'empereur et le paladin."

66. *Roland: Days of Wrath*, afterword.

67. For an overview of the Guillaume d'Orange cycle, see, in this volume, 32–35.

68. See Bennett, *Carnaval héroïque*, 12–13, for a summary of recent research on the formation of the Guillaume cycle.

69. Frappier, *Cycle de Guillaume d'Orange*, 2: 193; my translation.

70. A *charroi* is a convoy of carts used to transport merchandise. All quotations from the *Charroi de Nîmes* are from the edition by Duncan McMillan. English translations are my own.

71. The manuscripts, which do present a number of variants, have generally been divided into four "families." See the introductions to the *Charroi*, ed. McMillan, 14–26, and the *Prise d'Orange*, ed. Régnier, 7–13.

72. Among Heinemann's numerous studies of the *Charroi*'s formal features, see "L'art de la laisse" and "Existe-t-il une chanson de geste aussi brillante?" The *Charroi* also features prominently in *L'art métrique*.

73. On the historical foundations of the Guillaume cycle, see, in this volume, 32.

74. Frappier, *Cycle de Guillaume d'Orange*, 2: 189–91; Brault, "The Road Not Taken," 15; Payen, "Le *Charroi de Nîmes*: Comédie épique?" 899.

75. Bédier, *Les légendes épiques*, 1: 364–94. On Bédier's "individualist" theory, see, in this volume, 4–5.

76. Though Payen characterizes the text as "realistic," it is more useful to think in terms of Barthes's "reality effect." See Payen, "Le *Charroi de Nîmes*: Comédie épique?," 897–900; Barthes, "L'effet de réel."

77. See Frappier, *Cycle de Guillaume d'Orange*, 2: 191–92.

78. In v. 190 I adopt the variant from ms. B2; see *Charroi*, ed. McMillan, Notes, 136.

79. See Heinemann, "Le jeu d'échos," esp. 9. The hemistich appears seven times: vv. 60, 311, 322, 396, 467, 531, 543.

80. See Brault, "The Road Not Taken."

81. See Duby, "Dans la France du nord-ouest au XIIe siècle."

82. See Payen, "Le *Charroi de Nîmes*: Comédie épique?," 900; "Verelst, "Le *locus horribilis*."

83. See Brault, "The Road Not Taken."

84. See Payen, "Le *Charroi de Nîmes*: Comédie épique?"

85. Bennett, *Carnaval héroïque*, 7.

86. Corbellari, *Guillaume d'Orange*, 125.

87. Bennett, *Carnaval héroïque*, 75.

88. See note 16 to chapter 2.

89. The sequence begins in the final lines of the lengthy laisse 26. Only laisses 27 and 28 are strictly parallel.

90. See Corbellari, *Guillaume d'Orange*, 147–48.

91. Suard, "Le motif du déguisement," 343, 346.

92. Bennett, *Carnaval héroïque*, 20–27. Bennett explains (22–26) that he does not apply a strict Bakhtinian approach, which would preclude consideration of the chansons de geste.

93. All quotations from the *Prise d'Orange* are from Lachet's bilingual Old French/modern French edition. English translations are my own.

94. For an account of these critical views, see Lachet, *Parodie courtoise*, 7–8.

95. See Jauss, *Toward an Aesthetic of Reception*, esp. 93–96.

96. See, for example, Lachet, *Parodie courtoise*; Bennett, *"La Chanson de Guillaume" and "La Prise d'Orange"*; Kinoshita, *Medieval Boundaries*, chap. 2, "The Politics of Courtly Love: *La Prise d'Orange* and the Conversion of the Saracen Queen."

97. See Lachet's introduction to his edition/translation, 47–53; Colby-Hall, "Lost Epics."

98. For a perceptive discussion of onomastics in the *Prise*, see Kinoshita, *Medieval Boundaries*, 52–53, 61–62.

99. See Alain Labbé's monumental study, *L'architecture des palais et des jardins dans les chansons de geste*, 235–329.

100. Lachet, *Parodie courtoise*, 31.

101. "Aufrique" refers to the Africa of the Romans, a region encompassing areas of modern Tunisia and Libya.

102. Labbé, *L'architecture des palais et des jardins*, 55–57, 321–25.

103. The portrait of Blanchefleur in Chrétien de Troyes's *Conte du graal* is

the most dramatic depiction of the red/white complexion motif, which reappears in the form of blood on snow and the bleeding lance in the Grail scene. See Bennett, *"La Chanson de Guillaume" and "La Prise d'Orange*, 81–82.

104. See Kinoshita, *Medieval Boundaries*, 54.

105. In the *Chanson de Guillaume*, the hero is said to speak "salmoneis" (Hebrew?), "tieis" (German), "barbarin" (Berber), "grezeis" (Greek), "aleis" (Welsh?), and "hermin" (Armenian), as well as other languages not named (vv. 2170–72). In the *Aliscans* version of the same episode, the languages are limited to Greek and "sarrazinois" (vv. 1748–51).

106. Some actualizations of the polyglot motif do involve facilitated communication between Christians and Saracens, notably between Saracen Princesses and their beloved Western knights. See Jones, "Polyglots in the *chansons de geste*," 301–5.

107. Among the numerous studies devoted to the Saracen Princess/Queen motif, see de Weever, *Sheba's Daughters*; Bancourt, *Les Musulmans*, 571–826; Daniel, *Heroes and Saracens*, 69–93; Kay, *Chansons de Geste in the Age of Romance*, 25–48; Combarieu, "Un personnage épique: La jeune Musulmane;" Ramey, *Christian, Saracen and Genre*, 39–49.

108. Lachet, *Parodie courtoise*, 91–93. See *Chanson de Guillaume*, vv. 2591–94; *Enfances Guillaume*, vv. 1979–82.

109. Lachet, *Parodie courtoise*, 35–36.

110. Lachet compares the three works to panels in a triptych. See his introduction to the *Prise d'Orange*, 55.

111. Love from afar, or *amor de lonh*, is a stock feature of courtly lyric and is particularly associated with the troubadour Jaufré Rudel.

112. Variations on the expression "La seue amor me destreint et justise" may be found in numerous lyric and romance works. See *Prise d'Orange*, ed. Lachet, 109n289.

113. Ibid., 69–70.

114. Lachet, *Parodie courtoise*, 201–4. Lachet points out that although the Christian knights are threatened with violence and terrifying creatures, they never experience these hardships in the AB version. Later reworkings do reintroduce the *locus horribilis*: Guillaume and his companions are thrown into a dark cell full of reptiles and vermin (203).

115. Corbellari, *Guillaume d'Orange*, 142.

116. For an overview of the Guillaume legend's posterity, see the epilogue.

117. Wolfram's adaptation also includes material from a version of *Aliscans*.

118. For a detailed study of the *Roman de Guillaume d'Orange*, see Suard, *Guillaume d'Orange: Étude du roman en prose*.

119. Corbellari, *Guillaume d'Orange*, 203–24.

120. Ibid., 224–34.

121. All quotations from *Raoul de Cambrai* are based on Sarah Kay's edition (text and facing English translation) with only very minor changes. In particular, I have simplified the punctuation, eliminating the brackets around text supplied by the editor and material in parentheses that, in Kay's judgment, should be suppressed. Another excellent resource is the 1996 version that reproduces Kay's edition with a facing modern French translation by William W. Kibler.

122. See Calin, "*Raoul de Cambrai*: Un univers en décomposition."

123. François Suard in "Le romanesque dans *Raoul de Cambrai*" and Jean Subrenat in "*Raoul de Cambrai* et son public," among others, have sought to demonstrate the underlying cohesiveness of *Raoul*'s disjointed composition, as we shall see below.

124. For the sake of efficiency, I adopt the labels used by Kibler in his edition of *Raoul*.

125. Kay's title for this section is "Raoul II."

126. There is some confusion about Aalais's genealogy in the text. See Kay's edition of *Raoul*, 13n6.

127. The size of Raoul's heart signifies great valor and vitality. See Kay's edition, 199n87.

128. This recalls the conflicting interpretations of Ganelon's role in Roland's death. See above, 68–69, 73–74.

129. BnF fr. 2493 dates from the thirteenth century. It contains lacunae, particularly near the beginning of the poem. Some lost passages have been reconstituted with the help of the other two manuscripts: a sixteenth-century copy of the first 250 lines by the antiquarian Claude Fauchet (BnF fr. 24726) and two fragments found in the Bibliothèque Royale de Bruxelles, fr. IV 621. For complete descriptions of the manuscripts, see Kay's and Kibler's introductions.

130. For a detailed explanation of the arguments underlying this account, see Michel Rouche's historical introduction to *Histoire de Raoul*, the Berger-Suard translation, as well as the introductions to Kay's and Kibler's editions of *Raoul*.

131. William W. Kibler includes in the final reworking the opening section of the poem devoted to Louis's injustice. See his "Les fins de *Raoul de Cambrai*," 21.

132. See Rouche's introduction to *Histoire de Raoul*, 16–19.

133. For a more detailed discussion of origins, see Kay's and Kibler's introductions to *Raoul*.

134. See the introduction to Kibler's edition, 20, and Subrenat, *"Raoul de Cambrai* et son public."

135. See, for example, vv. 131–32, 322–23, 360–62, 419–24, 603–5, 958–59.

136. See Bezzola, "De Roland à Raoul de Cambrai."

137. vv. 1093, 1098.

138. vv. 1381–1404.

139. See esp. Bezzola, "De Roland à Raoul de Cambrai."

140. Boutet, *Raoul de Cambrai entre l'épique et le romanesque*, 6–7. On the emerging notion of the self, see Spence, *Texts and the Self*.

141. I acknowledge here my debt to François Suard's essay *"Raoul de Cambrai* et l'exaltation du tragique." Suard examines the poem's network of characters in terms of "couples" whose interactions are doomed to failure.

142. See Calin, *"Raoul de Cambrai:* Un univers en décomposition," 20.

143. Micheline de Combarieu du Grès argues that Raoul's later misdeeds reveal a latent evil, an innate desire for domination. See her "Raoul, 'li desreez,'" 47.

144. See also vv. 176.v–.vii: "Notre empereres esploita mallement, / de Cambrésis saisi le tenement / et au Mansel en fi saisissement" [Our emperor acted wrongly, he seized the fief of Cambrésis and invested Giboin with it].

145. See also vv. 648–50.

146. Combarieu demonstrates the complexity of Guerri's character, attributing to him a "lyric existence" that softens his warrior nature. See her "Guerri *li Sors:* Les enjeux du personnage."

147. Labbé, "Raoul et la voix des mères."

148. In his tirade, Raoul haughtily orders his mother to retire to her chambers and indulge in food and drink, the only activity befitting a woman (vv. 925–31).

149. On Raoul's vitriolic responses to Aalais and Marsent, see Calin, *In Defense of French Poetry*, 59–61.

150. See esp. Matarasso, *Recherches historiques et littéraires*.

151. This form of public reparation dates from Carolingian times and was known as *harmiscara*. See *Raoul*, ed. Kay, 111n45.

152. My translation, which is more literal than Kay's: "Raoul, dear lord, you can be praiseworthy, and then in other ways you lay yourself open to censure."

153. On the obsession with land, see Calin, *"Raoul de Cambrai:* Un univers en décomposition," 22–23.

154. Kelly, *The Hero's Place*, esp. 9–13.

155. Origny as a *locus amoenus* savagely destroyed is discussed in Baumgartner, "Quelques remarques sur l'espace et le temps," 15–16, and Calin, "*Raoul de Cambrai*: Un univers en décomposition," 23–24.

156. Cf. vv. 1347, 1678–79, 1708–9, and passim. Baumgartner, "Quelques remarques sur l'espace et le temps," 15, affirms that this formulation serves as a veritable motif specific to this song, or what Heinemann would call an "internal echo."

157. On the death of Bernier, see Kay, "Life of the Dead Body," esp. 106–8.

158. See esp. Subrenat, "*Raoul de Cambrai* et son public"; Suard, "Le romanesque dans *Raoul de Cambrai*."

159. Subrenat, "*Raoul de Cambrai* et son public," 19.

160. Suard, "Le romanesque dans *Raoul de Cambrai*," 45–46.

161. Kibler, "Les fins de *Raoul de Cambrai*," 15, 22.

162. Baumgartner, "Quelques remarques sur l'espace et le temps," 14.

163. See, in this volume, 44.

164. See Jones, "Recasting *Raoul de Cambrai*."

165. Hugo, *La Légende des Siècles*, 327.

166. All quotations from *Ami et Amile* are from Dembowski's edition. English translations are my own.

167. Calin, *The Epic Quest*, 116.

168. For a discussion of the various versions of *Ami et Amile*, see Leach's edition of the Middle English romance *Amis and Amiloun*, ix–xxxii.

169. *Rodulfi Tortarii Carmina*, Epistula II, vv. 29–30, 117–18. Leach includes an English translation as an appendix to *Amis and Amiloun*, 101–5.

170. Leach uses the term "romantic" in the introduction to *Amis and Amiloun*, ix. Rosenberg renamed the category "secular" in his introduction to *Ami and Amile*, 3.

171. The earliest manuscript dates from 1330, but Leach believes that it "represents a form of the story" dating back to the twelfth century (*Amis and Amiloun*, xx).

172. For the Anglo-Norman poem, see *Amys e Amillyoun*, ed. Fukui; the miracle play *Miracle de Nostre Dame d'Amis et d'Amille* appears in the *Miracles de Nostre Dame par personnages*, 1–67.

173. *Amis and Amiloun*, ed. Leach, xvi. A version of the *Vita* is included in Kölbing's edition of *Amis and Amiloun*, xcvii–cx.

174. For a summary of the debate, see Asher, "*Amis et Amiles*": An Exploratory Survey; *Ami et Amile*, ed. Dembowski, xi, note 2; Calin, *The Epic Quest*, 58–66; Rosenberg introduction to *Ami and Amile*, 1–2.

175. *Amis and Amiloun*, ed. Leach, xxxii–xxxvi.

176. Bédier, *Les légendes épiques*, 2: 170–96.

177. A major proponent of this theory is Francis Bar: see his source study in *Les épîtres latines de Raoul le Tourtier*, 27–108.

178. Gaunt, *Gender and Genre*, 47. He cites vv. 3068–79. The *s* at the end of Old French *amis* marks the nominative singular.

179. See Legros, *L'amitié dans les chansons de geste*, 19–59.

180. Ibid., 20–27, 48–49.

181. Ibid., 403.

182. Krappe, "The Legend of Amicus and Amelius," 153–54.

183. Sinclair, "The Imaginary Body," quotation 194.

184. *Ami and Amile*, 18–19.

185. The presence of parallel and inverted episodes has been widely noted; see, for example, Calin, *The Epic Quest*, 75; Kay, "Seduction and Suppression," 137.

186. See Hyatte, *The Arts of Friendship*, 124; Legros, *L'amitié dans les chansons de geste*, 288–94.

187. Gaunt, *Gender and Genre*, 48.

188. See Calin, *The Epic Quest*, 85–87.

189. Ibid., 84–85; Ribémont, "Épopée médiévale et questions de droit," 257.

190. In Béroul's romance, Iseut mounts on the back of Tristan, who is disguised as a leper, to cross the muddy Mal Pas. Thus she is able to swear truthfully that she has had no men between her legs other than King Mark and the "leper" who transported her. See *Tristan et Iseut*, vv. 3882–3940, 4197–4216.

191. Mickel, "The Question of Guilt," 33.

192. Ibid., 35.

193. See Calin, *The Epic Quest*, 87–90.

194. Gaunt, *Gender and Genre*, 46.

195. The only hint of discord occurs when Amile informs Ami of his predicament at Charlemagne's court. Ami cannot resist reminding his companion that he, Ami, had warned of Hardré's treacherous nature (vv. 994–1003).

196. Kay, "Seduction and Suppression," 137; Kay, *Chansons de Geste in the Age of Romance*, 153, 238; Johnson, *Once There Were Two True Friends*, 29–30.

197. Legros, *L'amitié dans les chansons de geste*, 292.

198. See in particular Kay, "Seduction and Suppression"; Zink, "Lubias et Belissant"; Calin, "Women and Their Sexuality."

199. Kay, "Seduction and Suppression," 131. Kay argues that the feudal model leads to the suppression of women while the clerical model informs

the women characters' access to sexual agency. In the case of both Lubias and Belissant, suppression wins out by the end of the narrative.

200. In this case Hardré, who denounces the lovers. Kay broadens the scope of Belissant's rebellion, referring to the "Father's law" undermined by Belissant's seduction. See "Seduction and Suppression," 140.

201. Zink, "Lubias et Belissant," 15–17. Zink finds that the *chansons de toile* are like fragments of chansons de geste that isolate and give lyric expression to the sentimental encounters of epic. Another example of the epic-lyric juncture is the character Beatrice, daughter of the king of Cologne, who pursues the eponymous hero of *Gerbert de Metz*, a mercenary in her father's army, in a passage that echoes lyric motifs of woman's song (vv. 3748–57).

202. Calin, "Women and Their Sexuality," 81. See also Duby, "Dans la France du nord-ouest au XIIe siècle."

203. See, for example, Calin, *The Epic Quest*, 110; Kay, *Chansons de Geste in the Age of Romance*, 236–38.

204. *Tristan et Iseut*, vv. 1981–2100.

205. "With us" is ambiguous, but the following laisse confirms the meaning "in our house"; see vv. 2768–69.

206. Le Saux, "Quand le héros devient malade," 12; *Ami and Amile*, 21–22; Calin, *The Epic Quest*, 72.

207. Pichon, "La lèpre dans *Ami et Amile*," 53–54. A contemporary Occitan romance, *Jaufré*, gives a much more vivid portrait of the disease. See Le Saux, "Quand le héros devient malade," 3–4.

208. Le Saux points out, however, that at the time *Ami et Amile* was composed, leper colonies afforded a more secure environment than that depicted in the story ("Quand le héros devient malade," 6).

209. Pichon, "La lèpre dans *Ami et Amile*," 54.

210. Le Saux, "Quand le héros devient malade," 5.

211. Calin, "Women and Their Sexuality," 87.

212. Pichon, "La lèpre dans *Ami et Amile*," 63–65.

213. Sinclair, "The Imaginary Body," 203.

214. The joint death and burial are, of course, reminiscent of legends surrounding famous lovers such as Tristan and Iseut and the unnamed lovers in Marie de France's "Les deux amants."

215. The antecedent of "Que" in v. 3503 is somewhat ambiguous; it may refer to Ami's fame or to the song of Ami and Amile.

216. See Dembowski's introduction to the edition of *Jourdain de Blaye*, xi.

217. On Delvau's adaptation, see Guidot, "De la chanson de geste au roman

populaire." The text of *Milles et Amys* is in Delvau, *Collection des romans*, 1: 193–240.

218. All quotations from *Huon de Bordeaux* are from Kibler and Suard's bilingual Old French/modern French edition. English translations are my own.

219. See, in this volume, 23–24.

220. For a detailed summary of research on source material, see *Huon de Bordeaux*, ed. Ruelle, 68–82; Rossi, "*Huon de Bordeaux*," 33–90.

221. *Huon de Bordeaux*, ed. Ruelle, 74. Another obvious source is the *Lai du Cor*, in which the magic horn doubles as a test of virtue and fidelity; *Huon de Bordeaux* splits this talisman's function into two objects, the horn and the cup.

222. Rossi, "*Huon de Bordeaux*," 35–36, 88–90.

223. *Huon de Bordeaux*, ed. Ruelle, 75–76.

224. Rossi, "*Huon de Bordeaux*," 90.

225. See Calin, *The Epic Quest*, 177–79; Rossi, "*Huon de Bordeaux*," 213–89.

226. On ignorance as an extenuating circumstance, see Jones, "Je ne soz queil homme j'oz ocis."

227. See Carbasse, *Introduction historique au droit pénal*, 186. With respect to intentionality, Huon's case may be compared to Guinevere's inadvertent poisoning of Gaheris in the *Mort Artu*. See Bloch, *Medieval French Literature and Law*, 28–32.

228. See Rossi, "*Huon de Bordeaux*," 296–315.

229. Ibid., 303–6.

230. See Jones, "Les chansons de geste et l'Orient," 634–38.

231. See Calin, *The Epic Quest*, 208–9.

232. See Berthelot, "*Huon de Bordeaux* ou l'irruption de la féerie," 841. Berthelot argues that otherworldly intervention is not an "invasive" technique: Huon often acts independently of Auberon, even disobeying him at times during the quest.

233. See Rossi, "*Huon de Bordeaux*," 370.

234. Sebille has been the giant's captive for seven years. Kibler and Suard note that nothing in the text would indicate that Sebille was sexually assaulted (*Huon de Bordeaux*, 271n1), but it is surely no accident that she chooses to aim her weapon between the giant's legs.

235. The word *estrument* means "instrument" in Old French.

236. See Suard, "Le motif du déguisement."

237. On humor in *Huon de Bordeaux*, see Calin, *The Epic Quest*, 215–32, and Rossi's response in "*Huon de Bordeaux*," 423–59.

238. Calin, *The Epic Quest*, 215–28.

239. Ibid., 228.

240. The first 79 lines of manuscript P are in alexandrine verse. See the Kibler-Suard edition of *Huon*.

241. On epic technique in *Huon*, see Rossi, "*Huon de Bordeaux*," 121–204.

242. See *Huon de Bordeaux*, ed. Kibler and Suard, xxxv. No manuscript of the prose version has survived; Michel Raby based his critical edition on the print version.

243. Tressan's version may be found in the *Œuvres choisies*, 8: 138–268; Delvau's version may be found in the *Collection des romans*, 1: 145–91. For a comparison of the Tressan and Delvau versions, see Guidot, "*Huon de Bordeaux: l'épisode de l'embuscade liminaire.*"

244. On the reworkings of *Huon de Bordeaux*, see Caroline Cazanave's thorough study, *D'Esclarmonde à Croissant*; on theater in particular, see her "Huon de Bordeaux au théâtre."

245. Cazanave, "Huon de Bordeaux à la sauce enfantine."

Epilogue

Translation of the epigraph from Philippe de Vigneulles's *Chronique*, 1: 177, is my own.

1. Several recent volumes in the Klincksieck series Les Grandes Figures du Moyen Âge trace the reception of popular epic heroes from the Middle Ages to the present. See Durand-Le Guern and Ribémont, *Charlemagne, empereur et mythe d'Occident*; Corbellari, *Guillaume d'Orange*; Suard, *Roland ou Les avatars d'une folie héroïque*. On *Renaut de Montauban/Les Quatre Fils Aymon*, see Baudelle-Michels, *Les avatars d'une chanson de geste*.

2. Bibliographical entries for this epilogue are limited to works quoted; reference sources are provided for each language tradition.

3. See Godzich and Kittay, *The Emergence of Prose*; Spiegel, *Romancing the Past: The Rise of Vernacular Prose Historiography in Thirteenth-Century France*.

4. See Spiegel, *Romancing the Past*, 55–61.

5. One exception is the late thirteenth-century reworking of the first part of the Crusade cycle, published under the title *Godefroi de Buillon*.

6. Wauquelin, *La Belle Hélène de Constantinople*, 14, my translation.

7. See Jones, *Philippe de Vigneulles and the Art of Prose Translation*, 11, 25–35.

8. *Le Roman de Guillaume d'Orange*, 1: 1; my translation.

9. Suard, "Le passage à la prose."

10. Léon Gautier famously referred to the works as "cette méchante prose qui est parfois si instructive" [this awful prose that is occasionally so instructive] (*Les épopées françaises*, 2: 600); my translation.

11. In 1939 Georges Doutrepont published a major inventory, *Les mises en prose des épopées et des romans chevaleresques*. Currently an international research team is undertaking a revision and updating of Doutrepont's work: see the journal *Moyen Français* 63 (2008) and 64 (2009). See also François Suard's seminal study *Guillaume d'Orange: Étude du roman en prose*.

12. Rasmussen, *La prose narrative française du XVe siècle*, 26–54.

13. The verse model used by the Burgundian translator has not survived, but extant verse versions serve as a useful reference point for comparative study.

14. *Garin le Loherenc*, my translation.

15. *Guerin le Loherain*, 104, my translation.

16. On the literature of the Burgundian court, see Quéruel, "Des mises en prose aux romans de chevalerie dans les collections bourguignonnes."

17. Wauquelin, *La Belle Hélène de Constantinople*, xxix–xxxii.

18. Jones, *Philippe de Vigneulles and the Art of Prose Translation*, 11.

19. Suard, *Le passage à la prose*, 2.

20. Wauquelin, *La Belle Hélène de Constantinople*, 14.

21. Suard, *Guide de la chanson de geste*, 323–32.

22. Ibid., 329. The Roland material survived in reworkings, notably the *Galien* versions. On the prose version of Aude's death, see Palumbo, "Une mise en prose de la belle Aude au XIIIe siècle."

23. Suard, *Guide de la chanson de geste*, 315. For a thorough inventory of the prose works, see pages 313–59.

24. Schwam-Baird, "Terror and Laughter in the Images of the Wild Man" and "The Romance Epic Hero, the Mercenary, and the Ottoman Turk."

25. Guidot, "Formes tardives de l'épopée médiévale," 589.

26. Everson, "Charlemagne in Italy," ¶6; *La Geste Francor*, 18.

27. *La Geste Francor*, 18.

28. *La Geste Francor*, 21.

29. For a rigorous typology of Franco-Italian material, see Holtus, "L'état actuel des recherches," 147–49. A complete catalogue of Franco-Italian works may be found in Holtus and Wunderli, *Franco-italien et épopée franco-italienne*.

30. See the magisterial two-volume edition of *La Geste Francor* by Leslie Zarker Morgan.

31. Everson, "Charlemagne in Italy," ¶14.

32. *L'Entrée d'Espagne*, v. 1046. On Roland as "baron révolté" in the *Entrée*, see Bradley-Cromey, *Authority and Autonomy*, 27–56.

33. See Holtus and Wunderli, *Franco-italien et épopée franco-italienne*, 189–90. The authors claim that part of the work may be a reworking of *Huon de Bordeaux*, a possibility echoed by Suard in *Guide de la chanson de geste*, 379. However, Leslie Zarker Morgan sees little connection between *Ugo* and *Huon* other than the "impossible mission" motif. I am grateful to Professor Morgan for her thorough summary of the unedited text of the Berlin ms. of *Ugo*.

34. See Everson, "Charlemagne in Italy," ¶10–24. Everson divides the content of Italian epic production into "narrative strands" that are developed by different formal modes: epic laisses, ottava rima, prose.

35. Everson, "Charlemagne in Italy," ¶19–20. On Andrea's style, see Allaire, *Andrea da Barberino and the Language of Chivalry*.

36. Everson, "Charlemagne in Italy," ¶26–63. See also Everson, *The Italian Romance Epic*, and, in this volume, 78. The tradition extended well into the seventeenth century. On later print editions and reworkings of French epic material in Italy, see Beer, *Romanzi di cavalleria*.

37. On the epic tradition in the Iberian Peninsula, see Horrent, *L'épopée dans la péninsule ibérique*.

38. Ibid., 45.

39. See Deyermond, "The Problem of Lost Epics."

40. For the Latin text and French translation, see the *Chanson de Roland*, ed. Moignet, 293–94.

41. For a summary of the chronicle accounts of Bernardo del Carpio, see Tolan, "The Battle of Roncesvalles as National Polemic."

42. Suard, *Guide de la chanson de geste*, 365.

43. Skårup, "La matière de France dans les pays du Nord," 10–11. Skårup hesitatingly includes the *Moniage Guillaume* in the list, noting, however, that it is likely not a direct translation of the French poem. For a cross-cultural reading of the Old Norse *Roland*, see Rikhardsdottir, *Medieval Translations and Cultural Discourse*, 53–75.

44. On the reception of French epics in German-speaking areas, see Hennings, *Französische Heldenepik im deutschen Sprachraum*.

45. Spiewok, "Le *Rolandslied* et le *Karl* du Stricker," 91.

46. Ibid., 92.

47. Jean-Charles Herbin has recently unearthed and edited, along with Thomas Falmagne, a 40-line decasyllabic fragment of a lost chanson de geste

devoted to Charlemagne's *enfances*, a version of the model used by the *Karl-meinet* poet. See Herbin and Falmagne, "Fragments."

48. Suard, *Guide de la chanson de geste*, 373–74.

49. Morrison, "Women Writers and Women Rulers," 27–35.

50. On the Middle Dutch reception of chansons de geste, see the series of articles in *Olifant* 23.1, 24.1, 26.1, 26.2. Bart Besamusca provides a helpful overview in "Medieval Dutch Charlemagne Romances."

51. Besamusca, "Medieval Dutch Charlemagne Romances," 168–69.

52. For a complete list and description of these texts, see Besamusca, "Medieval Dutch Charlemagne Romances," 171–82.

53. Ibid., 172.

54. Ibid., 173.

55. Ibid., 178; see Spijker, "*Renout van Montalbaen.*"

56. Besamusca, "Medieval Dutch Charlemagne Romances," 182–83.

57. See Suard, *Guide de la chanson de geste*, 369.

58. See, in this volume, 114.

59. Suard, *Guide de la chanson de geste*, 369.

60. See, in this volume, 135; *Huon de Bordeaux*, ed. Kibler and Suard, xxxv–xxxvi. On the rich and enduring tradition of *Huon de Bordeaux*, see Cazanave, *D'Esclarmonde à Croissant*.

61. For example, Rikhardsdottir, *Medieval Translations and Cultural Discourse*; Everson, *The Italian Romance Epic*.

62. Rikhardsdottir, *Medieval Translations and Cultural Discourse*, 2.

63. Striking examples are *Huon de Bordeaux* (see, in this volume, 135) and the *Quatre Fils Aymon* (see Baudelle-Michels, *Les avatars d'une chanson de geste*).

64. *Li romans de Garin le Loherain*, 2: 239n3; Gautier, *Les épopées françaises*, 1: 534–42. In the first edition, Gautier's pronouncement was more forceful: "Et la *Chanson de Roland* vaut l'*Iliade!*"

65. *Garin le Loherain . . . en nouveau langage*, 368–69.

66. Redman, *The Roland Legend in Nineteenth-Century French Literature*.

67. Ibid., 206–7.

68. See, in this volume, 4–5.

69. Warren, *Creole Medievalism*. The arguments advanced in this important study are highly nuanced, demonstrating the complex "dislocations between Réunion and France, and between past and present" (xii).

70. Ibid., chap. 5.

71. Corbellari, *Guillaume d'Orange*, 212. See also his *Joseph Bédier*, 573–616, for an edition of the longer version.

72. Corbellari, *Guillaume d'Orange*, 212–13.

73. Cazanave, *D'Esclarmonde à Croissant*, 253, and "Huon de Bordeaux au théâtre."

74. I summarize here Suard's account in *Roland ou Les avatars d'une folie héroïque*, 358–61. He reproduces portions of Gentet-Ravasco's "texte de présentation." The performance was directed by Pierre Sarzacq.

75. On the Cassenti film, see, in this volume, 79. An earlier and even more obscure film version is the 1913 Gaumont production *Roland à Roncevaux*, attributed to Louis Feuillade. See Amy de La Bretèque, *L'imaginaire médiéval dans le cinéma occidental*, 227–43, on the French epic tradition in cinema. On structural and aesthetic links between epic and cinema, see Lacy, "Épopée et cinéma."

76. See Cazanave and Houssais, *Grands textes du moyen âge à l'usage des petits*, especially the articles by Castellani, Henrard, Baudelle-Michels, and Cazanave.

Chansons de Geste—Dates and Versification

1. According to Suard, *Guide de la chanson de geste*, 255. No complete critical edition exists.

GLOSSARY

This list identifies fictional characters from the chansons de geste studied in chapter 3, "Selected Works," pertinent historical figures and entities, and literary terms.

Adenet le Roi. Thirteenth-century poet, author of the chansons de geste *Beuvon de Conmarchis*, the *Enfances Ogier*, and *Berte as grans piés*.

Albigensian Crusade. Series of military expeditions initiated by the papacy and undertaken between 1209 and 1229 to extirpate the Cathar heresy in what is now southern France; subject of the *Canso de la Crozada* (*Chanson de la Croisade Albigeoise*).

Alice. Name of several epic heroines, including the mother of Raoul de Cambrai, the mother of Hervis de Metz, and the wife of Garin le Lorrain.

Ami. Name meaning "friend"; in *Ami et Amile*, faithful companion of Amile and husband of the treacherous Lubias.

Amile. In *Ami et Amile*, faithful friend of Ami and husband of Belissant, Charlemagne's daughter.

amistiet. In the chansons de geste, most often a military, diplomatic, or judicial alliance. The Old French word was seldom used in the sense of the modern French *amitié*.

assonance. In the context of the chansons de geste, repetition of the same stressed (tonic) vowel at the end of each line of a given stanza.

Auberon. Fairy king in *Huon de Bordeaux*; likely prototype of Shakespeare's Oberon in *A Midsummer Night's Dream*.

Aude. Oliver's sister and Roland's fiancée, who dies upon learning of Roland's death.

Beatrice. Name of several epic heroines including the wife of Hervis in *Hervis de Metz*, the wife of Begon in *Garin le Lorrain*, and the wife of Bernier in *Raoul de Cambrai*.

Bédier, Joseph (1864–1938). Renowned French philologist and academician, author of the four-volume *Légendes épiques*, representative of the "individualist" position in the controversy over the origins of the chansons de geste.

Belissant. Daughter of Charlemagne who seduces and marries Amile in *Ami et Amile*.

Bernier. Companion and vassal of Raoul de Cambrai. He kills Raoul in single combat.

Berte as grans piés (Big-Footed Bertha, 720–783). Bertrada of Laon, wife of Pepin the Short and mother of Charlemagne; eponymous heroine of a chanson de geste by Adenet le Roi.

Bertrand de Bar-sur-Aube. Author of a version of *Girart de Vienne* and perhaps *Aymeri de Narbonne*. One of the few named authors of chansons de geste, Bertrand is known for his division of epic material into three *gestes* or cycles.

Bibliothèque Bleue. Series of mass-produced, inexpensive volumes sold by itinerant peddlers from the seventeenth to the nineteenth century. So named for their blue covers, they were an important vehicle for the continued transmission of epic narratives.

Bibliothèque Universelle des Romans. Series of 112 volumes created by the Marquis de Paulmy, appearing in 1774–89 and including versions of chansons de geste by the Count of Tressan.

Bramimonde. In the *Chanson de Roland*, the Saracen queen of Saragossa, wife of Marsile. Converting to Christianity, she takes the name Julianne.

caesura. Pause in a poetic line. In epic caesura, decasyllabic lines are typically divided after the fourth syllable and alexandrine (12-syllable) lines after the sixth syllable.

chanson d'aventures. Subgenre of the chanson de geste, arising in the thirteenth century, that combines conventional epic conflict with narrative devices associated with adventure romance. The term was coined by William W. Kibler.

Charlemagne (742–814). Son of Pepin the Short and Bertrada; from 771, sole king of the Franks; crowned emperor of the Romans in 800.

Associated with a substantial cycle of chansons de geste, the epic
figure Charlemagne is idealized in some songs and disparaged in
others. Primarily known as the aged and benign uncle of Roland in
the *Chanson de Roland*, he is a weak and unjust monarch in *Huon de
Bordeaux*.

Charles Martel (686–741). Frankish military chief and mayor of the
palace, father of Pepin the Short and grandfather of Charlemagne. He
appears in a number of chansons de geste, including *Garin le Lorrain*
and *Girart de Roussillon*.

Charlot. Conniving and treacherous son of Charlemagne, killed by
Huon in *Huon de Bordeaux*.

cycle. Group of chansons de geste related by the heroes' lineage or by
thematic considerations. Most prominent are the Charlemagne,
Guillaume d'Orange, Crusade, Lorraine, and "rebellious baron" cycles.

dérimage (derhyming). Prose rendering of an earlier verse narrative.
The term tends to designate an adaptation limited to derhyming and
linguistic updating, without substantial reworking of the narrative.
Also see *mise en prose*.

Elisabeth of Lorraine-Vaudémont, Countess of Nassau-Saarbrücken
(ca. 1395–1456). Early woman writer who adapted four chansons de
geste into German: *Herzog Herpin* (*Lion de Bourges*), *Huge Scheppel*
(*Hugues Capet*), *Die Könige Sebille* (*Reine Sebile*), and *Loher und
Maller* (*Lohier et Malart*).

enchaînement (linking). Narration of the same action at the end of one
laisse and the beginning of the following laisse, creating a lyric bridge
between the two laisses.

enfances. Prequel recounting the early exploits of an epic hero already
known through one or more chansons de geste.

epic of revolt. See "rebellious baron" cycle.

Esclarmonde. In *Huon de Bordeaux*, daughter of the Saracen Gaudisse
and bride of Huon. In the sequel titled *Esclarmonde*, she becomes a
fairy queen.

faide. Blood feud; private war of revenge.

fief. Land accorded by the lord to his vassal in exchange for service.

formula. Group of words, comprising a hemistich or a line, that is
regularly employed to express a given narrative detail.

formulaic style. Style of narrative poetry employing highly conventional, stereotyped language and narrative content.

Franco-Italian. Hybrid, artificial literary language used in the copying, adaptation, and composition of chansons de geste in northeastern Italy from the mid-thirteenth to the early fifteenth century. Texts fall across a wide spectrum, with varying degrees of Italianization.

Ganelon. Roland's stepfather, a member of the lineage of Doon de Mayence, a family of traitors. Found guilty of betraying Roland and Charlemagne, he is executed at the end of the *Chanson de Roland*.

geste (n.f.). Heroic deeds; a family or lineage; a chronicle or account; a group of epic songs about a particular lineage. This last meaning is roughly synonymous with "cycle."

Guerri the Red. Uncle of Raoul de Cambrai.

Guibourc. Originally named Orable, wife of the Saracen Thibaut. In the *Prise d'Orange* she falls in love with Guillaume d'Orange, converts to Christianity, taking the name Guibourc at baptism, and marries Guillaume.

Guillaume d'Orange. Old French epic hero, surnamed "Guillaume Fierebrace" (of the strong arms) and "Guillaume au cort nés" (of the short nose), at the center of a prominent cycle of chansons de geste. He is loosely based on the historical figure Guillaume of Toulouse (ca. 755–812).

Guilhem de Tudela. Poet from Navarre, working in Montauban in the early thirteenth century, who composed the first part of the Occitan *Canso de la Crozada* (*Chanson de la Croisade Albigeoise*).

Huon de Bordeaux. Eponymous hero of a chanson de geste. After slaying Charlemagne's son Charlot in self-defense, he undertakes a series of adventures, aided by the fairy king Auberon.

individualist. Proponent of the theory that the chansons de geste were composed by individual poets of genius, who drew their inspiration from local legends preserved along pilgrimage routes.

Jehan Bodel. Poet and dramatist from Arras working in the late twelfth century; author of lyric poetry, fabliaux, the *Jeu de Saint Nicolas*, and a chanson de geste of the Charlemagne cycle, the *Chanson des Saisnes*.

jongleur. Itinerant performer whose repertory included chansons de geste and saints' lives as well as acrobatics, juggling, and other forms of entertainment.

judicium Dei (judgment of God). Judicial combat: ordeal in the form of a duel, the outcome of which is determined by God, used to determine innocence or guilt, or to settle various types of disputes.

laisse. Standard strophic unit of the chansons de geste; stanza of varying length, the boundaries of which are determined by assonance (in the earlier texts) or rhyme (in later epics).

Louis. In the Guillaume cycle, Louis I the Pious (778–840), son of Charlemagne; in *Raoul de Cambrai*, a composite figure based on Louis the Pious, Louis II the Stammerer (846–879), and Louis IV d'Outremer (920–954).

Lubias. Niece of the traitor Hardré and treacherous wife of Ami in *Ami et Amile*.

Malabron. Shapeshifter in the service of Auberon who metamorphoses into a sea creature to carry Huon across the Red Sea and later to free him from the desert island.

Marsile. Saracen king of Saragossa, slain by Roland at the battle of Roncevaux.

matière de France. Narrative material of France, primary source material for the chanson de geste; distinguished from the matter of Britain (associated with the *lais* and Arthurian romance) and the matter of Rome (which furnished the romances of antiquity). See Jehan Bodel's prologue to the *Chanson des Saisnes*.

mise en prose. Prose rendering of an earlier verse narrative. Approximately half of the extant chansons de geste were adapted into prose from the fourteenth to the sixteenth century.

moniage. Episode or work relating an epic hero's retirement to a monastery.

motif. Conventional narrative unit expressing a given content in a standard configuration. Examples include single lance combat, epic prayers, and laments over a slain hero.

mouvance (textual mobility). As formulated by Paul Zumthor in *Essai de poétique médievale*, the inherent instability of the medieval work, which exists as a dynamic interplay of variants and reworkings.

Naimes. Sage counselor to Charlemagne in the *Chanson de Roland*, *Huon de Bordeaux*, and other works.

Oliver. Roland's companion and Aude's brother, who perishes at the Battle of Roncevaux.

ottava rima. Form of narrative poetry consisting of eight hendecasyllabic verses with an *abababcc* rhyme scheme. The most widespread nonlyric form used in medieval and Renaissance Italian literature, it was an important vehicle of vernacular epic material in Italy from the fourteenth century onward.

parallel laisses. Series of two or more laisses presenting an analogous action in a similar form.

Paris, Gaston (1839–1903). French philologist, professor at the Collège de France and member of the Académie Française; renowned scholar of medieval literature and proponent of the "traditionalist" theory on the origins of the chansons de geste.

Pepin the Short (d. 768). Son of Charles Martel and father of Charlemagne; mayor of the palace and subsequently king of the Franks. He appears in the chansons de geste of the Lorraine cycle as a weak and unjust monarch.

Philip the Good, Duke of Burgundy (1396–1467). Patron of artists and writers, admirer of chivalric literature, who commissioned prose translations of several chansons de geste, including *Girart de Roussillon* and *La Belle Hélène de Constantinople* by Jean Wauquelin, and the compilation *L'Histoire de Charles Martel* copied by David Aubert.

Philippe de Vigneulles (1471–ca. 1528). Cloth merchant of Metz who composed a *Chronicle* and a prose translation of the Lorraine cycle, as well as a journal and a version of the *Cent Nouvelles nouvelles*.

Rainouart. Guibourc's brother, a giant who appears in several chansons de geste of the Guillaume cycle and assists Guillaume in defeating the Saracens at l'Archamp.

Raoul de Cambrai. Eponymous hero of a chanson de geste of the "rebellious baron" cycle.

"rebellious baron" cycle, or **epic of revolt.** Group of poems depicting barons who rebel against royal authority. The cycle includes *Raoul de Cambrai, Girart de Roussillon, Renaut de Montauban,* and *Ogier le Danois.*

Roland. In the *Chanson de Roland,* nephew of Charlemagne who, betrayed by Ganelon, dies at the Battle of Roncevaux. Early exploits are recounted in other poems of the Charlemagne cycle, including *Aspremont.*

Saracen. All-purpose designation for the enemies of Christianity, but most often denoting a Muslim adversary; in many chansons de geste, interchangeable with "pagan" and "Turk."

similar laisses. Series of two or more laisses presenting the same action from a slightly different perspective, with little or no narrative progress.

traditionalist. Proponent of the theory that the chansons de geste were the products of a long oral tradition, a collaborative venture involving the reworking of individual songs by generations of itinerant poets.

Tressan, Louis-Élisabeth de la Vergne, Count of (1705–1783). Adapter and publisher of chansons de geste in the Bibliothèque Universelle des Romans series.

Turold. Name appearing at the end of the *Chanson de Roland* in an ambiguous passage that identifies "Turoldus" (a typical Anglo-Norman name) as the one who "declinet"—a polyvalent word that might signify "composes," "transcribes," "copies," "transmits," "recites," and so on.

Turpin. Archbishop of Reims, who combines priestly and warrior functions. In the *Chanson de Roland* he grants absolution to Charlemagne's knights and declares them holy martyrs. He perishes at the battle of Roncevaux.

Twelve Peers. Charlemagne's most distinguished barons, including Roland and Oliver. The number twelve has symbolic value (i.e., the twelve apostles) rather than historical accuracy.

Wauquelin, Jean. Translator (1440–52) at the court of Philip the Good of Burgundy, where he was also charged with the purchase, binding, and restoration of books. He translated into prose two chansons de geste, *Girart de Roussillon* and *La Belle Hélène de Constantinople*; other notable works are the *Chroniques de Hainaut* and a prosification of Philippe de Beaumanoir's *La Manekine*.

SELECT BIBLIOGRAPHY

Abbreviations

CUERMA   Centre Universitaire d'Études et de Recherches Médiévales
                   d'Aix-en-Provence
SATF   Société des Anciens Textes Français

Primary Sources

The reader is reminded that in medieval usage, surnames are subordinate to given names; thus, for instance, Jehan Bodel and Johannes de Grocheio are both listed under *J*.

Adenet le Roi. *Berte as grans piés*. Edited by Albert Henry. Geneva: Droz, 1982.

Aliscans. Edited by Claude Régnier. Translated by Jean Subrenat. Paris: Champion, 2007. [Bilingual Old French/modern French.]

Ami and Amile: A Medieval Tale of Friendship, Translated from the Old French. Translated by Samuel Danon and Samuel N. Rosenberg. York, S.C.: French Literature Publications, 1981.

Ami et Amile: Chanson de geste. Edited by Peter F. Dembowski. Paris: Champion, 1969.

Ami et Amile: Chanson de geste traduite en français moderne. Translated by Joël Blanchard and Michel Quereuil. Paris: Champion, 1985.

Amis and Amiloun. Edited by Eugen Kölbing. Heilbronn: Gebr. Henninger, 1884.

Amis and Amiloun. Edited by MacEdward Leach. London: Early English Text Society, Oxford University Press, 1937.

Amys e Amillyoun. Edited by Hideka Fukui. London: Anglo-Norman Text Society, 1990.

Anseïs von Karthago. Edited by Johannes Alton. Tübingen: Niemeyer, 1892.

Anseÿs de Mes, According to Ms. N. Edited by Herman J. Green. Paris: Presses Modernes, 1939.

Ariosto, Ludovico. *Orlando Furioso.* Translated by Guido Waldman. New York: Oxford University Press, 1974.

Aspremont: Chanson de geste du XIIe siècle. Edited and translated by François Suard. Paris: Champion, 2008. [Bilingual Old French/modern French.]

Aye d'Avignon: Chanson de geste anonyme. Edited by S. J. Borg. Geneva: Droz, 1967.

Aymeri de Narbonne. Edited by Hélène Gallé. Paris: Champion, 2007.

Aymeri of Narbonne: A French Epic Romance. Translated by Michael A. H. Newth. New York: Italica, 2005.

La Bataille Loquifer. Edited by Monica Barnett. Oxford: Blackwell, 1975.

Le Bâtard de Bouillon. Edited by Robert Francis Cook. Geneva: Droz, 1972.

Baudouin de Sebourc. Edited by Larry S. Crist and Robert Francis Cook. 2 vols. Paris: SATF, 2002.

La Belle Hélène de Constantinople: Chanson de geste du XIVe siècle. Edited by Claude Roussel. Geneva: Droz, 1995.

Bertrand de Bar-sur-Aube. *Girart de Vienne.* Edited by Wolfgang van Emden. Paris: Société des Anciens Textes Français, 1977.

Boiardo, Matteo Maria. *Orlando Innamorato (Orlando in Love).* Translated by Charles Stanley Ross. Berkeley: University of California Press, 1989.

The "Canso d'Antioca": An Occitan Epic Chronicle of the First Crusade. Edited by Carol Sweetenham and Linda M. Paterson. Burlington, Vt.: Ashgate, 2003.

Cassenti, Frank, dir. *La Chanson de Roland.* Gaumont, 1978.

La Chanson d'Antioche. Edited by Jan A. Nelson. Vol. 4 of Nelson and Mickel, *Old French Crusade Cycle.* 2003.

La Chanson d'Antioche: Chanson de geste du dernier quart du XIIe siècle. Edited and translated by Bernard Guidot. Paris: Champion, 2011. [Bilingual Old French/modern French.]

The "Chanson d'Antioche": An Old French Account of the First Crusade. Translated by Susan B. Edgington and Carol Sweetenham. Burlington, Vt.: Ashgate, 2011.

"*La Chanson de Doon de Nanteuil:* Fragments inédits." Edited by Paul Meyer. *Romania* 13 (1884): 1–26.

La Chanson de Girart de Roussillon. Edited by Mary Hackett. Translated by Micheline de Combarieu du Grès and Gérard Gouiran. Collection Lettres

Gothiques, Livre de Poche. Paris: Librairie Générale Française, 1993. [Bilingual Old French/modern French.]

La Chanson de Godin. Edited by Françoise Meunier. Louvain: Bibliothèque de l'Université, 1958.

La Chanson de Guillaume (La Chançun de Willame). Edited and translated by Philip E. Bennett. London: Grant & Cutler, 2000. [Bilingual Old French/English.]

La Chanson de Jérusalem. Edited by Nigel R. Thorp. Vol. 6 of Nelson and Mickel, *Old French Crusade Cycle.* 1992.

La Chanson de Roland. Edited and translated by Ian Short. 2nd ed. Collection Lettres Gothiques, Livre de Poche. Paris: Librairie Générale Française, 1990. [Bilingual Old French/modern French.]

La Chanson de Roland: Texte original et traduction. Edited and translated by Gérard Moignet. Paris: Bordas, 1967. [Bilingual Old French/modern French.]

La Chanson de Roland/The Song of Roland: The French Corpus. General editor Joseph J. Duggan. 3 vols. Turnhout: Brepols, 2005.

Le Charroi de Nîmes: An English Translation with Notes. Translated by Henri Godin. Oxford: Blackwell, 1936.

Le Charroi de Nîmes: Chanson de geste du XIIe siècle éditée d'après la rédaction AB. Edited by Duncan McMillan. 2nd ed. Paris: Klincksieck, 1978.

Les Chétifs. Edited by Geoffrey M. Myers. Vol. 5 of Nelson and Mickel, *Old French Crusade Cycle.* 1981.

La Chevalerie d'Ogier de Danemarche. Edited by Mario Eusebi. Milan: Istituto Editoriale Cisalpino, 1963.

La Chevalerie Ogier. Vol. 1, *Enfances.* Edited by Muriel Ott. Paris: Champion, 2013.

La Chevalerie Vivien. Edited by Duncan McMillan. 2 vols. Aix-en-Provence: CUERMA, 1997.

"Le Chevalier au cygne" and "La Fin d'Elias." Edited by Jan A. Nelson. Vol. 2 of Nelson and Mickel, *Old French Crusade Cycle.* 1985.

Le Couronnement de Louis: Chanson de geste du XIIe siècle. Edited by Ernest Langlois. 2nd ed. Paris: Champion, 1925.

Cuvelier. *La Chanson de Bertrand du Guesclin.* Edited by Jean-Claude Faucon. 3 vols. Toulouse: Éditions Universitaires du Sud, 1990.

Le Cycle de Guillaume d'Orange. Edited and translated by Dominique Boutet. Collection Lettres Gothiques, Livre de Poche. Paris: Librairie Générale Française, 1996. [Bilingual Old French/modern French. Contains excerpts of *Les Enfances Guillaume, Le Couronnement de Louis, Le Charroi de Nîmes, La Prise d'Orange, Les Enfances Vivien, La Chevalerie Vivien, Aliscans, La Bataille Loquifer, Le Moniage Rainouart, Le Moniage Guillaume,* and *La Chanson de Guillaume.*]

Daurel et Beton. Edited by Arthur S. Kimmel. Chapel Hill: University of North Carolina Press, 1971.

Delvau, Alfred. *Collection des romans de chevalerie mis en prose française moderne.* 4 vols. Paris: Bachelin-Deflorenne, 1869.

"'De tradicione Guenonis': An Edition with Translation." Edited by William D. Paden and Patricia Harris Stäblein. *Traditio* 44 (1988): 201–51.

Doon de Maience. Edited by Alexandre Pey. Paris: Vieweg, 1858.

"*Les Enfances Godefroi*" *and* "*Le Retour de Cornumarant.*" Edited by Emanuel J. Mickel. Vol. 3 of Nelson and Mickel, *Old French Crusade Cycle.* 1999.

Les Enfances Guillaume: Chanson de geste du XIIIe siècle. Edited by Patrice Henry. Paris: SATF, 1935.

Les Enfances Renier. Edited by Delphine Dalens-Marekovic. Paris: Champion, 2009.

Les Enfances Vivien. Edited by Magali Rouquier. Geneva: Droz, 1997.

L'Entrée d'Espagne: Chanson de geste franco-italienne. Edited by Antoine Thomas. 1913. New York: Johnson Reprint, 1968.

Esclarmonde, Clarisse et Florent, Yde et Olive: Drei Fortsetzungen der "Chanson von Huon de Bordeaux" nach der einzigen Turiner Handschrift zum erstenmal veröffentlicht. Edited by Max Schweigel. Marburg: N. G. Elwert, 1889.

Esclarmonde, Clarisse et Florent, Yde et Olive I, Croissant, Yde et Olive II, Huon et les géants: Sequels to "Huon de Bordeaux" as Contained in Turin MS L.II.14: An Edition. Edited by Barbara Anne Brewka. Ph.D. diss., Vanderbilt University, 1977.

Der festländische Bueve de Hantone. Edited by Albert Stimming. 5 vols. Dresden: Gesellschaft für romanische Literatur, 1911–20.

Fierabras: Chanson de geste du XIIe siècle. Edited by Marc Le Person. Paris: Champion, 2003.

Florence de Rome: Chanson d'aventure du premier quart du XIIIe siècle. Edited by A. Wallensköld. 2 vols. SATF. Paris: Firmin Didot, 1907–9.

Folque de Candie, von Herbert le Duc de Danmartin. Edited by Oskar Schultz-Gora. 4 vols. Dresden: Gesellschaft für romanische Literatur, 1909–66.

Le "Galien" de Cheltenham. Edited by David M. Dougherty and Eugene B. Barnes. Amsterdam: Benjamins, 1981.

Garin le Loherain: Chanson de geste composée au XIIe siècle par Jean de Flagy, mise en nouveau langage. Translated by Paulin Paris. Paris: Hetzel, 1862.

Garin le Loherenc. Edited by Anne Iker-Gittleman. 3 vols. Paris: Champion, 1996.

Gaufrey. Edited by François Guessard and Henri Michelant. Paris: Vieweg, 1859.

Gaydon: Chanson de geste du XIIIe siècle. Edited and translated by Jean Subrenat. Louvain: Peeters, 2007. [Bilingual Old French/modern French.]

Gerbert de Mez: Chanson de geste du XIIe siècle. Edited by Pauline Taylor. Namur: Facultés Universitaires; Louvain: Nauwelaerts; Lille: Giard, 1952.

La Geste du Chevalier au cygne. Edited by Edmond A. Emplaincourt. Vol. 9 of Nelson and Mickel, *Old French Crusade Cycle.* 1989.

La Geste Francor: Edition of the Chansons de geste of MS. Marc. Fr. XIII (=256). Edited by Leslie Zarker Morgan. 2 vols. Tempe: Arizona Center for Medieval and Renaissance Studies, 2009.

Girart d'Amiens. *L'Istoire le Roy Charlemaine.* Edited by Daniel Métraux. 3 vols. Lewiston, N.Y.: Edwin Mellen Press, 2003.

Girart de Roussillon. Edited by Mary Hackett. 3 vols. SATF. Paris: Picard, 1953–55.

Godefroi de Buillon. Edited by Jan Boyd Roberts. Vol. 10 of Nelson and Mickel, *Old French Crusade Cycle.* 1996.

Gormont et Isembart: Fragment de chanson de geste du XIIe siècle. Edited by Alphonse Bayot. 3rd ed. Paris: Champion, 1931.

Guerin le Loherain: Édition critique et commentaire par Valérie Naudet de la prose de David Aubert extraite des "Histoires de Charles Martel." Aix-en-Provence: Université de Provence, 2005.

Guibert d'Andrenas. Edited by Muriel Ott. Paris: Champion, 2004.

Gui de Bourgogne. Edited by François Guessard and Henri Michelant. Paris: Vieweg, 1858.

Gui de Nanteuil: Chanson de geste. Edited by James R. McCormack. Geneva: Droz; Paris: Minard, 1970.

Guillaume d'Orange: Four Twelfth-Century Epics. Translated by Joan M. Ferrante. New York: Columbia University Press, 1974. [Contains *Le Couronnement de Louis, La Prise d'Orange, Aliscans,* and *Le Moniage Guillaume.*]

Guillaume de Tudèle and Anonymous. *La Chanson de la Croisade Albigeoise.* Edited by Eugène Martin-Chabot. Translated by Henri Gougaud. 1984. Collection Lettres Gothiques, Livre de Poche. Paris: Librairie Générale Française, 1989. [Bilingual Old French/modern French.]

Heroes of the French Epic: Translations from the "Chansons de Geste." Translated by Michael Newth. Woodbridge, Suffolk: Boydell, 2005. [Contains English translations of *Gormont et Isembart*, the *Chanson de Guillaume*, the *Voyage de Charlemagne*, *Raoul de Cambrai*, *Girart de Vienne*, and the *Narbonnais.*]

Hervis de Mes: Chanson de geste anonyme. Edited by Jean-Charles Herbin. Geneva: Droz, 1992.

Histoire de Raoul de Cambrai et de Bernier, le bon chevalier: Chanson de geste du XIIe siècle. Translated by Roger Berger and François Suard, with a historical introduction by Michel Rouche. Troesnes: Corps 9 Éditions, 1986.

Hugo, Victor. *La Légende des siècles.* 1859. Paris: Garnier, 1974.

Huon de Bordeaux. Edited by Pierre Ruelle. Brussels: Presses Universitaires de Bruxelles; Paris: Presses Universitaires de France, 1960.

Huon de Bordeaux: Chanson de geste du XIIIe siècle, publiée d'après le ms. Paris BNF fr. 22555. Edited and translated by William W. Kibler and François Suard. Paris: Champion, 2003. [Bilingual Old French/modern French.]

Jean Renart. *Le Roman de la Rose ou de Guillaume de Dole.* Edited by Félix Lecoy. Paris: Champion, 1962.

Jehan Bodel. *La Chanson des Saisnes.* Edited by Annette Brasseur. 2 vols. Geneva: Droz, 1989.

The Jérusalem Continuations. Part I, *La Chrétienté Corbaran.* Part II, *La Prise d'Acre, La Mort Godefroi, La Chanson des Rois Baudouin.* Edited by Peter Grillo. Vol. 7 of Nelson and Mickel, *Old French Crusade Cycle.* 1984–87.

The Jérusalem Continuations: The London-Turin Version. Edited by Peter Grillo. Vol. 8 of Nelson and Mickel, *Old French Crusade Cycle.* 1994.

Johannes de Grocheio. "Johannes de Grocheio on Secular Music: A Corrected Text and a New Translation." Translated from *De musica* (ca. 1300) by Christopher Page in *Music and Instruments of the Middle Ages: Studies on Text and Performance*, chap. 20, pp. 17–41. Brookfield, Vt.: Variorum, 1997.

Jourdain de Blaye (Jourdains de Blavies): Chanson de geste. Edited by Peter F. Dembowski. Rev. ed. Paris: Champion, 1991.

The Journey of Charlemagne to Jerusalem and Constantinople. Edited and translated by Jean-Louis G. Picherit. Birmingham, Ala.: Summa, 1984. [Bilingual Old French/English.]

Karlamagnús Saga: The Saga of Charlemagne and His Heroes. Translated by Constance B. Hieatt. 3 vols. Toronto: Pontifical Institute of Medieval Studies, 1975–80.

Les Lais de Marie de France. Edited by Jean Rychner. Paris: Champion, 1966.

Lion de Bourges: Poème épique du XIVe siècle. Edited by William W. Kibler, Jean-Louis G. Picherit, and Thelma S. Fenster. 2 vols. Geneva: Droz, 1980.

Mainet: Fragments d'une chanson de geste du XIIe siècle. Edited by Gaston Paris. *Romania* 4 (1875): 304–37.

Maugis d'Aigremont, chanson de geste. Edited by Philippe Vernay. Berne: Franck, 1980.

Miracles de Nostre Dame par personnages. Vol. 4. Edited by Gaston Paris and Ulysse Robert. SATF. Paris: Firmin Didot, 1879.

Le Moniage Guillaume: Chanson de geste du XIIe siècle; Édition de la rédaction longue. Edited by Nelly Andrieux-Reix. Paris: Champion, 2003.

Le Moniage Rainouart. Edited by Gerald A. Bertin. 3 vols. SATF. Paris: Picard, 1973–2004.

La Mort Aymeri de Narbonne. Edited by Paolo Rinoldi. Milan: Unicopli, 2000.

La Naissance du Chevalier au cygne. Edited by Emanuel J. Mickel and Jan A. Nelson. Vol. 1 of Nelson and Mickel, *Old French Crusade Cycle.* 1977.

Les Narbonnais. Edited by Hermann Suchier. 2 vols. 1898. New York: Johnson Reprints, 1965.

Nelson, Jan A., and Emanuel J. Mickel, gen. eds. *The Old French Crusade Cycle.* 10 vols. Tuscaloosa: University of Alabama Press, 1977–2003.

Niccolò da Verona. *Opere.* Edited by Franca Di Ninni. Venice: Marsilio, 1992.

Otinel. Edited by François Guessard and Henri Michelant. Paris: Vieweg, 1858.

Parise la Duchesse: Chanson de geste du XIIIe siècle. Edited by May Plouzeau. Aix-en-Provence: CUERMA, Université de Provence, 1986.

Philippe de Vigneulles. *La Chronique de Philippe de Vigneulles.* Edited by Charles Bruneau. 4 vols. Metz: Société d'histoire et d'archéologie de la Lorraine, 1927–33.

———. *Yonnet de Metz: Mise en prose de Philippe de Vigneulles (1515–1528) d'après le manuscrit h, avec en regard la version remaniée en vers du manuscrit N (Arsenal 3143—XIVe siècle).* Edited by Jean-Charles Herbin. Paris: Société des Anciens Textes Français, 2011.

"The Pilgrimage of Charlemagne" and "Aucassin and Nicolette." Edited and translated by Glyn S. Burgess and Anne Elizabeth Cobby. New York: Garland, 1988. [Bilingual Old French/English.]

Priest Konrad's "Song of Roland." (*Rolandslied.*) Translated by J. W. Thomas. Columbia, S.C.: Camden House, 1994.

La Prise de Cordres et de Sebille. Edited by Magaly Del Vecchio-Drion. Paris: Champion, 2011.

La Prise d'Orange: Chanson de geste de la fin du XIIe siècle. Edited by Claude Régnier. 4th ed. Paris: Klincksieck, 1969.

La Prise d'Orange: Chanson de geste (fin XIIe–début XIIIe siècle). Edited and translated by Claude Lachet. Paris: Champion Classiques, 2010. [Bilingual Old French/modern French.]

Prose des Loherains (Ms. Arsenal 3346). Edited by Jean-Charles Herbin. Valenciennes: Presses Universitaires de Valenciennes, 1995.

The Pseudo-Turpin: Edited from Bibliothèque Nationale, Fonds Latin, MS. 17656, with an Annotated Synopsis. Edited by H. M. Smyser. Cambridge, Mass.: Mediaeval Academy of America, 1937.

Raffaele da Verona. *Aquilon de Bavière: Roman franco-italien en prose (1379–1407)*. Edited by Peter Wunderli. 3 vols. Tübingen: Niemeyer, 1982–2007.

Raoul de Cambrai. Edited and translated by Sarah Kay. Oxford: Clarendon, 1992. [Bilingual Old French/English.]

Raoul de Cambrai: Chanson de geste du XIIe siècle. Edited by Sarah Kay. Translated and annotated by William W. Kibler. Collection Lettres Gothiques, Livre de Poche. Paris: Librairie Générale Française, 1996. [Bilingual Old French/modern French.]

Renaut de Montauban: Édition critique du manuscrit Douce. Edited by Jacques Thomas. Geneva: Droz, 1989.

Renaut de Montauban: Édition critique du ms. de Paris, BN. fr. 764 (R). Edited by Philippe Verelst. Ghent: Rijksuniversiteit te Gent, 1988.

Robert the Monk's History of the First Crusade: Historia Iherosolimitana. Translated by Carol Sweetenham. Burlington, Vt.: Ashgate, 2005.

Rodulfi Tortarii Carmina. Edited by Marbury B. Ogle and Dorothy M. Schullian. Rome: American Academy in Rome, 1933.

Roland: Days of Wrath. Comic book by Shane L. Amaya, Fabio Moon, and Gabriel Ba. Santa Barbara: Terra Major, 1999.

Le Roland occitan. Edited and translated by Gérard Gouiran and Robert Lafont. Paris: Christian Bourgeois, 1991. [Bilingual Occitan/modern French.]

Le Roman d'Auberon. Edited by Jean Subrenat. Geneva: Droz, 1973.

Le Roman de Flamenca: Un art d'aimer occitanien du XIIIe siècle. Edited by René Nelli. Toulouse: Institut d'études occitanes, 1966.

Le Roman de Guillaume d'Orange. Edited by Madeleine Tyssens, Nadine Henrard, and Louis Gemenne. Paris: Champion, 2000.

The Romance of Horn, by Thomas. Edited by Mildred K. Pope. 2 vols. Oxford: Blackwell, for the Anglo-Norman Text Society, 1955–64.

Li romans de Garin le Loherain, publié pour la première fois. Edited by Paulin Paris. 2 vols. 1833–35; Geneva: Slatkine Reprints, 1969.

Roncesvalles: Un nuevo cantar de gesta español del siglo XIII. Edited by Ramón

Menéndez Pidal. 1917. In *Textos Medievales Españoles*, 7–99. Madrid: Espasa-Calpe, 1976.

Saladin: Suite et fin du deuxième Cycle de la croisade. Edited by Larry S. Crist. Paris: Minard; Geneva: Droz, 1972.

Le Siège de Barbastre. Edited by Bernard Guidot. Paris: Champion, 2000.

The Song of Aspremont (La Chanson d'Aspremont). Translated by Michael A. Newth. New York: Garland, 1989.

The Song of Roland. Translated by Glyn Burgess. London: Penguin, 1990.

The Song of Roland: Translations of the Versions in Assonance and Rhyme of the "Chanson de Roland." Translated by Joseph J. Duggan and Annalee C. Rejhon. Turnhout: Brepols, 2012.

Songs of the Troubadours and Trouvères: An Anthology of Poems and Melodies. Edited by Samuel N. Rosenberg, Margaret Switten, and Gérard Le Vot. New York: Garland, 1998.

Tressan, Louis-Élisabeth de La Vergne, comte de. *Œuvres choisies du comte de Tressan.* Vol. 8, *Corps d'extraits de romans de chevalerie, avec figures.* Paris: Rue et Hôtel Serpente, 1788.

Tristan de Nanteuil: Chanson de geste inédite. Edited by Keith V. Sinclair. Assen, Netherlands: Van Gorcum, 1971.

Tristan et Iseut: Les poèmes français, la saga norroise. Edited and translated by Daniel Lacroix and Philippe Walter. Collection Lettres Gothiques, Livre de Poche. Paris: Librairie Générale Française, 1989. [Bilingual Old French/ modern French.]

Valentin et Orson: An Edition and Translation of the Fifteenth-Century Romance Epic. Edited and translated by Shira Schwam-Baird. Tempe: Arizona Center for Medieval and Renaissance Studies, 2011. [Bilingual Middle French/English.]

La Vengeance Fromondin. Edited by Jean-Charles Herbin. Paris: Société des Anciens Textes Français, 2005.

Vigny, Alfred de. *Œuvres complètes.* Edited by F. Baldensperger. 2 vols. Paris: Gallimard, 1948–50.

Villon, François. *The Poems of François Villon.* Translated by Galway Kinnell. Boston: Houghton Mifflin, 1977.

Vivien de Monbranc. Edited by Wolfgang van Emden. Geneva: Droz, 1987.

Le Voyage de Charlemagne à Jérusalem et à Constantinople. Edited by Paul Aebischer. Geneva: Droz, 1965.

Wace. *The History of the Norman People: Wace's "Roman de Rou."* Translated by Glyn S. Burgess, with notes by Burgess and Elisabeth van Houts. Woodbridge, Suffolk: Boydell, 2004.

———. *Le Roman de Rou.* Edited by Anthony J. Holden. 3 vols. SATF. Paris: Picard, 1970–73.

Wauquelin, Jehan. *La Belle Hélène de Constantinople: Mise en prose d'une chanson de geste.* Edited by Marie-Claude de Crécy. Geneva: Droz, 2002.

William of Malmesbury. *Gesta Regum Anglorum = The History of the English Kings.* Edited and translated by R. A. B. Mynors, completed by R. M. Thomson and M. Winterbottom. 2 vols. Oxford: Clarendon, 1998–99.

Wolfram von Eschenbach. *Willehalm.* Edited by Werner Schröder. Translated by Dieter Kartschoke. Berlin: De Gruyter, 1989. [Bilingual Middle High German/modern German.]

Secondary Sources

Akbari, Suzanne Conklin. *Idols in the East: European Representations of Islam and the Orient, 1100–1450.* Ithaca, N.Y.: Cornell University Press, 2008.

Allaire, Gloria. *Andrea da Barberino and the Language of Chivalry.* Gainesville: University Press of Florida, 1997.

———. "Noble Saracen or Muslim Enemy? The Changing Image of the Saracen in Late Medieval Italian Literature." In *Western Views of Islam in Medieval and Early Modern Europe: Perception of Other.* Edited by David R. Blanks and Michael Frassetto. New York: St. Martin's Press, 1999. 173–84.

Amy de La Bretèque, François. *L'imaginaire médiéval dans le cinéma occidental.* Paris: Champion, 2004.

Asher, J. A. "*Amis et Amiles*": An Exploratory Survey. *Auckland University College Bulletin* 39 (1953).

Au carrefour des routes d'Europe: La chanson de geste; Actes du Xe Congrès de la Société Rencesvals. 2 vols. Aix-en-Provence: CUERMA, 1987.

Baldwin, John W. *Aristocratic Life in Medieval France: The Romances of Jean Renart and Gerbert de Montreuil, 1190–1230.* Baltimore: Johns Hopkins University Press, 2000.

———. "The Image of the *Jongleur* in Northern France around 1200." *Speculum* 72 (1997): 635–63.

Bancourt, Paul. *Les Musulmans dans les chansons de geste du cycle du Roi.* 2 vols. Aix-en-Provence: Université de Provence, 1982.

Bar, Francis. *Les épîtres latines de Raoul le Tourtier (1065?–1114?): Étude de sources; La légende d'Ami et Amile.* Paris: Droz, 1937.

Barthes, Roland. "L'effet de réel." *Communications* 11 (1968): 84–89.

Baudelle-Michels, Sarah. *Les avatars d'une chanson de geste: De "Renaut de Montauban" aux "Quatre Fils Aymon."* Paris: Champion, 2006.

———. "Les *Quatre Fils Aymon* racontés aux petits." In Cazanave and Houssais, *Grands textes*, 342–62.

Baumgartner, Emmanuèle. "Quelques remarques sur l'espace et le temps dans *Raoul de Cambrai*." In *La chanson de geste et le mythe carolingien: Mélanges René Louis*, edited by André Moisan, 2: 1010–19. Saint-Père-sous-Vézelay: Musée archéologique régional, 1982.

———. "Texte de prologue et statut du texte." In *Essor et fortune*, 2: 465–73.

Baumgartner, Emmanuèle, and Laurence Harf-Lancner. *Raoul de Cambrai: L'impossible révolte*. Paris: Champion, 1999.

Bédier, Joseph. *"La Chanson de Roland" commentée par Joseph Bédier*. 1927. Paris: Piazza, 1968.

———. *Les légendes épiques: Recherches sur la formation des chansons de geste*. 3rd ed. 4 vols. Paris: Champion, 1926–29.

Beer, Marina. *Romanzi di cavalleria: Il "Furioso" e il romanzo italiano del primo Cinquecento*. Biblioteca del Cinquecento. Rome: Bulzoni, 1987.

Bennett, Philip E. *Carnaval héroïque et écriture cyclique dans la geste de Guillaume d'Orange*. Paris: Champion, 2006.

———. *"La Chanson de Guillaume" and "La Prise d'Orange."* Critical Guides to French Texts. London: Grant & Cutler, 2000.

———. *The Cycle of Guillaume d'Orange or Garin de Monglane: A Critical Bibliography*. Research Bibliographies and Checklists: New Series. Woodbridge, Suffolk: Tamesis, 2004.

Bennett, Philip E., Anne Elizabeth Cobby, and Graham Runnalls, eds. *Charlemagne in the North: Proceedings of the Twelfth International Conference of the Société Rencesvals*. Edinburgh: Société Rencesvals British Branch, 1993.

Berthelot, Anne. "*Huon de Bordeaux* ou l'irruption de la féerie dans la geste." In Luongo, *L'épopée romane*, 2: 829–42.

Berthelot, Anne, and Leslie Zarker Morgan, eds. "Acts of the Seventeenth International Congress of the Société Rencesvals." Special issue, *Olifant* 25.1–2 (2008).

Besamusca, Bart. "Middle Dutch Charlemagne Romances: An Overview." *Olifant* 26.2 (2011): 167–93.

Bezzola, Reto R. "De Roland à Raoul de Cambrai." In *Mélanges de philologie romane et de littérature médiévale offerts à Ernest Hoepffner*, 195–213. Paris: Belles Lettres, 1949.

Black, Patricia. "The Gendered World of the *Chanson de Guillaume*." *Olifant* 21 (1997): 41–63.

Bloch, R. Howard. *Etymologies and Genealogies: A Literary Anthropology of the French Middle Ages*. Chicago: University of Chicago Press, 1983.

——. *Medieval French Literature and Law*. Berkeley: University of California Press, 1977.

Boutet, Dominique. "Au carrefour des cycles épiques: La chanson de *Doon de Mayence*." In *Plaist vos oïr bone cançon vaillant? Mélanges de langue et de littérature médiévales offerts à François Suard*, edited by Dominique Boutet, Marie-Madeleine Castellani, Françoise Ferrand, and Aimé Petit, 1: 101–9. Lille: Université Charles de Gaulle–Lille, 1999.

——. *La chanson de geste: Forme et signification d'une écriture épique du moyen âge*. Paris: Presses Universitaires de France, 1993.

——. "The *Chanson de geste* and Orality." In *Medieval Oral Literature*, edited by Karl Reichl, 353–70. Berlin: De Gruyter, 2012.

——, ed. "*Raoul de Cambrai*" entre l'épique et le romanesque: Actes du Colloque du Groupe de recherche sur l'épique (20 novembre 1999). Littérales 25. Nanterre: Centre des Sciences de la Littérature, Université Paris X, 2000.

Bradley-Cromey, Nancy. *Authority and Autonomy in "L'Entrée d'Espagne."* New York: Garland, 1993.

Brault, Gerard J. "Le portrait des Sarrasins dans les chansons de geste, image projective?" In *Au carrefour des routes*, 1: 301–11.

——. "The Road Not Taken in the *Charroi de Nîmes*." In *Guillaume d'Orange and the Chanson de geste: Essays Presented to Duncan McMillan*, edited by Wolfgang van Emden and Philip E. Bennett, 15–21. Reading: Société Rencesvals British Branch, 1984.

——. "*Sapientia* dans la *Chanson de Roland*." *French Forum* 1 (1976): 99–118.

——. *The Song of Roland: An Analytical Edition*. Vol. 1, *Introduction and Commentary*. University Park: Pennsylvania State University Press, 1978.

——. "Structure et sens de la *Chanson de Roland*." *French Review* 45, spec. issue 3 (1971): 1–12.

Bulletin bibliographique de la Société Rencesvals pour l'étude des épopées romanes. Paris: Nizet, 1958–.

Burger, André. *Turold, poète de la fidélité: Essai d'explication de la "Chanson de Roland."* Geneva: Droz, 1977.

Burland, Margaret Jewett. *Strange Words: Retelling and Reception in the Medieval Roland Tradition*. Notre Dame: University of Notre Dame Press, 2007.

Busby, Keith. *Codex and Context: Reading Old French Verse Narrative in Manuscript*. 2 vols. Amsterdam: Rodopi, 2002.

Calin, William C. *The Epic Quest: Studies in Four Old French Chansons de Geste*. Baltimore: Johns Hopkins University Press, 1966.

——. *In Defense of French Poetry: An Essay in Revaluation*. University Park: Pennsylvania State University Press, 1987.

———. *A Muse for Heroes: Nine Centuries of the Epic in France.* Toronto: University of Toronto Press, 1983.

———. *The Old French Epic of Revolt: "Raoul de Cambrai," "Renaud de Montauban," "Gormond et Isembard."* Geneva: Droz, 1962.

———. "*Raoul de Cambrai*: Un univers en décomposition." In *Actes du VIe Congrès de la Société Rencesvals*, 427–38. Aix-en-Provence: CUERMA, 1974.

———. "Rapports entre chanson de geste et roman au treizième siècle." In *Essor et fortune*, 2: 407–24.

———. "Women and Their Sexuality in *Ami et Amile*: An Occasion to Deconstruct?" *Olifant* 16 (1991): 77–89.

Calin, William C., and Joseph J. Duggan. "Un débat sur l'épopée vivante." *Olifant* 8 (1981): 227–316.

Carbasse, Jean-Marie. *Introduction historique au droit pénal.* Paris: Presses Universitaires de France, 1990.

Castellani, Marie-Madeleine. "Le félon, l'empereur et le paladin." In Cazanave and Houssais, *Grands textes*, 33–53.

Cazanave, Caroline. *D'Esclarmonde à Croissant: Huon de Bordeaux, l'épique médiéval et l'esprit de suite.* Besançon: Presses Universitaires de Franche-Comté, 2007.

———. "*Huon de Bordeaux* à la sauce enfantine." In Cazanave and Houssais, *Grands textes*, 123–61.

———. "*Huon de Bordeaux* au théâtre (les temps modernes)." In *Études médiévales*, edited by Danielle Buschinger, 71–102. Amiens: Université de Picardie–Jules Verne, 1999.

Cazanave, Caroline, and Yvon Houssais, ed. *Grands textes du moyen âge à l'usage des petits.* Besançon: Presses Universitaires de Franche-Comté, 2010.

Colby-Hall, Alice. "In Search of the Lost Epics of the Lower Rhône Valley." *Olifant* 8 (1981): 339–51.

Coleman, Joyce. *Public Reading and the Reading Public in Late Medieval England and France.* Cambridge: Cambridge University Press, 1996.

Combarieu du Grès, Micheline de. "Guerri *li Sors*: Les enjeux du personnage." In Boutet, *"Raoul de Cambrai" entre l'épique et le romanesque*, 123–52.

———. *L'idéal humain et l'expérience morale chez les héros des chansons de geste: Des origines à 1250.* 2 vols. Aix-en-Provence: Université de Provence, 1979.

———. "Un personnage épique: La jeune Musulmane." In *Mélanges de langue et de littérature françaises du moyen-âge offerts à Pierre Jonin*, 181–96. Aix-en-Provence: CUERMA, 1979.

———. "Raoul, 'li desreez.'" In Hüe, *"L'orgueil a desmesure,"* 27–60.

Cook, Robert Francis. *"Chanson d'Antioche," chanson de geste: Le cycle de la Croisade est-elle épique?* Amsterdam: Benjamins, 1980.

———. "Les épopées de la Croisade." In Van Dijk and Noomen, *Aspects de l'épopée romane*, 93–110.

———. *The Sense of the "Song of Roland."* Ithaca, N.Y.: Cornell University Press, 1987.

———. "Unity and Esthetics of the Late *Chansons de geste.*" *Olifant* 11 (1986): 103–14.

Corbellari, Alain. *Guillaume d'Orange ou la naissance du héros médiéval.* Paris: Klincksieck, 2011.

———. *Joseph Bédier: Écrivain et philologue.* Geneva: Droz, 1997.

Cowell, Andrew. *The Medieval Warrior Aristocracy: Gifts, Violence, Performance, and the Sacred.* Cambridge: D. S. Brewer, 2007.

Crosland, Jessie Raven. *The Old French Epic.* Oxford: Blackwell, 1951.

Daniel, Norman. *Heroes and Saracens: An Interpretation of the Chansons de Geste.* Edinburgh: Edinburgh University Press, 1984.

Denis, Françoise. *Barons et chevaliers dans "Raoul de Cambrai": Autopsie d'un phénomène de glissement.* New York: Peter Lang, 1989.

de Weever, Jacqueline. *Sheba's Daughters: Whitening and Demonizing the Saracen Woman in Medieval French Epic.* New York: Garland, 1998.

Deyermond, Alan. "The Problem of Lost Epics: Evidence and Criteria." In *Al que en buen hora naçio: Essays on the Spanish Epic and Ballad in Honour of Colin Smith*, edited by Brian Powell and Geoffrey West, 27–43. Liverpool: Liverpool University Press, 1996.

Doutrepont, Georges. *Les mises en prose des épopées et des romans chevaleresques du XIVe au XVIe siècle.* 1939. Geneva: Slatkine Reprints, 1969.

Duby, Georges. "Dans la France du nord-ouest au XIIe siècle: Les 'jeunes' dans la société aristocratique." *Annales* 19 (1964): 835–46.

———. *The Three Orders: Feudal Society Imagined.* Trans. Arthur Goldhammer. Chicago: University of Chicago Press, 1982.

Dufournet, Jean, ed. *"Ami et Amile": Une chanson de geste de l'amitié; Études.* Paris: Champion, 1987.

Duggan, Joseph J. "L'épisode d'Aude dans la tradition en rime de la *Chanson de Roland.*" In Bennett, Cobby, and Runnalls, *Charlemagne in the North*, 273–79.

———. "Franco-German Conflict and the History of French Scholarship on the *Song of Roland.*" In *Hermeneutics and Medieval Culture*, edited by Patrick J. Gallacher and Helen Damico, 97–106. Albany: State University of New York Press, 1989.

———. "Medieval Epic as Popular Historiography: Appropriation of Historical Knowledge in the Vernacular Epic." In *La littérature historiographique des origines à 1500*, 285–312. Grundriss der romanischen Literaturen des Mittelalters 11/1. Heidelberg: Carl Winter, 1986.

———. *The Romances of Chrétien de Troyes.* New Haven, Conn.: Yale University Press, 2001.

———. *"The Song of Roland": Formulaic Style and Poetic Craft.* Berkeley: University of California Press, 1973.

Durand-Le Guern, Isabelle, and Bernard Ribémont. *Charlemagne: Empereur et mythe d'Occident.* Paris: Klincksieck, 2009.

Les épopées romanes. General editors Rita Lejeune, Jeanne Wathelet-Willem, and Henning Krauss. Grundriss der Romanischen Literaturen des Mittelalters 3. Heidelberg: Carl Winter, 1981–.

Essor et fortune de la chanson de geste dans l'Europe et l'Orient latin: Actes du IXe Congrès international de la Société Rencesvals. 2 vols. Modena: Mucchi, 1984.

Everson, Jane E. "The Epic Tradition of Charlemagne in Italy." *Cahiers de recherches médiévales et humanistes* 12 (2005): 45–81. crm.revues.org/2192.

———. *The Italian Romance Epic in the Age of Humanism: The Matter of Italy and the World of Rome.* New York: Oxford University Press, 2001.

Faral, Edmond. *Les jongleurs en France au moyen âge.* Paris: Champion, 1910.

Farnham, Fern. "Romanesque Design in the *Chanson de Roland.*" *Romance Philology* 18 (1964): 143–64.

Farnsworth, William Oliver. *Uncle and Nephew in the Old French Chansons de Geste: A Study in the Survival of Matriarchy.* New York: Columbia University Press, 1913.

Farrier, Susan E. *The Medieval Charlemagne Legend: An Annotated Bibliography.* New York: Garland, 1993.

Fenster, Thelma S. "The Family Romance of *Aye d'Avignon.*" *Romance Quarterly* 33 (1986): 11–22.

Frappier, Jean. *Les chansons de geste du cycle de Guillaume d'Orange.* 2 vols. Paris: Société d'édition d'enseignement supérieur, 1955–65.

Gaunt, Simon. *Gender and Genre in Medieval French Literature.* Cambridge: Cambridge University Press, 1995.

Gautier, Léon. *Les épopées françaises: Étude sur les origines et l'histoire de la littérature nationale.* 2nd ed. 4 vols. 1878–92. Osnabrück: Zeller, 1966.

Gittleman, Anne Iker. *Le style épique de "Garin le Loherain."* Geneva: Droz, 1967.

Godzich, Wlad, and Jeffrey Kittay. *The Emergence of Prose: An Essay in Prosaics.* Minneapolis: University of Minnesota Press, 1987.

Goody, Jack. *The Development of the Family and Marriage in Europe.* Cambridge: Cambridge University Press, 1983.

Grisward, Joël H. *Archéologie de l'épopée médiévale.* Paris: Payot, 1981.

Guidot, Bernard. *Chanson de geste et réécritures.* Orléans: Paradigme, 2008.

———. "Le crime, les hommes et Dieu dans *La Chanson d'Antioche*." In Ribémont, *Crimes et châtiments,* 29–53.

———. "De la chanson de geste au roman populaire: Quelques aperçus fondés sur *Milles et Amys,* réécriture d'Alfred Delvau." In *The Chanson de Geste and Its Reception: Essays Presented to Philip E. Bennett by Members of the Société Rencesvals,* edited by Marianne J. Ailes, Anne Elizabeth Cobby, and Peter S. Noble, 55–72. Edinburgh: Société Rencesvals British Branch, 2012.

———. "L'extension cyclique de la Geste des Lorrains: Abandons, résurgences, irradiation." In *Chanson de geste et réécritures,* 92–117.

———. "Formes tardives de l'épopée médiévale: Mises en prose, imprimés, livres populaires." In Luongo, *L'épopée romane,* 2: 579–610.

———. "*Huon de Bordeaux* et l'épisode de l'embuscade liminaire chez Tressan et chez Delvau." In *Chanson de geste et réécritures,* 398–406.

———. *Recherches sur la chanson de geste au XIIIe siècle d'après certaines œuvres du cycle de Guillaume d'Orange.* 2 vols. Aix-en-Provence: Université de Provence, 1986.

Haidu, Peter. *The Subject of Violence: The "Song of Roland" and the Birth of the State.* Bloomington: Indiana University Press, 1993.

Harney, Michael. *Kinship and Polity in the "Poema de Mio Cid."* West Lafayette, Ind.: Purdue University Press, 1993.

Heinemann, Edward A. "L'art de la laisse dans le *Charroi de Nîmes.*" In *"Contez me tout": Mélanges de langue et de littérature médiévales offerts à Herman Braet,* edited by Catherine Bel, Pascale Dumont, and Frank Willaert, 217–28. Louvain: Peeters, 2006.

———. *L'art métrique de la chanson de geste: Essai sur la musicalité du récit.* Geneva: Droz, 1993.

———. "Existe-t-il une chanson de geste aussi brillante que le *Charroi de Nîmes?*" In Van Dijk and Noomen, *Aspects de l'épopée romane,* 461–69.

———. "Le jeu d'échos associés à l'hémistiche *Non ferai sire* dans le *Charroi de Nîmes.*" *Romania* 112 (1991): 1–17.

Hennings, Thordis. *Französische Heldenepik im deutschen Sprachraum: Die*

Rezeption der Chansons de Geste im 12. und 13. Jahrhundert. Heidelberg: Winter, 2008.

Henrard, Nadine, ed. *Cinquante ans d'études épiques: Actes du Colloque anniversaire de la Société Rencesvals.* Geneva: Droz, 2008.

———. "Le cycle de Guillaume d'Orange ou les *Aliscans* rajeunis." In Cazanave and Houssais, *Grands textes,* 57–80.

Herbin, Jean-Charles. "*Anseÿs de Gascogne* et la Flandre." In "Picard d'hier et d'aujourd'hui," *Bien dire et bien aprandre* (Centre d'Études Médiévales et Dialectales de Lille 3) 21 (2003): 207–28.

———. "*Auberi le Bourguignon,* personnage de *Garin le Loherain.*" In Ott, *L'épopée médiévale et la Bourgogne,* 67–81.

———. "Variations, vie et mort des Loherains: Réflexions sur la gestation et les paradoxes d'un grand cycle épique." *Cahiers de recherches médiévales et humanistes* 12 (2005): 147–74. crm.revues.org/2242.

———. "*Yonnet de Metz.*" In *Les mises en prose,* edited by Aimé Petit, 31–45. Ateliers 35. Lille: Centre de Gestion de l'Édition Scientifique, 2006.

Herbin, Jean-Charles, and Thomas Falmagne. "Fragments d'une chanson de geste perdue (*Les Enfances Charlemagne?*)." *Romania* 130 (2012): 473–92.

Hindley, Alan, and Brian J. Levy. *The Old French Epic: An Introduction; Texts, Commentaries, Notes.* Louvain: Peeters, 1983.

Hogetoorn, Corrie. "Bevis of Hampton." In *A Dictionary of Medieval Heroes,* edited by Willem Pieter Gerritsen and Anthony G. van Melle, translated by Tanis M. Guest, 62–64. Woodbridge, Suffolk: Boydell, 1998.

Holtus, Günter. "L'état actuel des recherches sur le franco-italien: Corpus de textes et description linguistique." In Suard, *La chanson de geste: Écriture* . . . , 147–71.

Holtus, Günter, and Peter Wunderli. *Franco-italien et épopée franco-italienne.* In *Les épopées romanes,* t. 1–2, fasc. 10.

Horrent, Jacques. *L'épopée dans la péninsule ibérique.* In *Les épopées romanes,* t. 1–2, fasc 9.

Hüe, Denis, ed. *"L'orgueil a desmesure": Études sur "Raoul de Cambrai."* Orléans: Paradigme, 1999.

Hyatte, Reginald. *The Arts of Friendship: The Idealization of Friendship in Medieval and Early Renaissance Literature.* Leiden: Brill, 1994.

Jauss, Hans-Robert. *Toward an Aesthetic of Reception.* Translated by Timothy Bahti. Minneapolis: University of Minnesota Press, 1982.

Johnson, Edward Joe. *Once There Were Two True Friends: Or Idealized Male Friendship in French Narrative from the Middle Ages through the Enlightenment.* Birmingham, Ala.: Summa, 2003.

Jones, Catherine M. "Les chansons de geste et l'Orient." In Luongo, *L'épopée romane*, 2: 629–45.

———. "The Death of Bégon Revisited." In *"Por le soie amisté": Essays in Honor of Norris J. Lacy*, edited by Keith Busby and Catherine M. Jones, 235–46. Amsterdam: Rodopi, 1999.

———. "'Je ne soz queil homme j'oz ocis': Ignorance et innocence dans *Huon de Bordeaux* et *Garin le Lorrain*." In Ribémont, *La faute dans l'épopée médiévale*, 123–36.

———. *The Noble Merchant: Problems of Genre and Lineage in "Hervis de Mes."* Chapel Hill: Department of Romance Languages, University of North Carolina, 1993.

———. "Of Giants and Griffons: Narrative and Lineal Dysfunctions in *Gaufrey*." In *"Moult a sans et vallour": Studies in Medieval French Literature in Honor of William W. Kibler*, edited by Monica L. Wright, Norris J. Lacy, and Rupert T. Pickens, 207–18. Amsterdam: Rodopi, 2012.

———. *Philippe de Vigneulles and the Art of Prose Translation.* Cambridge: D. S. Brewer, 2008.

———. "Polyglots in the *chansons de geste*." In *"De sens rassis": Essays in Honor of Rupert T. Pickens*, edited by Keith Busby, Bernard Guidot, and Logan E. Whalen, 297–307. Amsterdam: Rodopi, 2005.

———. "Recasting *Raoul de Cambrai*: The Loherain Version." *Olifant* 14 (1989): 3–18.

———. "Roland versus Oliver." In Kibler and Morgan, *Approaches to Teaching the "Song of Roland*," 201–6.

———. "'Se je fusse hons': Les guerrières dans *Anseÿs de Mes*." In Bennett, Cobby, and Runnalls, *Charlemagne in the North*, 291–97.

Kay, Sarah. *The Chansons de Geste in the Age of Romance: Political Fictions.* Oxford: Clarendon, 1995.

———. "The Character of Character in the *Chansons de Geste*." In *The Craft of Fiction: Essays in Medieval Poetics*, edited by Leigh A. Arrathoon, 475–98. Rochester, Mich.: Solaris, 1984.

———. "The Epic Formula: A Revised Definition." *Zeitschrift für französische Sprache und Literatur* 93 (1983): 170–89.

———. "The Life of the Dead Body: Death and the Sacred in the *chansons de geste*." In "Corps mystique, corps sacré: Textual Transfigurations of the Body from the Middle Ages to the Seventeenth Century," *Yale French Studies* 86 (1994): 94–108.

———. "La représentation de la féminité dans les chansons de geste." In Bennett, Cobby, and Runnalls, *Charlemagne in the North*, 223–40.

———. "Seduction and Suppression in *Ami et Amile*." *French Studies* 44 (1990): 129–42.

Kelly, Molly Robinson. *The Hero's Place: Medieval Literary Traditions of Space and Belonging*. Washington, D.C.: Catholic University of America Press, 2009.

Kibler, William W. "La chanson d'aventures." In *Essor et fortune*, 2: 509–15.

———. "Les fins de *Raoul de Cambrai*." In Boutet, *"Raoul de Cambrai" entre l'épique et le romanesque*, 13–23.

———. "Relectures de l'épopée." In *Au carrefour des routes*, 1: 103–40.

———. "Rencesvals: The Event." In Kibler and Morgan, *Approaches to Teaching the "Song of Roland,"* 53–56.

Kibler, William W., and Leslie Zarker Morgan, eds. *Approaches to Teaching the "Song of Roland."* New York: Modern Language Association of America, 2006.

Kibler, William W., and Grover Zinn, eds. *Medieval France: An Encyclopedia*. New York: Garland, 1995.

Kinoshita, Sharon. *Medieval Boundaries: Rethinking Difference in Old French Literature*. Philadelphia: University of Pennsylvania Press, 2006.

Krappe, A. H. "The Legend of Amicus and Amelius." *Modern Language Review* 18 (1923): 152–61.

Kullmann, Dorothea. "Le contexte idéologique de *Girart de Roussillon*: Quelques remarques sur la partie finale du poème." In Berthelot and Morgan, "Acts of the Seventeenth International Congress," 271–82.

Labbé, Alain. *L'architecture des palais et des jardins dans les chansons de geste: Essai sur le thème du roi en majesté*. Paris: Champion; Geneva: Slatkine, 1987.

———. "Raoul et la voix des mères: Parole féminine et pouvoir masculin dans *Raoul de Cambrai*." In Boutet, *"Raoul de Cambrai" entre l'épique et le romanesque*, 105–21.

Lachet, Claude. *La "Prise d'Orange" ou la parodie courtoise d'une épopée*. Paris: Champion, 1986.

Lacy, Norris J. "Épopée et cinéma." *Olifant* 25 (2006): 83–96.

Lafont, Robert. *La Geste de Roland*. 2 vols. Paris: L'Harmattan, 1991.

Leclercq, Armelle. *Portraits croisés: L'image des Francs et des Musulmans dans les textes sur la Première Croisade; Chroniques latines et arabes, chansons de geste françaises des XIIe et XIIIe siècles*. Paris: Champion, 2010.

Lecouteux, Claude. *Mélusine et le Chevalier au cygne*. Paris: Imago, 1997.

Le Gentil, Pierre. "Les chansons de geste: Le problème des origines." *Revue d'histoire littéraire de la France* 70 (1970): 992–1006.

Legros, Huguette. *L'amitié dans les chansons de geste à l'époque romane*. Aix: Université de Provence, 2001.

Lejeune, Rita. "La naissance du couple littéraire Roland et Olivier." In "Mélanges Grégoire," vol. 2, *Annuaire de l'institut de philologie et d'histoire orientales et slaves* 10 (1950): 371–401.

———. *Recherches sur le thème: Les chansons de geste et l'histoire*. Liège: Faculté de philosophie et lettres, 1948.

Le Saux, Françoise. "Quand le héros devient malade: Le lépreux dans *Ami et Amile* et *Amys e Amillyoun*." In *Epidemics and Sickness in French Literature and Culture*, edited by Christopher Lloyd, 3–14. Durham, England: University of Durham, 1995.

Leverage, Paula. *Reception and Memory: A Cognitive Approach to the chansons de geste*. Amsterdam: Rodopi, 2010.

Lord, Albert B. *The Singer of Tales*. Edited by Stephen Mitchell and Gregory Nagy. 2nd ed. Cambridge, Mass.: Harvard University Press, 2000.

Luongo, Salvatore, ed. *L'épopée romane au moyen âge et aux temps modernes: Actes du XIVe Congrès International de la Société Rencesvals*. 2 vols. Naples: Fridericiana Editrice Universitaria, 2001.

Maddox, Donald. "The 'Archaeology' of Medieval Epic." *Olifant* 14 (1989): 101–14.

Malicote, Sandra. *Image and Imagination: Picturing the Old French Epic*. Lanham, Md.: University Press of America, 2010.

Martin, Jean-Pierre. "*Beuves de Hantone* entre roman et chanson de geste." In *Le romanesque dans l'épique*, edited by Dominique Boutet, 97–112. Littérales 31. Nanterre: Université de Paris X, 2002.

———. *Les motifs dans la chanson de geste: Définition et utilisation*. Lille: Centre d'Études Médiévales et Dialectales, Université de Lille III, 1992.

———. "Sur les prologues des chansons de geste: Structures rhétoriques et fonctions discursives." *Le Moyen Âge* 93 (1987): 185–201.

Matarasso, Pauline. *Recherches historiques et littéraires sur "Raoul de Cambrai."* Paris: Nizet, 1962.

McKitterick, Rosamond. *Charlemagne: The Formation of a European Identity*. Cambridge: Cambridge University Press, 2008.

Menéndez Pidal, Ramón. *"La Chanson de Roland" et la tradition épique des Francs*. 2nd ed. Translated by Irénée-Marcel Cluzel. Paris: Picard, 1960.

Métraux, Daniel. "Le *Charlemagne* de Girart d'Amiens: Vers un empereur modèle." *Cahiers de recherches médiévales et humanistes* 14 (2007): 201–7.

Mickel, Emanuel J. *Ganelon, Treason, and the "Chanson de Roland."* University Park: Pennsylvania State University Press, 1989.

———. "The Question of Guilt in *Ami et Amile*." *Romania* 106 (1985): 19–35.

Middle Dutch Charlemagne Romances. Special series devoted to Middle Dutch adaptations of the chansons de geste. *Olifant* 23.1, 24.1, 26.1–2.

Moisan, André. *Répertoire des noms propres de personnes et de lieux cités dans les chansons de geste françaises et les œuvres étrangères dérivées*. 5 vols. Geneva: Droz, 1986.

Morrison, Susan Signe. "Women Writers and Women Rulers: Rhetorical and Political Empowerment in the Fifteenth Century." *Women in German Yearbook* 9 (1993): 25–48.

Nichols, Stephen G. *Formulaic Diction and Thematic Composition in the "Chanson de Roland."* Chapel Hill: University of North Carolina Press, 1961.

———. *Romanesque Signs: Early Medieval Narrative and Iconography*. New Haven, Conn.: Yale University Press, 1983.

Ott, Muriel, ed. *L'épopée médiévale et la Bourgogne*. Dijon: Éditions Universitaires de Dijon, 2006.

Palumbo, Giovanni. "Une mise en prose de la belle Aude au XIIIe siècle. Édition du ms. BnF. fr. 1621." In *Quant l'ung amy pour l'autre veille: Mélanges de moyen français offerts à Claude Thiry*. Edited by Tania Van Hemelryck and Maria Colombo Timelli. Turnhout: Brepols, 2008. 147–62.

———. "Le 'Roman de la Belle Aude' dans les versions rimées de *La Chanson de Roland*." *Olifant* 25 (2006): 339–52.

Paris, Gaston. *Histoire poétique de Charlemagne*. 2nd ed. 1865. Paris: Bouillon, 1905.

Parmly, Ruth. *The Geographical References in the Chanson de Garin le Loherain*. New York: Institute of French Studies, Columbia University, 1935.

Parry, Milman. "Studies in the Epic Technique of Oral Verse-Making. I. Homer and Homeric Style." *Harvard Studies in Classical Philology* 41 (1930): 73–147.

Payen, Jean-Charles. "Le *Charroi de Nîmes*: Comédie épique?" In *Mélanges de langue et de littérature du moyen âge et de la Renaissance offerts à Jean Frappier*, 2: 891–902. Geneva: Droz, 1970.

———. *Le motif du repentir dans la littérature française médiévale: Des origines à 1230*. Geneva: Droz, 1967.

———. "Une poétique du génocide joyeux: Devoir de violence et plaisir de tuer dans *La Chanson de Roland*." *Olifant* 6 (1979): 226–36.

Picherit, Jean-Louis. "Les Sarrasins dans *Tristan de Nanteuil*." In *Au carrefour des routes*, 2: 941–57.

Pichon, Geneviève. "La lèpre dans *Ami et Amile*." In Dufournet, *Ami et Amile*, 51–66.

Poirion, Daniel. "Chanson de geste ou épopée? Remarques sur la définition d'un genre." *Travaux de linguistique et de littérature* 10 (1972): 7–20.

Quéruel, Danielle. "Des mises en prose aux romans de chevalerie dans les collections bourguignonnes." In *Rhétorique et mise en prose au XVe siècle: Actes du VIe Colloque International sur le moyen français*, edited by Sergio Cigada and Anne Slerca, 173–93. Milan: Vita e Pensiero, 1991.

Ramey, Lynn Tarte. *Christian, Saracen and Genre in Medieval French Literature*. New York: Routledge, 2001.

Rasmussen, Jens. *La prose narrative française du XVe siècle: Étude esthétique et stylistique*. Copenhagen: Munksgaard, 1958.

Redman, Harry, Jr. *The Roland Legend in Nineteenth-Century French Literature*. Lexington: University Press of Kentucky, 1991.

Ribémont, Bernard. "La chanson de geste, une 'machine judiciaire'?" Introduction to *Crimes et châtiments*, vii–xxv.

———. "Epopée médiévale et questions de droit: Règlement de conflits, Résolution des tensions; Le cas d'*Ami et Amile* et de *Jourdain de Blaye*." *Romanistische Zeitschrift für Literaturgeschichte / Cahiers d'histoire des littératures romanes* 31 (2007): 249–61.

———, ed. *Crimes et châtiments dans la chanson de geste*. Paris: Klincksieck, 2008.

———, ed. *La faute dans l'épopée médiévale: Ambiguïté du jugement*. Rennes: Presses Universitaires de Rennes, 2011.

Rikhardsdottir, Sif. *Medieval Translations and Cultural Discourse: The Movement of Texts in England, France and Scandinavia*. Cambridge: D. S. Brewer, 2012.

Riley-Smith, Jonathan. *The Crusades: A History*. 2nd ed. New Haven, Conn.: Yale University Press, 2005.

Riquer, Martín de. *Les chansons de geste françaises*. 2nd ed. Translated by Irénée-Marcel Cluzel. Paris: Nizet, 1957.

Rossi, Marguerite. "*Huon de Bordeaux*" et l'évolution du genre épique au XIIIe siècle. Paris: Champion, 1975.

Roussel, Claude. *Conter de geste au XIVe siècle: Inspiration folklorique et écriture épique dans "La Belle Hélène de Constantinople."* Geneva: Droz, 1998.

Ruggieri, Ruggero M. *Il processo di Gano nella "Chanson de Roland."* Florence: Sansoni, 1936.

Rychner, Jean. *La chanson de geste: Essai sur l'art épique des jongleurs*. Geneva: Droz; Lille: Giard, 1955.

Schenck, Mary Jane. "The Baligant Episode." In Kibler and Morgan, *Approaches to Teaching the "Song of Roland,"* 213–19.

———. "If There Wasn't 'a' *Song of Roland*, Was There a 'Trial' of Ganelon?" *Olifant* 22 (2003): 143–57.

Schwam-Baird, Shira. "The Romance Epic Hero, the Mercenary, and the Ottoman Turk Seen Through the Lens of *Valentin et Orson* (1489)." *Medievalia et Humanistica* 34 (2008): 105–27.

———. "Terror and Laughter in the Images of the Wild Man: The Case of the 1489 *Valentin et Orson*." *Fifteenth-Century Studies* 27 (2002): 238–56.

Siciliano, Italo. *Les chansons de geste et l'épopée: Mythes, histoire, poèmes*. Turin: Società editrice internazionale, 1968.

Sinclair, Finn. "The Imaginary Body: Framing Identity in *Ami et Amile*." *Neophilologus* 92 (2008): 193–204.

Skårup, Povl. "La matière de France dans les pays du Nord." In Bennett, Cobby, and Runnalls, *Charlemagne in the North*, 5–20.

Spence, Sarah. *Texts and the Self in the Twelfth Century*. Cambridge: Cambridge University Press, 1996.

Spiegel, Gabrielle M. *Romancing the Past: The Rise of Vernacular Prose Historiography in Thirteenth-Century France*. Berkeley: University of California Press, 1993.

Spiewok, Wolfgang. "Le *Rolandslied* et le *Karl* du Stricker." In Bennett, Cobby, and Runnalls, *Charlemagne in the North*, 89–93.

Spijker, Irene. "Renout van Montalbaen." *Olifant* 23.1 (2004): 27–43.

Suard, François. *La chanson de geste*. Paris: Presses Universitaires de France, 1993.

———. "L'épopée française tardive (XIVe–XVe siècles)." In *Études de philologie romane et d'histoire littéraire offertes à Jules Horrent*, edited by Jean-Marie d'Heur and Nicoletta Cherubini, 449–58. Liège: Comité d'Honneur, 1980.

———. *Guide de la chanson de geste et de sa postérité littéraire (XIe–XVe siècle)*. Paris: Champion, 2011.

———. *Guillaume d'Orange: Étude du roman en prose*. Paris: Champion, 1979.

———. "Le motif du déguisement dans quelques chansons du cycle de Guillaume d'Orange." *Olifant* 7 (1980): 343–58.

———. "Le passage à la prose." *Cahiers de recherches médiévales et humanistes* 12 (2005): 29–43.

———. "*Raoul de Cambrai* et l'exaltation du tragique." In *Première journée valenciennoise de médiévistique*, edited by Jean-Charles Herbin, 113–30. Valenciennes: Presses Universitaires de Valenciennes, 1999.

———. "*Renaut de Montauban*: Enjeux et problèmes de la chanson du XIIIe siècle." In *Entre épopée et légende: "Les Quatre Fils Aymon" ou "Renaut de Montauban*," edited by Danielle Quéruel, 1: 17–49. Langres–Saints-Geosmes: Dominique Guéniot, 2000.

———. *Roland ou Les avatars d'une folie héroïque*. Paris: Klincksieck, 2012.

———. "Le romanesque dans *Raoul de Cambrai*." In Boutet, *"Raoul de Cambrai" entre l'épique et le romanesque*, 45–63.

———, ed. *La chanson de geste: Écriture, intertextualités, translations*. Littérales 14. Nanterre: Centre des Sciences de la Littérature, Université Paris X, 1994.

Subrenat, Jean. "*Raoul de Cambrai* et son public au 'siècle' de Philippe II Auguste." In Vallecalle, *"Raoul de Cambrai,"* 9–20.

Sunderland, Luke. *Old French Narrative Cycles: Heroism Between Ethics and Morality*. Cambridge: D. S. Brewer, 2010.

Sweetenham, Carol. "How History Became Epic but lost its Identity on the Way: The Half-Life of First Crusade Epic in Romance Literature." In Berthelot and Morgan, "Acts of the Seventeenth International Congress," 435–52.

Taylor, Andrew. "Was There a Song of Roland?" *Speculum* 76 (2001): 28–65.

Tolan, John. "The Battle of Roncesvalles as National Polemic." In *Bridging the Atlantic: Toward a Reassessment of Iberian and Latin American Cultural Ties*, edited by Marina Pérez de Mendiola, 15–29. Albany: State University of New York Press, 1996.

Tuffrau, Paul. *La Légende de Guillaume d'Orange, renouvelée*. Paris: Piazza, 1920.

Tyssens, Madeleine. *La Geste de Guillaume d'Orange dans les manuscrits cycliques*. Paris: Belles Lettres, 1967.

Vallecalle, Jean-Claude. "*Aquilon de Bavière* ou l'ambiguïté de l'innocence." In Ribémont, *La faute dans l'épopée médiévale*, 159–75.

———, ed. *"Raoul de Cambrai": Ouvrage dirigé par Jean-Claude Vallecalle*. Paris: Ellipses, 1999.

Vance, Eugene. *Reading "The Song of Roland."* Englewood Cliffs, N.J.: Prentice-Hall, 1970.

Van der Have, J. Bert. *Roman der Lorreinen: De fragmenten en het geheel*. Schiedam: Scriptum, 1990.

Van Dijk, Hans, and Willem Noomen, eds. *Aspects de l'épopée romane*. Groningen: Egbert Forsten, 1995.

Verelst, Philippe. "Le *locus horribilis*: Ébauche d'une étude." In Suard, *La chanson de geste: Écriture . . .* , 41–57.

Warren, Michelle R. *Creole Medievalism: Colonial France and Joseph Bédié's Middle Ages*. Minneapolis: University of Minnesota Press, 2011.

Weill, Isabelle. "Auberi, un Bourguignon exilé, dans la chanson d'*Auberi le Bourgoin*." In Ott, *L'épopée médiévale et la Bourgogne*, 167–76.

Weiss, Judith. "'The Courteous Warrior': Epic, Romance and Comedy in *Boeve de Haumtone*." In *Boundaries in Medieval Romance*, edited by Neil Cartlidge, 149–60. Cambridge: D. S. Brewer, 2008.

Windelberg, Marjorie, and D. Gary Miller. "How (Not) to Define the Epic Formula." *Olifant* 8 (1980–81): 29–50.

Woods, Ellen Rose. *"Aye d'Avignon": A Study of Genre and Society*. Geneva: Droz, 1978.

Zink, Michel. "Lubias et Belissant dans la chanson d'*Ami et Amile*." *Littératures* 17 (1987): 11–24.

Zumthor, Paul. *Essai de poétique médiévale*. Paris: Seuil, 1972.

———. *La lettre et la voix: De la "littérature" médiévale*. Paris: Seuil, 1987.

INDEX

Cantar de Rodlane, 5, 143
Cantari di Aspromonte, 142
Cantilènes, 4
Cassenti, Franck, 79, 147
Chanson d'Antioche, 9, 45, 46–47, 48, 56
Chanson d'aventures, defined, 23–24;
  examples of, 31, 37, 43, 48, 49, 51, 52, 56,
  109, 124, 125, 134, 161n81
Chanson de Bertrand du Guesclin, 54–55
Chanson de Godin, 135
Chanson de Guillaume, 11, 33–34, 93, 94, 145
Chanson de Jérusalem, 47, 48
Chanson de Roland, 60–79; adaptations,
  79, 140, 141–42, 143, 144, 145, 147; AOI,
  11; artistry, 5, 12, 14–15, 24, 67–71, 146;
  authorship, 3; Charlemagne in, 72–73,
  130; dating, 5; death of Roland, 14, 34, 71;
  démesure, 69–71; feudal relationships,
  19; formulaic style, 5–6; homosocial
  bonds, 50, 119; horn scenes, 69–70, 128;
  laisse length, 134–35; manuscripts, 60,
  64, 77, 112, 153n10, 162n1, 162n2; narrator,
  19; Ogier le Danois in, 36; place in Char-
  lemagne cycle, 29; propaganda and, 21,
  79; relationship to history, 3–4, 9, 63–64;
  Romanticism and, 78–79, 146; structure,
  64–66; summary, 61–62; treason, 68–69;
  tree imagery, 92; trial scene, 73–75;
  uncle-nephew relationship, 23; versions,
  77–78; women characters, 75–77
Chanson des Rois Baudouin, 49
Chanson des Saisnes, 2, 3, 30, 143
Chansons de geste: adaptations outside
  France, 141–45; authorship, 3; defined,
  1–3; form and style, 10–19, 156n19; law
  and, 20–21; modern adaptations, 78–79,
  97, 135, 146–47; and music, 1, 6–7, 11, 12,
  153n1; narrative repertory, 19–25; narra-
  tive voice, 18–19; origins, 3–6; prologues,
  18–19; prose versions, 3, 24, 39, 44, 49,
  52, 54, 55, 56, 97, 124, 135, 137–41; recep-
  tion and transmission, 6–9; sources
  and relationship to history, 9–10; versus
  romance, 23–24; women's roles, 22

Chansons de toile, 76, 121, 172n201
Charlemagne, cycle of, 26–27, 28–31, 145;
  historical figure, 4, 7, 63. See also Chan-
  son de Roland, Huon de Bordeaux
Charles Martel (fictionalized character),
  27, 39, 42, 82, 142, 159n39
Charroi de Nîmes, 33, 80–89, 95; comic
  elements, 85–89; geographical precision,
  82; laisse technique, 82–83; manuscripts,
  80; prologue, 32; prose version, 97; re-
  lationship to history, 82; royal injustice,
  19, 20, 82–84, 107; summary, 81–82
Chétifs, 21, 47–48
Chevalerie, 147
Chevalerie Ogier de Danemarche, 20, 35,
  36, 128
Chevalerie Vivien, 34
Chevalier au cygne, 48, 49, 140
Chevalier au cygne et Godefroi de Bouil-
  lon, 49
Children's literature, 147
Chrétien de Troyes, 133; Chevalier au lion,
  128; Conte du Graal, 166n103
Chrétienté Corbaran, 48
Cinema, 79, 147
Coleman, Joyce, 154n29
Comédie Française, 147
Compagnie Picrokole, 147
Conversio Othgerii militis, 36
Cook, Robert Francis, 46, 49, 53, 68, 70,
  163n18
Corbellari, Alain, 85, 96
Couronnement de Louis, 33, 80, 83, 95,
  158n16
Croissant, 135
Crusade cycle, 28, 45–49, 140
Crusades, 7, 9, 21, 45–47, 49
Cuvelier, 54
Cycles, formation, 22–23; 26–28. See also
  Blaye, cycle of; Charlemagne, cycle of;
  Crusade cycle; Geste, defined; Guillaume
  d'Orange, cycle of; Lorraine cycle; Nan-
  teuil, cycle of; Rebellious Baron cycle;
  Renaut de Montauban, cycle of

Catherine M. Jones, Josiah Meigs Distinguished Professor of French and Provençal at the University of Georgia, is the author of *The Noble Merchant: Problems of Genre and Lineage in Hervis de Mes* and *Philippe de Vigneulles and the Art of Prose Translation*.

New Perspectives on Medieval Literature: Authors and Traditions

EDITED BY R. BARTON PALMER AND TISON PUGH

This series offers compact, comprehensive, and up-to-date studies of important medieval authors and traditions written by leading scholars. These volumes will appeal to undergraduate and graduate students, academics, and general readers interested in the vibrant world of medieval literature. Our philosophy in New Perspectives on Medieval Literature is that good scholarship should excite both interest in and accessibility to a field of study, and this principle of combining the scholarship of teaching with student learning informs our editorial decisions.

An Introduction to Christine de Pizan, by Nadia Margolis (2011; first paperback edition, 2012)

An Introduction to the "Gawain" Poet, by John M. Bowers (2012; first paperback edition, 2013)

An Introduction to British Arthurian Narrative, by Susan Aronstein (2012; first paperback edition, 2014)

An Introduction to Geoffrey Chaucer, by Tison Pugh (2013)

An Introduction to the Chansons de Geste, by Catherine M. Jones (2014)